Whillans's Tax Tables

Finance Act 2018 Edition

Edited by

Claire Hayes CTA

Shilpa Veerappa ATT

Tolley®

Members of the LexisNexis Group worldwide

United Kingdom	RELX (UK) Limited trading as LexisNexis, 1–3 Strand, London WC2N 5JR
Australia	Reed International Books Australia Pty Ltd trading as LexisNexis, Chatswood, New South Wales
Austria	LexisNexis Verlag ARD Orac GmbH & Co KG, Vienna
Benelux	LexisNexis Benelux, Amsterdam
Canada	LexisNexis Canada, Markham, Ontario
China	LexisNexis China, Beijing and Shanghai
France	LexisNexis SA, Paris
Germany	LexisNexis GmbH, Dusseldorf
Hong Kong	LexisNexis Hong Kong, Hong Kong
India	LexisNexis India, New Delhi
Italy	Giuffrè Editore, Milan
Japan	LexisNexis Japan, Tokyo
Malaysia	Malayan Law Journal Sdn Bhd, Kuala Lumpur
New Zealand	LexisNexis NZ Ltd, Wellington
Singapore	LexisNexis Singapore, Singapore
South Africa	LexisNexis Butterworths, Durban
USA	LexisNexis, Dayton, Ohio

First published in 1948

Published by LexisNexis
This is a Tolley title

A CIP Catalogue record for this book is available from the British Library.

ISBN for this volume: 9781474307840

Printed and bound by CPI Group (UK) Ltd, Croydon, CR0 4YY

Visit LexisNexis at www.lexisnexis.co.uk

Foreword

Since 1948, when George Whillans produced the first edition of his tax tables this publication, which still bears his name, has provided tax practitioners with concise, quick and easily accessible information about rates, allowances and other useful information across all the main taxes. This Finance Act 2018 edition includes all relevant measures in the 2018 Finance Act and other changes since the Budget edition was published in February. In particular, the additions include the HMRC exchanges rates at 31 March 2018 and the VAT fuel scale charges at 1 May 2018.

Andrew Hubbard

Editor-in-chief *Taxation Magazine*

Disclaimer

While every care has been taken to ensure the accuracy of this work, no responsibility for loss or damage occasioned to any person acting or refraining from action as a result of any statement in it can be accepted by the authors, editor or publisher.

Administration

Bank base rates

Period	Rate
from 2 November 2017	**0.50%**
4 August 2016–1 November 2017	0.25%
5 March 2009–3 August 2016	0.50%

Due dates for tax

Capital gains tax

Generally

Normally 31 January following end of year of assessment. (TMA 1970 s 59B)

Non-resident CGT disposals

30 days after the date of completion of sale if not registered for self-assessment. (TMA 1970 s 59AA)

(See also *Extended due dates* under **Income tax**, see p 2.)

Corporation tax

SEE TOLLEY'S TAX COMPUTATIONS **115.1**.

Must be paid electronically for tax due on or after 1 April 2011.

Generally (TMA 1970 s 59D)

9 months and 1 day after end of accounting period.

Instalments for large and very large companies (TMA 1970 s 59E; SI 1998/3175; SI 2017/1072)

A '**large company**' is any company whose augmented profits (see p 65) for the accounting period exceed £1.5m (but from 1 April 2019, do not exceed £20m, see below), both thresholds being proportionately reduced for accounting periods of less than 12 months and divided by 1 plus the number of any active 51% group companies (before 1 April 2015, associated companies). Any company which pays the bank levy is also a large company unless, from 1 April 2019, it exceeds the £20m threshold resulting in it being a very large company (see below). A company is not a large company in respect of an accounting period if its total liability for that period is not more than £10,000, or if its profits for an accounting period are £10m or less (both limits proportionately reduced for accounting periods of less than 12 months) and it was not a large company (or from 1 April 2019, a very large company, see below) in the 12 months preceding that accounting period. For most large companies (those with no ring fence profits) the amount of each instalment for a 12 month accounting period will be one quarter of its total liability. The amount of each instalment for any accounting period longer than 3 months but shorter than 12 months is calculated using the formula 3 x CTI/n where CTI is the amount of a company's total liability for that accounting period, and n is the number of months in the accounting period. The due dates of instalments are as follows:

1st instalment: 6 months and 13 days from start of accounting period (or date of final instalment if earlier);
2nd instalment: 3 months after 1st instalment, if length of accounting period allows;
3rd instalment: 3 months after 2nd instalment, if length of accounting period allows;
Final instalment: 3 months and 14 days from end of accounting period.

For accounting periods beginning on or after 1 April 2019 revised payment dates will apply to a '**very large company**' which is one whose augmented profits exceed £20m (proportionately reduced for accounting periods of less than 12 months and divided by 1 plus the number of any active 51% group companies). A company is not a very large company in respect of an accounting period if its total liability for that period is not more than £10,000 (proportionately reduced for accounting periods of less than 12 months). The due dates of instalments are as follows:

1st instalment: 2 months and 13 days from start of accounting period (or date of final instalment if earlier);
2nd instalment: 3 months after 1st instalment, if length of accounting period allows;
3rd instalment: 3 months after 2nd instalment, if length of accounting period allows;
Final instalment: 3 months after 3rd instalment, if length of accounting period allows.

Close companies: tax on loans or benefits to participators

9 months and 1 day after the end of the accounting period. To be included in instalment payments for large and very large companies (see above) (TMA 1970 s 59E(11)).

Income tax

SEE TOLLEY'S TAX COMPUTATIONS **26.1**.

Payments on account (TMA 1970 s 59A; SSCBA 1992 ss 11A, 16; SI 1996/1654)

A payment on account is required where a taxpayer was assessed to income tax in the immediately preceding year to an amount exceeding the amount of tax deducted at source in respect of that year (subject to a de minimis limit, see below).

The payment on account (which includes Class 4 NIC) is made in 2 equal instalments due on:

(a) 31 January during the year of assessment, and
(b) 31 July in the following year of assessment.

No payments on account are required where either:

(a) the aggregate of the liability (including Class 4 NIC) for the preceding year (net of tax deducted at source) is less than £1,000; or
(b) more than 80% of the taxpayer's income tax and Class 4 NIC liability for the preceding year was met by tax deducted at source (including PAYE).

Note that payments on account are not required for Class 2 NIC.

Final payment (TMA 1970 s 59B, Sch 3ZA)

Balance of income tax due for a year of assessment (after deducting payments on account, tax deducted at source if any and (before 2016–17) credits in respect of dividends, etc) is due on:

31 January following end of year of assessment (TMA 1970 s 59B(4)).

From 2015–16 Class 2 NIC is also due through the self-assessment system no later than 31 January following end of year of assessment.

Extended due dates:

(a) If a taxpayer has given notice of liability within 6 months of the end of the year of assessment, but a notice to make a return is not given until after 31 October following the end of the year of assessment, the due date is 3 months after the notice is given (TMA 1970 s 59B(3)).
(b) If tax is payable as a result of a taxpayer's notice of amendment, an HMRC notice of correction or an HMRC notice of closure following enquiry, in each case given less than 30 days before the due date (or the extended due date at (a) above), the due date is on or before the day following the end of a 30-day period beginning on the day on which the notice is given (TMA 1970 s 59B(5), Sch 3ZA).
(c) If an assessment other than a self-assessment or simple assessment is made, tax payable under the assessment is due on the day following the end of a 30-day period beginning on the day on which notice of the assessment is given (TMA 1970 s 59B(6)).

The extensions under (b) and (c) do *not* alter the due date for *interest purposes* (see p 4).

Final tax payable under simple assessment:

(a) If a taxpayer is given notice of the simple assessment after 31 October following the end of the year of assessment, the due date is 3 months after the notice is given (TMA 1970 s 59BA(4)).
(b) In any other case, due date is no later than 31 January following end of year of assessment (TMA 1970 s 59BA(5)).

Harmonised interest regime see p 4.
Interest on overdue tax see p 5.
Interest on overpaid tax see p 5.
Penalties see p 12.
Remission of tax see p 6.

Inheritance tax

(IHTA 1984 s 226)

Chargeable transfers other than on death, made between:

6 April and 30 September	–	30 April in next year.
1 October and 5 April	–	6 months after end of month in which chargeable transfer is made.

Relevant property settlements periodic and exit charges

– 6 months after end of month in which chargeable event occurs. (For chargeable events before 6 April 2014, tax is payable as for chargeable transfers other than on death, see above).

Chargeable events following conditional exemption for heritage etc property and charge on disposal of trees or underwood before the second death:

– 6 months after end of month in which chargeable event occurs.

***Transfers on death*:**

Earlier of	(*a*)	6 months after end of month in which death occurs, and
	(*b*)	delivery of account by personal representatives.

***Tax or extra tax becoming payable on death*:**

Chargeable transfers and potentially exempt transfers within 7 years of death.

– 6 months after end of month in which death occurs.

PAYE and NIC

(SSCBA 1992 ss 11A, 15; SI 2001/1004; SI 2003/2682)

Employer's tax and Class 1 NIC payable under PAYE	In-year payments – 14 days after end of tax month or quarter to which it relates (extended to 17 days where payments are made by electronic means). Final payment for tax year – 19 April following deduction year (extended to 22 April where payments are made by electronic means).
Class 1A NIC	19 July following year in which contributions due (extended to 22 July where payments are made by electronic means).
PAYE settlement agreement and Class 1B NIC	19 October following year to which agreement relates (extended to 22 October where payments are made by electronic means).
Class 2 NIC	For 2015–16 onwards contributions based on an annual liability are due through the self-assessment system no later than 31 January following the tax year[1]. Previously due in 2 instalments on 31 January and 31 July. From April 2014 HMRC could collect outstanding Class 2 by an adjustment to PAYE codes.
Class 4 NIC	See under income tax on p 2.

[1] Those who do not pay through self-assessment will be sent a bill by HMRC. Voluntary payments may still be made. Class 2 will be abolished from April 2019, see p 117.

Paying HMRC

HMRC have a number of bank accounts. The respective accounts to which payments should be made from UK bank accounts for the main taxes are as follows:

Tax	Account name	Sort code	Account number
Self-assessment/ capital gains tax	HMRC Shipley	08 32 10	12001020
Self-assessment/ capital gains tax	HMRC Cumbernauld	08 32 10	12001039
Corporation tax	HMRC Shipley	08 32 10	12001020
Corporation tax	HMRC Cumbernauld	08 32 10	12001039
PAYE/ Class 1/ Class 1A NIC	HMRC Cumbernauld	08 32 10	12001039
Class 2 NIC[1]	HMRC NICO	08 32 20	12001004

[1] If taxpayer does not pay through self-assessment.

[2] Where both Shipley and Cumbernauld can apply and a taxpayer does not know which accounts office he normally pays, generally he should send payment to Cumbernauld. For details of other taxes see the list of taxes at www.gov.uk/topic/dealing-with-hmrc/paying-hmrc.

Harmonised interest regime

SEE TOLLEY'S TAX COMPUTATIONS **13.1, 222.1**.

(FA 2009 ss 101–104, Schs 53–54A; SI 2011/701; SI 2011/2391; SI 2013/280; SI 2013/2472; SI 2014/992; SI 2014/3269; SI 2015/974)

A harmonised interest regime is being phased in for all taxes and duties and currently applies to:

- income and capital gains tax self-assessment amounts including penalties from 31 October 2011,
- CIS late return penalties from 6 October 2011,
- tax agent dishonest conduct penalties from 1 April 2013,
- annual tax on enveloped dwellings and penalties from 1 October 2013,
- PAYE and CIS in-year amounts for 2014–15 onwards from 6 April 2014 (although from 6 October 2014 for in-year late filing penalties for employers with 50 or more employees, 6 March 2015 for in-year late filing penalties for employers with fewer than 50 employees, and 6 April 2015 for in-year late payment penalties),
- stamp duty reserve tax and penalties from 1 January 2015,
- diverted profits tax and penalties from 1 April 2015,
- Class 2 NIC from 6 April 2015.

For annual PAYE payments such as Classes 1A and 1B NIC HMRC will continue to charge interest on any amount which remains unpaid after the due date.

Appointed Day Orders will be made in due course to align the treatment of interest and penalties for inheritance tax purposes with other taxes (F(No 2)A 2015 s 15).

The measure provides for differential interest charged and paid by HMRC to be based around the Bank of England base rate. The current late payment rate is:

Late payment interest	*Rate*
from 21 November 2017	**3.00%**
23 August 2016–20 November 2017	2.75%
29 September 2009–22 August 2016	3.00%

The current repayment rate is:

Repayment interest	*Rate*
from 29 September 2009	**0.50%**

Late payment interest runs from the start date to the date of payment. The start date is generally the date on which the amount becomes due and payable, but special rules apply as follows:

Where an amount is due as a result of—

(a) an amendment or correction to an assessment or self-assessment; or
(b) an HMRC assessment in place of, or in addition to, an assessment made by the taxpayer; or
(c) an HMRC assessment in place of an assessment which ought to have been made by the taxpayer,

the start date is the date it would have been if the original assessment or self-assessment had been complete and accurate and made on the date (if any) by which it was required to be made, and the tax had been due and payable as a result of the original assessment or self-assessment.

Repayment interest runs from the start date until the date the payment or repayment is made. The start date in the case of an amount paid to HMRC is the later of—

(i) the date the amount was paid to HMRC; and
(ii) the date on which the amount became due and payable to HMRC (in a case where the amount has been paid in connection with a liability to make a payment to HMRC, and it is to be repaid by them).

The start date, in the case of an amount which has not been paid to HMRC and which is payable by virtue of a return or a claim having been submitted, is the later of—

(1) the date (if any) on which the return or claim was required to be submitted; and
(2) the date on which the return or claim was submitted.

The start date in the case of the carry back of losses or averaging claims is 31 January following the *later* tax year in relation to the claim.

Interest on overdue tax

See p 4 regarding the **harmonised interest regime** and the taxes to which this currently applies. The provisions on interest on overdue tax continue to apply to taxes where the harmonised interest regime does not yet apply, and applied to other taxes before the transition to the harmonised regime.

NICs Class 1, 1A, 1B, 4, stamp duty, stamp duty reserve tax and stamp duty land tax

These provisions apply to Class 1 NIC before 6 April 2014, and stamp duty reserve tax payable before 1 January 2015 only. The rules under FA 2009 ss 101 and 103 on p 4 have effect thereafter.

Interest runs from the due date (see p 2 for income tax and p 1 for capital gains tax) to the date of payment, on the amount outstanding. Interest is payable gross and is not tax deductible.

Period	*Rate*
from 21 November 2017	**3.00%**
23 August 2016–20 November 2017	2.75%
29 September 2009–22 August 2016	3.00%

Corporation tax

SEE TOLLEY'S TAX COMPUTATIONS 110.1.

Interest runs from the due date (see p 1) to the date of payment. For instalment payments by large and, for accounting periods beginning on or after 1 April 2019, very large companies, a special rate of interest runs from the due date to the earlier of the date of payment and nine months after the end of the accounting period (after which the normal rate applies).

Corporation tax self-assessment

Period	*Normal rate*
from 21 November 2017	**3.00%**
23 August 2016–20 November 2017	2.75%
29 September 2009–22 August 2016	3.00%

Period	*Special rate for instalment payments (except where still unpaid nine months after end of accounting period)*
from 13 November 2017	**1.50%**
15 August 2016–12 November 2017	1.25%
16 March 2009–14 August 2016	1.50%

Income tax on company payments

Period	*Rate*
from 21 November 2017	**3.00%**
23 August 2016–20 November 2017	2.75%
29 September 2009–22 August 2016	3.00%

Inheritance tax[1]

SEE TOLLEY'S TAX COMPUTATIONS 312.1 ONWARDS.

Interest runs from the due date[2] (see p 2) to the date of payment.

Period	*Rate*
from 21 November 2017	**3.00%**
23 August 2016–20 November 2017	2.75%
29 September 2009–22 August 2016	3.00%

1 Appointed Day Orders will be made in due course to align the treatment of interest and penalties for inheritance tax purposes with other taxes.

2 Where higher IHT is payable as a result of IHTA 1984 Sch A1 or the F(No 2)A 2017 domicile changes, interest runs from the last day of December 2017 if later than normal payment date.

Interest on overpaid tax

See p 4 regarding the **harmonised interest regime** and the taxes to which this currently applies. The provisions on interest on overpaid tax continue to apply to taxes where the harmonised interest regime does not yet apply, and applied to other taxes before the transition to the harmonised regime.

NICs Class 1, 1A, 1B, 4, stamp duty, stamp duty reserve tax and stamp duty land tax

These provisions apply to Class 1 NIC before 6 April 2014, and stamp duty reserve tax payable before 1 January 2015 only. The rules under FA 2009 ss 101 and 103 on p 4 have effect thereafter.

Calculated as simple interest on the amount of tax repaid. The supplement is tax-free.

Period	*Rate*
from 29 September 2009	**0.50%**

Inheritance tax

(IHTA 1984 s 235)

Repayments of inheritance tax or interest paid carries interest *from* the date of payment *to* the date on which the order for repayment is issued.

Period	*Rate*
from 29 September 2009	**0.50%**

Appointed Day Orders will be made in due course to align the treatment of interest and penalties for inheritance tax purposes with other taxes.

Companies

Corporation tax self-assessment

SEE TOLLEY'S TAX COMPUTATIONS 109.1.

Normal rates

Rates on overpaid corporation tax in respect of periods after normal due date (SI 1989/1297 reg 3BB).

Period	*Rate*
from 29 September 2009	**0.50%**

Special rates

For instalment payments by large and, for accounting periods beginning on or after 1 April 2019, very large companies and early payments by other companies, a special rate of interest runs from the date the excess arises (but not earlier than the due date of the first instalment) to the earlier of the date the repayment order is issued and nine months and one day after the end of the accounting period, after which the normal rate of interest (as above) applies.

Rates on overpaid instalment payments and on corporation tax paid early (but not due by instalments).

Period	*Rate*
from 21 September 2009	**0.50%**

Direct recovery of debt

(F(No 2)A 2015 Sch 8)

From 18 November 2015 HMRC are able to secure payment of tax and tax credit debts directly from debtors' bank and building society accounts (including funds held in cash in Individual Savings Accounts) that have a minimum aggregate credit of £5,000. HMRC will only take action against debtors who owe over £1,000 of debt, and will only put a hold on the funds in the affected account up to the value of the debt. Safeguards in place include a face-to-face visit with an HMRC officer, a specialist unit to deal with cases involving the vulnerable, and availability of appeal to the County Court.

Remission of tax

(Concession A19)

By concession, arrears of tax may be waived if they result from HMRC's failure to make proper and timely use of information supplied by the taxpayer or, where it affects the taxpayer's coding, by his or her employer. The concession also applies to information supplied by the Department for Work and Pensions affecting the taxpayer's entitlement to a retirement, disability or widow's pension. The concession only applies where the taxpayer could reasonably have believed that his or her affairs were in order and (unless the circumstances are exceptional) where the taxpayer is notified of the arrears more than 12 months after the end of the tax year in which HMRC received the information indicating that more tax was due.

Special relief

(TMA 1970 Sch 1AB para 3A; FA 1998 Sch 18 para 51BA)

A statutory 'special relief' is available which allows HMRC to give effect to a claim for repayment or discharge of an amount of tax that a person is liable to pay, but which the person believes is not due or, if it has been paid, was not due, where the usual time limits for such relief have expired. Relief is only available to taxpayers in receipt of an income tax or corporation tax self-assessment determination made by HMRC in the absence of a self-assessment return being submitted, and where the following specific conditions are met: (a) it would be unconscionable for HMRC to seek to recover the amount or to refuse to repay it if it has already been paid; (b) that the person's tax affairs are otherwise up to date, or arrangements have been put in place to HMRC's satisfaction, to bring them up to date as far as possible; and (c) the person has not previously claimed special relief, or its concessionary predecessor equitable liability, whether or not such a claim was successful. This latter condition may be waived in exceptional circumstances. There is no time limit for claiming the relief.

Certificates of tax deposit

From 23 November 2017 the scheme is closed for new purchases, but existing certificates will be honoured until 23 November 2023. Any certificates remaining after this date should be submitted to HMRC for refund. HMRC will seek to repay the balance of any certificate remaining unpaid and unclaimed. If they are unable to contact the current certificate holder after reasonable effort the balance will be forfeited.

Certificates were available to purchase by individuals, partnerships, individual partners, trustees, personal representatives and companies for the payment of income tax, Class 4 NIC, capital gains tax, inheritance tax, or petroleum revenue tax, but not payment of corporation tax, PAYE liabilities, or tax payable by companies etc on disposals of high value UK residential property, see p 65. Interest is paid gross and is chargeable to tax. It will only be paid for the first six years of a deposit. A deposit bears interest for the first year at the rate in force at the time of the deposit and for each subsequent year at the rate in force on the anniversary of the deposit. HMRC provide an interest calculator tool on their website.

Date of deposit	*Amount*	*Held for (mths in yr)*	*Pay't of tax %*	*Cashed %*
6.3.09–	Under £100,000	No limit	0.00	0.00
	£100,000 or over	under 1	0.00	0.00
		1–under 3	0.75	0.25
		3–under 6	0.75	0.25
		6–under 9	0.75	0.25
		9–12	0.75	0.25

Student loan deductions

Plan 1

	Percentage of income above the threshold	Threshold
2018–19	**9%**	**£18,330 per year £1,527 per month £352 per week**
2017–18	9%	£17,775 per year £1,481 per month £341 per week
2016–17	9%	£17,495 per year £1,457 per month £336 per week
2015–16	9%	£17,335 per year £1,444 per month £333 per week
2014–15	9%	£16,910 per year £1,409.16 per month £325.19 per week
2013–14	9%	£16,365 per year £1,363.75 per month £314.71 per week

Plan 2

	Percentage of income above the threshold	Threshold
2018–19	**9%**	**£25,000 per year £2,083 per month £480 per week**
2017–18	9%	£21,000 per year £1,750 per month £403 per week
2016–17	9%	£21,000 per year £1,750 per month £403 per week

Filing dates

Corporation tax

SEE TOLLEY'S TAX COMPUTATIONS 118.2.

(FA 1998 Sch 18 paras 14, 15; SI 2003/282 reg 3(2A))

The return must be filed on the latest of the following dates—

(a) 12 months from the end of the period for which the return is made;
(b) where the company makes up its accounts for a period not exceeding 18 months, 12 months from the end of that period;
(c) where the company makes up its accounts for a period exceeding 18 months, 30 months from the start of that period;
(d) 3 months from the date of issue of the notice requiring the return.

All company returns must be filed online. Computations and, in most cases, accounts must be submitted in iXBRL format. Micro-entities have the option to file simplified accounts.

Income tax and capital gains tax

(TMA 1970 ss 8, 8A, 12AA; SI 2003/2682 reg 186)

Basic position for paper returns.	On or before 31 October following end of tax year.
Basic position for electronic returns.	On or before 31 January following end of tax year.
Paper return and notice to file return issued after 31 July but on or before 31 October following end of tax year.	Within 3 months of date of notice.
Electronic return and notice to file return issued after 31 July but on or before 31 October following end of tax year.	On or before 31 January following end of tax year.
Paper or electronic return and notice to file return issued after 31 October following end of tax year.	Within 3 months of date of notice.
Paper return and taxpayer wishes tax underpayment of less than £3,000 to be coded out.	On or before 31 October following end of tax year.
Electronic return and taxpayer wishes tax underpayment of less than £3,000 to be coded out.	Before 31 December following end of tax year.

Non-resident capital gains tax

(TMA 1970 s 12ZB)

30 days after the date of completion of sale via online NRCGT return.

Withdrawal of self-assessment notice

(TMA 1970 s 8B)

HMRC may withdraw a notice to file a self-assessment tax return in certain circumstances. The statutory power has effect for returns for 2012–13 onwards. Penalties for failure to make a return may be cancelled.

Simple assessment

(TMA 1970 ss 28H–28J, 31AA)

From 2016–17 HMRC may make an assessment of an individual's or trustee's income tax or capital gains tax liability without that person first being required to complete a self-assessment return. HMRC will instead assess their tax liability on the basis of information already held. The assessment notice must include details of the information used and the amount of tax due. The assessment may be appealed or queried without formal appeal. HMRC may withdraw a simple assessment notice.

Penalties

Penalties — modernised penalty regime

A modernised penalty regime is being rolled out to all taxes and duties with the exception of tax credits. The penalty regime in force in respect of various defaults is set out below.

Inaccuracy in return or other document

(FA 2007 Sch 24 para 1; SI 2017/355; SI 2017/259)

Applies to	***Commencement date***	***Penalty details***
IT, CGT, CT, VAT, CIS, NIC Classes 1 and 4[1]	Return periods starting 1 April 2008 where the return is due to be filed on or after 1 April 2009	Penalty based on potential lost revenue Careless inaccuracy — 30% Deliberate but not concealed — 70% Deliberate and concealed — 100%
IHT, SDLT, SDRT, other taxes, levies and duties (except tax credits)	Return periods starting 1 April 2009 where the return is due to be filed on or after 1 April 2010, or where the liability arises on or after 1 April 2010; for IHT in respect of deaths from 1 April 2009	*Reductions for disclosure*[3] Unprompted disclosure minimum penalties nil, 20% and 30% Prompted disclosure minimum penalties 15%, 35% and 50%
Class 1A NIC	2010–11 returns	
Corporation tax credit, return by registered pension scheme	Return periods starting 1 April 2009 where the return is due to be filed on or after 1 April 2010	
Annual tax on enveloped dwellings	2013–14 returns	
Non-resident CGT	6 April 2015	
Class 2 NIC	6 April 2015	
Apprenticeship levy	6 April 2017	
IT, CGT but offshore matter Extended to IHT and offshore transfers (see note)[2]	6 April 2011 (see note)[2]	Penalties above are increased by either 0%, 50% or 100% depending on the territory concerned (see table on p 13 for a list of territories in each category) Statutory limits for reductions for disclosure apply

1 From 2013–14 for RTI purposes an inaccuracy in any full payment submission can attract a penalty. HMRC may issue one penalty notice for multiple inaccuracy penalties in a year.

2 From 1 April 2016 the offshore penalty regime is amended to include IHT. From 1 April 2017 for IHT transfers and from 6 April 2016 otherwise, the regime also applies to domestic offences where the proceeds are hidden offshore. From a date to be appointed the territory classification system will be updated to reflect the jurisdictions that adopt the new global standard of automatic tax information exchange and there will be four levels of penalty instead of three.

3 In December 2017 HMRC announced a restriction on quality of disclosure penalty reductions where taxpayers take 'a significant period (normally 3 years) to correct or disclose the inaccuracy'. They will restrict the penalty range by 10% above the minimum before working out the reductions. It is not clear when the 3-year period starts.

Inaccuracy in return or other document as a result of third party providing incorrect (or withholding) information

(FA 2007 Sch 24 para 1A)

Applies to	***Commencement date***	***Penalty details***
IT, CGT, CT, VAT, IHT, CIS, NIC Classes 1 and 4, SDLT, SDRT, other taxes, levies and duties (except tax credits)	1 April 2009 where the return is due to be filed on or after 1 April 2010	100% of potential lost revenue Subject to reduction for disclosure as for inaccuracies above
Class 1A NIC	2010–11 returns	
Annual tax on enveloped dwellings	2013–14 returns	

Failure to notify HMRC of an error in an assessment (within 30 days)

(FA 2007 Sch 24 para 2)

Applies to	***Commencement date***	***Penalty details***
IT, CGT, CT, VAT, CIS, NIC Classes 1 and 4	1 April 2008 where the return is due to be filed on or after 1 April 2009	30% of potential lost revenue *Reductions for disclosure*[1] Unprompted disclosure minimum penalty nil Prompted disclosure minimum penalty 15%
IHT, SDLT, SDRT, other taxes, levies and duties (except tax credits)	1 April 2009 where the return is due to be filed on or after 1 April 2010	
Class 1A NIC	2010–11 returns	
Annual tax on enveloped dwellings	2013–14 returns	

1 In December 2017 HMRC announced a restriction on quality of disclosure penalty reductions where taxpayers take 'a significant period (normally 3 years) to correct or disclose the inaccuracy'. They will restrict the penalty range by 10% above the minimum before working out the reductions. It is not clear when the 3-year period starts.

Failure to notify chargeability (includes failure to register for VAT)

(FA 2008 Sch 41; SI 2017/259)

Applies to	***Commencement date***	***Penalty details***
IT, CGT, NIC Class 4[2]	2009–10	Penalty based on potential lost revenue Failure to notify — 30% Deliberate but not concealed — 70% Deliberate and concealed — 100% *Reductions for disclosure*[3] Unprompted disclosure minimum penalties nil (within 12 months late), 10% (more than 12 months late), 20% and 30% Prompted disclosure minimum penalties 15%, 35%, 50%
CT	Accounting periods ending on or after 31 March 2010	
Other taxes, levies and duties (not IHT, SDLT, SDRT)	Obligations arising on or after 1 April 2010	
Diverted profits tax	Accounting periods beginning on or after 1 April 2015	
IT, CGT but offshore matter Extended to offshore transfers (see note)[1]	6 April 2011 (see note)[1]	Penalties above are increased by either 0%, 50% or 100% depending on the territory concerned (see table on p 13 for a list of territories in each category) Statutory limits for reductions for disclosure apply

1 From 6 April 2016 the offshore penalty regime is amended to apply to domestic offences where the proceeds are hidden offshore. From a date to be appointed the territory classification system will be updated to reflect the jurisdictions that adopt the new global standard of automatic tax information exchange and there will be four levels of penalty instead of three.

2 Before 6 April 2015, there were similar provisions for Class 2 NIC but in separate legislation.

3 In December 2017 HMRC announced a restriction on quality of disclosure penalty reductions where taxpayers take 'a significant period (normally 3 years) to correct or disclose the inaccuracy'. They will restrict the penalty range by 10% above the minimum before working out the reductions. It is not clear when the 3-year period starts.

Failure to make returns on time

(FA 2009 Sch 55; FA 2010 Sch 1; SI 2003/2682; SI 2017/259)

Applies to	***Commencement date***	***Penalty details***
Bank Payroll Tax	31 August 2010	Initial penalty £100 Failure continues for more than three months — with notice — £10 per day for up to 90 days Six months late — greater of 5% of the tax due and £300 12 months late — same penalty as for 6 months late unless deliberately withholding the return Deliberate withholding of the return more than 12 months — 70% of tax due (minimum £300) Deliberate and concealed withholding of the return more than 12 months — 100% of tax due (minimum £300) *Reductions for disclosure*[7] Unprompted disclosure minimum penalty 20% and 30% Prompted disclosure minimum penalties 35% and 50%
IT, CGT, NIC Class 4[5]	6 April 2011	
Return by Registered Pension scheme	1 April 2011	
Annual tax on enveloped dwellings	2013–14 returns due 1 October 2013	
Stamp duty reserve tax	1 January 2015	
Class 2 NIC	6 April 2015	
Non-resident CGT[6]	26 March 2015	Penalties as above *except* the £10 daily penalty
CIS returns	6 October 2011	Initial penalty £100 After two months — £200 Six months late — greater of 5% of the tax due and £300 12 months late — same penalty as for 6 months late unless deliberately withholding the return Deliberate withholding of the return more than 12 months — 70% of tax due (minimum £1,500) Deliberate and concealed withholding of the return more than 12 months — 100% of tax due (minimum £3,000) *Reductions for disclosure*[7] Unprompted disclosure minimum penalty 20% and 30% Prompted disclosure minimum penalties 35% and 50% Special rules apply to the first returns made on registration for CIS so that the maximum total penalty that can apply for the initial and second fixed penalties for all such returns is £3,000. Subsequent tax-geared penalties may still be incurred. Where a CIS return only relates to persons registered for 'gross payment' a tax-geared penalty after 6 months or 12 months cannot apply. In these cases the person is liable to the fixed amount penalty.
PAYE Real Time Information. Failure during a tax month to make a return on or before the filing date (normally the date employee is paid)	6 October 2014 in relation to 2014–15 onwards for employers with 50 or more employees 6 March 2015 for employers with fewer than 50 employees[1]	First failure in a tax year — nil Second and subsequent failure in tax year 1–9 employees — £100 10–49 employees — £200 50–249 employees — £300 250 or more employees — £400[2] Failure continues for more than three months — with notice — 5% of tax due New employers only: A failure in the 'initial period'[3] — nil

continued on next page

Applies to	Commencement date	Penalty details
IT, CGT but offshore matter Extended to offshore transfers (see note)[4]	6 April 2011(see note)[4]	Penalties above for a return later than 12 months which has been withheld are increased by either 0%, 50% or 100% depending on the territory concerned (see table on p 13 for a list of territories in each category) Statutory limits for reductions for disclosure apply

1 For 2013–14 the rules in the PAYE table on p 15 under 'failure to submit year-end PAYE returns' apply.
2 Before 6 April 2018 employers did not incur penalties for delays of up to 3 days in filing PAYE information. HMRC take a more proportionate approach and concentrate on the more serious defaults on a risk-assessed basis.
3 A penalty will not be issued to a new employer if their first FPS is received within 30 days of making the first payment to their employee(s) (known as the 'initial period'). After that, normal penalties rules will apply if there is a failure to file on time.
4 From 6 April 2016 the offshore penalty regime is amended to apply to domestic offences where the proceeds are hidden offshore. From a date to be appointed the territory classification system will be updated to reflect the jurisdictions that adopt the new global standard of automatic tax information exchange and there will be four levels of penalty instead of three. Proposed to be extended to IHT failures.
5 HMRC will accept reasonable excuses from taxpayers who are generally compliant without further investigation.
6 Does not apply to an elective return made under TMA 1970 s 12ZBA. HMRC confirmed in June 2017 that they no longer issue the £10 daily penalty and such past penalties will be withdrawn.
7 In December 2017 HMRC announced a restriction on quality of disclosure penalty reductions where taxpayers take 'a significant period (normally 3 years) to correct or disclose the inaccuracy'. They will restrict the penalty range by 10% above the minimum before working out the reductions. It is not clear when the 3-year period starts.

Failure to pay tax on time

(FA 2009 Sch 56; FA 2010 Sch 1)

Applies to	Commencement date	Penalty details
PAYE[1], NIC Class 1, CIS[2], student loan deductions.	2010–11 liabilities (on a risk assessed basis at present)	Penalty based on number of late payments in a year applied to the amounts paid late 1 late payment — nil 2, 3, 4 late payments — 1% 5, 6, 7 late payments — 2% 8, 9, 10 late payments — 3% 11, 12 late payments — 4% Any amount paid 6 months late — 5% Any amount paid 12 months late — 5%
NIC Class 1A and 1B (SI 2001/1004 reg 67B)	2010–11	31 days late — 5% 6 months late — 5% 12 months late — 5%
Bank Payroll Tax	31 August 2010	1 day late — 5% 5 months late — 5% 11 months late — 5%
Tax due by Registered Pension schemes	Payments due 30 September 2010	31 days late — 5% 6 months late — 5% 12 months late — 5%
IT, CGT payable under self-assessment	6 April 2011 for self-assessment for 2010–11 onwards	31 days late — 5% 6 months late — 5% 12 months late — 5%
Annual tax on enveloped dwellings	2013–14 payments due 31 October 2013	31 days late — 5% 6 months late — 5% 12 months late — 5%
Stamp duty reserve tax	1 January 2015	31 days late — 5% 6 months late — 5% 12 months late — 5%
Class 2 NIC	6 April 2015	31 days late — 5% 6 months late — 5% 12 months late — 5%

1 It had been intended to charge automatic in-year late payment penalties for RTI from 6 April 2015 but HMRC confirmed that late payment penalties will continue to be reviewed on a risk-assessed basis rather than be issued automatically. From 2014–15 a 'tolerance' of £100 has been introduced for PAYE in-year late payment penalties. Where the difference between the total of all the amounts that the employer is due to pay to HMRC for a tax period and the amount paid over for that period is no more than £100 the employer will not be liable to a late payment penalty.
2 From 2014–15 a 'tolerance' of £100 has been introduced for CIS in-year late payment penalties. Where the

difference between the amount that the contractor is due to pay to HMRC for a tax period and the amount paid over for that period is no more than £100 the contractor will not be liable to a late payment penalty.

Offshore penalties — territory categories[8]

Category 1

Anguilla	Estonia	Japan	Poland
Aruba	Finland	Korea, South	Portugal[4]
Australia	France[2]	Latvia	Romania
Belgium	Germany	Liechtenstein (from 24 July 2013)[7]	Slovakia
Bulgaria	Greece	Lithuania	Slovenia
Canada	Guernsey[3]	Malta	Spain[5]
Cayman Islands	Hungary	Montserrat	Sweden
Cyprus	Ireland	Netherlands (not including Bonaire, Sint Eustatius and Saba)	Switzerland (from 24 July 2013)[7]
Czech Republic	Isle of Man	New Zealand (not including Tokelau)	USA (not including overseas territories and possessions)[6]
Denmark (not including Faroe Islands or Greenland)[1]	Italy	Norway	

1 Faroe Islands and Greenland are in Category 2.
2 Includes overseas Departments of France; the overseas collectivities of France are in Category 2.
3 Includes Alderney and Sark.
4 Includes Madeira and the Azores.
5 Includes the Canary Islands and other overseas territories of Spain.
6 The overseas territories and possessions of the USA are in Category 2.
7 SI 2013/1618 changed the level of penalties which may be charged for 14 specified countries from 24 July 2013. This is to reflect the entry into force of tax information exchange and enhanced tax cooperation agreements with those countries. Liechtenstein and Switzerland were previously in Category 2.
8 From a date to be set by Treasury Order the territory classification system will be updated to reflect the jurisdictions that adopt the new global standard of automatic tax information exchange.

Category 2

Territories not listed in Categories 1 or 3 (other than the UK) will be in Category 2. Crown Dependencies and Overseas Territories of the UK are, unless listed, in Category 2.

Category 3

Albania	Costa Rica	Kyrgyzstan	(Before 24 July 2013) *Saint Lucia*[2]
Algeria	Curaçao	Lebanon	(Before 24 July 2013) *Saint Vincent and the Grenadines*[2]
Andorra	Cuba	Macau[1]	(Before 24 July 2013) *San Marino*[2]
(Before 24 July 2013) *Antigua and Barbuda*[2]	Democratic People's Republic of Korea	Marshall Islands	Seychelles
(Before 24 July 2013) *Armenia*[2]	(Before 24 July 2013) *Dominica*[2]	(Before 24 July 2013) *Mauritius*[2]	Sint Maarten
(Before 24 July 2013) *Bahrain*[2]	Dominican Republic	Micronesia, Federated States of	Suriname
(Before 24 July 2013) *Barbados*[2]	Ecuador	Monaco	Syria
(Before 24 July 2013) *Belize*[2]	El Salvador	Nauru	Tokelau
Bonaire, Sint Eustatius and Saba	Gabon	Nicaragua	Tonga
Brazil	(Before 24 July 2013) *Grenada*[2]	Niue	Trinidad and Tobago
Cameroon	Guatemala	Palau	United Arab Emirates
Cape Verde	Honduras	Panama	Uruguay
Colombia	Iran	Paraguay	
Congo, Republic of	Iraq	Peru	
Cook Islands	Jamaica	(Before 24 July 2013) *Saint Kitts and Nevis*[2]	

1 China and Hong Kong are in Category 2.
2 SI 2013/1618 changed the level of penalties which may be charged for 14 specified countries from 24.7.13. This is to reflect the entry into force of tax information exchange and enhanced tax cooperation agreements with those countries. 12 of the countries highlighted in this table are in Category 2 from 24.7.13.

Offshore assets moves

(FA 2015 Sch 21; SI 2015/866; SI 2017/989)

Applies to	Commencement date	Penalty details
Offshore assets move from a specified territory to a non-specified territory where IT, CGT or IHT penalty under FA 2007 Sch 24 para 1, FA 2008 Sch 41, or FA 2009 Sch 55 above already applies for a deliberate failure (see table below for a list of specified territories)	27 March 2015	50% of amount of original penalty

Offshore assets move penalties — specified territories

Andorra	Curaçao	Japan	Qatar
Anguilla	Cyprus	Jersey	Romania
Antigua and Barbuda	Czech Republic	Korea, South	Russia
Argentina	Denmark	Kuwait[1]	Saint Kitts and Nevis
Aruba	Dominica	Latvia	Saint Lucia
Australia	Estonia	Lebanon[1]	Saint Vincent and the Grenadines
Austria	Faroe Islands	Liechtenstein	Samoa
The Bahamas	Finland	Lithuania	San Marino
Bahrain[1]	France	Luxembourg	Saudi Arabia
Barbados	Germany	Macau	Seychelles
Belgium	Ghana[1]	Malaysia	Singapore
Belize	Gibraltar	Malta	Sint Maarten
Bermuda	Greece	Marshall Islands	Slovak Republic
Brazil	Greenland	Mauritius	Slovenia
British Virgin Islands	Grenada	Mexico	South Africa
Brunei Darussalam	Guernsey	Monaco	Spain
Bulgaria	Hong Kong	Montserrat	Sweden
Canada	Hungary	Nauru[1]	Switzerland
Cayman Islands	Iceland	Netherlands (including Bonaire, Sint Eustatius and Saba)	Trinidad and Tobago
Chile	India	New Zealand (not including Tokelau)	Turkey
China	Indonesia	Niue	Turks and Caicos Islands
Colombia	Ireland	Norway	United Arab Emirates
Cook Islands[1]	Isle of Man	Panama[1]	Uruguay
Costa Rica	Israel	Poland	Vanuatu[1]
Croatia	Italy	Portugal	

1 Added from 3.11.17 when Albania and USA (excluding overseas territories and possessions) removed.

Deliberate enablers of offshore evasion or non-compliance

Applies to	Commencement date	Penalty details
A person who has enabled another person (Q) to commit a relevant offence in relation to IT, CGT or IHT, or to engage in conduct which makes Q liable to a penalty under FA 2007 Sch 24 para 1, FA 2008 Sch 41, FA 2009 Sch 55, or FA 2015 Sch 21 above, provided certain other conditions are met (FA 2016 Sch 20; SI 2016/1249).	1 January 2017	For penalties other than under FA 2015 Sch 21, the higher of— (a) 100% of potential lost revenue; and (b) £3,000 For penalties under FA 2015 Sch 21, the higher of— (a) 50% of potential lost revenue in respect of the original tax non-compliance; and (b) £3,000 Reductions available for disclosure

Asset-based penalty for offshore inaccuracies and failures

Applies to	Commencement date	Penalty details
A person to whom a CGT, IHT or asset-based IT penalty under FA 2007 Sch 24 para 1, FA 2008 Sch 41, or FA 2009 Sch 55 above already applies for a deliberate failure in relation to an offshore matter or transfer for a tax year in which the potential lost revenue exceeds £25,000 (FA 2016 Sch 22; SI 2017/277).	2016–17 onwards for CGT and IT Transfers of value on or after 1 April 2017 for IHT	The lower of— (a) 10% of the value of the asset; and (b) 10 times the offshore potential lost revenue (as defined) Reductions available for disclosure

Personal tax and corporation tax

Offence	*Penalty*
Failure to render return for corporation tax (FA 1998 Sch 18 paras 17, 18).	(*a*) £100 if up to three months late (£500 if previous two returns also late); (*b*) £200 if over three months late (£1,000 if previous two returns also late); (*c*) if failure continues, on final day for delivery of return or, if later, 18 months after return period, 10% of tax unpaid 18 months after return period (20% of tax unpaid at that date if return not made within two years of return period).
Failure to maintain records supporting personal and trustees' returns of partnership returns (TMA 1970 s 12B).	Up to £3,000.
Fraudulently or negligently making an incorrect statement in connection with a claim to reduce payments on account (TMA 1970 s 59A(6)).	Up to the amount (or additional amount) payable on account if a correct statement had been made.
Deliberately or recklessly failing to pay corporation tax due in respect of total liability of company for accounting period, or fraudulently or negligently making claim for repayment (TMA 1970 s 59E(4); SI 1998/3175 reg 13).	Penalty not exceeding twice amount of interest charged under SI 1998/3175 reg 7.

PAYE

Offence	*Penalty*
Failure to submit return P9D or P11D (benefits in kind) by due date (6 July following subsequent tax years) (TMA 1970 s 98(1)).	(*a*) Initial penalty up to £300; and (*b*) continuing penalty up to £60 for each day on which the failure continues.
Failure to submit information in connection with mandatory e-filing from 2004–05 onwards (SI 2003/2682 as amended by 2009/2029 reg 14).	Penalty based on number of employees not exceeding £3,000 for 1,000 or more employees.
Failure to submit returns P11D(b) (Class 1A NIC returns) by due date (6 July following tax year, but by concession until 31 March 2013, 19 July applied) (SI 2001/1004 reg 81(2)).	(*a*) First 12 months: penalty of £100 for each 50 employees (or part thereof) for each month the failure continues (but total penalty not to exceed total Class 1A NIC due); (*b*) failures exceeding 12 months: a penalty not exceeding the amount of Class 1A NIC due and unpaid after 19 July following tax year.

Offence	*Penalty*
Repealed provisions	
Failure to submit year-end PAYE returns final FPS, or EPS, or EYU as applicable, formerly P14 (individual end of year summary), P35 (annual return), P38 or P38A (supplementary returns for employees not on P35) by due date (19 May following tax year) (TMA 1970 s 98A).	(*a*) *First 12 months: penalty of £100 for each 50 employees (or part thereof) for each month the failure continues;* (*b*) *failures exceeding 12 months: penalty up to amount of PAYE or NIC due and unpaid after 19 April following tax year.* ***Replaced by penalty under FA 2009 Sch 55 from 6 October 2014 for 2014–15 onwards.***

Inheritance tax returns and information[1]

Offence	*Penalty*
Failure to deliver an account within 12 months of death (unless tax is less than £100 or there is a reasonable excuse) (IHTA 1984 s 245).	(*a*) Initial penalty of £100 (or the amount of tax payable if less); (*b*) further penalty up to £60 (where penalty determined by court or tribunal) for each day on which the failure continues; (*c*) if failure continues after six months after the date on which account is due, and proceedings not commenced, a further penalty of £100 (or amount of tax payable if less); and (*d*) if failure continues one year after end of the period in which account is due, and IHT is payable, a penalty not exceeding £3,000.
Failure to submit account or notify HMRC under IHTA 1984 s 218A if a disposition on a death is varied within six months of the variation and additional tax is payable (IHTA 1984 s 245A(1A), (1B)).	(*a*) Initial penalty up to £100; (*b*) further penalty up to £60 (if determined by court or tribunal) for each day on which the failure continues; (*c*) up to £3,000 if failure continues after 12 months from date notification is due.
Failure to provide information etc under IHTA 1984 s 218 concerning a settlement by a UK-domiciled settlor with non-resident trustees (IHTA 1984 s 245A(1)).	(*a*) Initial penalty up to £300; and (*b*) further penalty up to £60 (where penalty determined by court or tribunal) for each day on which the failure continues.
Person other than the taxpayer fraudulently or negligently delivering, furnishing or producing incorrect accounts, information or documents (IHTA 1984 s 247(3); FA 2004 s 295(4), (9)).	Up to £3,000.
Repealed provisions	
Incorrect return etc: Assisting in or inducing the delivery, furnishing or production of any account, information or document knowing it to be incorrect (IHTA 1984 s 247(4)).	*Up to £3,000.* ***Repealed with effect from 1 April 2013. See now tax agent dishonest conduct penalties under FA 2012 Sch 38 (see p 18).***

1 Appointed Day Orders will be made in due course to align the treatment of interest and penalties for inheritance tax purposes with other taxes.

Special returns of information

Offence	*Penalty*
Failure to comply with a notice to deliver a return or other document, furnish particulars or make anything available for inspection under any of the provisions listed in column 1 of the table in TMA 1970 s 98.	(*a*) Initial penalty up to £300; (*b*) further penalty up to £60 for each day on which the failure continues.
Failure to furnish information, give certificates or produce documents or records under any of the provisions listed in column 2 of the table in TMA 1970 s 98.	(*a*) Initial penalty up to £300; and (*b*) further penalty up to £60 for each day on which the failure continues.
Failure to deduct income tax at source from payments of interest or royalties under ITA 2007 Part 15 where the exemption does not apply and the company did not believe or could not reasonably have believed that it would apply (TMA 1970 s 98(4A)–(4E)).	(*a*) Initial penalty up to £3,000; and (*b*) further penalty up to £600 for each day on which the failure continues.
Failure of an employment intermediary to furnish information or produce documents or records (TMA 1970 s 98(4F)).	(*a*) Initial penalty up to £3,000; and (*b*) further penalty up to £600 for each day on which the failure continues.
Advance pricing agreements: Fraudulently or negligently making a false or misleading statement in the preparation of, or application to enter into, any advance pricing agreement (TIOPA 2010 s 227).	Penalty up to £10,000.
Declaration of non-UK residence: Fraudulently or negligently making a false or misleading declaration of non-UK residence to a deposit-taker or building society under ITA 2007 ss 858-861 (TMA 1970 s 99B).	Penalty up to £3,000.

Offence	*Penalty*
Repealed provisions	
Fraudulently or negligently delivering any incorrect document, information etc required under the above provisions (TMA 1970 s 99; SI 2013/279).	*Penalty up to £3,000.* ***Repealed with effect from 1 April 2013. See now tax agent dishonest conduct penalties under FA 2012 Sch 38 (see p 18).***

Other offences by taxpayers, agents etc

Offence	*Penalty*
GAAR. Applies to arrangements entered into after 15 September 2016 if a taxpayer (or in some cases another person) submits a return, claim, or other document on the basis that a tax advantage arises from the tax arrangements and all or part of that tax advantage is later counteracted under the GAAR (FA 2013 s 212A).	60% of the value of the counteracted advantage.
Serial tax avoiders. Use of any avoidance schemes in the warning period after the defeat of a relevant scheme. Applies to defeats incurred after 15 September 2016 (FA 2016 Sch 18).	(*a*) 20% of the tax understated or overclaimed for the first defeat of a scheme used during the warning period; (*b*) 40% for the second such defeat; and (*c*) 60% for any subsequent defeats.
Falsification of documents. Intentionally falsifying, concealing or destroying documents required under TMA 1970 ss 20A (repealed with effect from 1 April 2013) or 20BA (TMA 1970 s 20BB).	On summary conviction, a fine up to the statutory maximum (£5,000); on conviction on indictment, imprisonment for a term not exceeding two years or a fine or both.
European Economic Interest Groupings– Offences in connection with the supply of information:	
(i) failure to supply information	Initial penalty up to £300 per member of the Grouping at the time of failure and after direction by the tribunal: continuing penalty up to £60 per member of the Grouping at the end of the day for each day on which the failure continues.
(ii) fraudulent or negligent delivery of an incorrect return, accounts or statement (TMA 1970 s 98B).	Up to £3,000 for each member of the Grouping at the time of delivery.
Certificates of non-liability to income tax: Fraudulently or negligently giving such a certificate for the purposes of receiving interest gross on a bank or building society account, or failing to comply with an undertaking given in such a certificate (TMA 1970 s 99A).	Penalty up to £3,000.
Refusal to allow a deduction of income tax at source (TMA 1970 s 106).	£50.
Construction Industry Scheme: (post 31 March 2007 scheme) Making false statements etc for the purpose of obtaining a gross payment certificate (FA 2004 s 72).	Up to £3,000.
Fraudulent evasion of income tax (TMA 1970 s 106A).	On summary conviction, imprisonment for up to six months or a fine up to the statutory maximum (£5,000) or both; on conviction on indictment, imprisonment for up to seven years or a fine or both.
Enterprise investment scheme relief: Issue by a company of a certificate of approval for such relief fraudulently or negligently or without the authority of HMRC (ITA 2007 s 207).	Not exceeding £3,000.
Failure of a company to maintain records (other than those only required for claims, etc, or dividend vouchers and certificates of income tax deducted where other evidence is available) (FA 1998 Sch 18 para 23).	Penalty not exceeding £3,000.

continued on next page

Offence	*Penalty*
Failure to notify notifiable proposals or notifiable arrangements, or failure to notify the client of the relevant scheme reference number under the provisions of FA 2004 ss 306–319 (TMA 1970 s 98C; SI 2007/3104; SI 2008/1935; SI 2010/3019; FA 2013 s 223; FA 2014 s 284; FA 2015 Sch 17).	(*a*) Up to 31 December 2010 an initial penalty not exceeding £5,000; (i) From 1 January 2011 in the case of provisions under FA 2004 ss 308(1) and (3), 309(1) and 310 up to £600 per day in 'initial period' (but a tribunal can determine a higher penalty up to £1 million); (ii) From 1 January 2011 in the case of provisions in FA 2004 ss 312(2), 312A(2), 313ZA, 313A, 313B, 313C, from 17 July 2013 in the case of provisions in ss 312B and 313ZB, and from 26 March 2015 in the case of ss 310C, 312A(2A), 313ZC, and 316A, an initial penalty up to £5,000. Where a disclosure order is made the amount in (i) above is increased up to £5,000 per day that failure continues from ten days after the order is made. (*b*) a continuing penalty not exceeding £600 for each day on which the failure continues after imposition of initial penalty. Where a disclosure order is made the amount is increased up to £5,000 per day that failure continues from ten days after the order is made.
Failure to notify scheme reference number etc under FA 2004 s 313(1); for second failure, occurring within three years from the date on which the first failure began; for subsequent failures, occurring within three years from the date on which the previous failure began. (TMA 1970 s 98C; FA 2004 s 315(1)).	Penalty not exceeding £5,000[1] in respect of each scheme to which the failure relates; penalty not exceeding £7,500[1] in respect of each scheme to which the failure relates; penalty not exceeding £10,000[1] in respect of each scheme to which the failure relates.
Failure to comply with HMRC investigatory powers under FA 2008 Sch 36. Failure to comply with an information notice within FA 2008 Sch 36 Pt 1 or deliberately obstructing an HMRC officer in the course of an inspection of business premises under FA 2008 Sch 36 Pt 2 which has been approved by the First-tier Tribunal. Applies to IT (including PAYE and CIS), CT, CGT, VAT and certain foreign taxes with effect from 1 April 2009. Extended to IHT, SDLT and other taxes from 1 April 2010, to Bank Payroll Tax (BPT) from 31 August 2010, to ATED from 17 July 2013; to pension scheme registration applications from 17 July 2014; and to Diverted Profits Tax from 1 April 2015.	(*a*) an initial penalty of £300; (*b*) if failure/obstruction continues, a further penalty up to £60 per day; (*c*) if failure/obstruction continues after penalty under (*a*) imposed, a tax-related amount determined by the Upper Tribunal.
Carelessly or deliberately providing inaccurate information or an inaccurate document in response to an information notice.	Up to £3,000 per inaccuracy.
Failure of a senior accounting officer to ensure a company maintains appropriate tax accounting arrangements (FA 2009 Sch 46).	£5,000.
Failure of a senior accounting officer to provide a certificate stating whether the company had appropriate tax accounting arrangements (FA 2009 Sch 46).	£5,000.
Failure to notify Commissioners of name of senior accounting officer (FA 2009 Sch 46).	£5,000.
Failure of a third party to notify the contact details of a debtor (FA 2009 Sch 49).	£300.
Failure to comply with data-holder notice (FA 2011 Sch 23).	(*a*) an initial penalty of £300. (*b*) if failure continues, a further penalty up to £60 per day. (*c*) increased daily penalty of up to £1,000 to be set by Tribunal if notice still not complied with within 30 days of a daily penalty being notified.
Tax agent failure to comply with file access notice (FA 2012 Sch 38).	(*a*) an initial penalty of £300. (*b*) if failure continues, a further penalty up to £60 per day.
Tax agent engaging in dishonest conduct (FA 2012 Sch 38).	£5,000 minimum to £50,0000 maximum subject to the quality of disclosure and compliance with any access notice, with possible special reduction of £5,000 penalty to nil at HMRC's discretion.
Failure to keep records for the purposes of the annual tax on enveloped dwellings (FA 2013 Sch 33).	Up to £3,000
Corrective action not taken in response to follower notice (FA 2014 s 208).	50% of value of the denied advantage (20% for relevant partners). May be reduced for co-operation.

Offence	Penalty
Failure to pay accelerated payment (FA 2014 s 226).	(*a*) Initial penalty of 5% of any amount unpaid at end of payment period (or where the accelerated payment relates to an instalment of IHT, 5% of any amount unpaid by the later due date of that instalment if applicable). (*b*) Further penalty of 5% of any amount unpaid after 5 months. (*c*) Further penalty of 5% of any amount unpaid after 11 months.
Failure of monitored promoter of a tax avoidance scheme, or their intermediary, to comply with various duties to notify clients, provide information or produce documents (FA 2014 Sch 35 para 2).	(*a*) Initial maximum penalty of £5,000, £7,500, £10,000, or £1,000,000 depending on failure. (*b*) Further daily penalty for each day on which failure continues of up to £10,000 where the maximum penalty could have been £1,000,000, or otherwise, £600.
Provision of inaccurate information or document by a monitored promoter of a tax avoidance scheme when complying with an information duty (FA 2014 Sch 35 para 4).	Maximum penalty of £5,000, £10,000, or £1,000,000 depending on duty being complied with.
Concealing, destroying etc documents required to be produced in connection with a monitored promoter of a tax avoidance scheme (FA 2014 s 280).	On summary conviction, a fine; on conviction on indictment, imprisonment for up to two years or a fine or both.
Failure of a company to provide a return in respect of a SIP, SAYE option, CSOP, EMI or other employee share scheme (ITEPA 2003 Sch 2 para 81C; Sch 3 para 40C; Sch 4 para 28C; Sch 5 para 57B; s 421JC).	(*a*) Initial penalty of £100. (*b*) Further penalty of £300 if failure continues for 3 months. (*c*) Further penalty of £300 if failure continues for 6 months. (*d*) Further penalty of £10 for each day that failure continues beyond 9 months (with notice).
Inaccurate return provided by a company, or return not filed electronically as required in respect of a SIP, SAYE option, CSOP, EMI or other employee share scheme (ITEPA 2003 Sch 2 para 81E; Sch 3 para 40E; Sch 4 para 28E; Sch 5 para 57C; s 421JD).	Up to £5,000.
Failure of a company to comply with the rules in respect of a SIP, SAYE option, or CSOP scheme (ITEPA 2003 Sch 2 para 81H–81I; Sch 3 para 40H–41I; Sch 4 para 28H–28I).	If scheme does not comply at all, penalty not exceeding twice the tax and NIC HMRC estimate has been 'saved'. Otherwise, up to £5,000.
Failure of a company to provide to HMRC a declaration under ITEPA 2003 Sch 5 para 44(6) by individual to whom an EMI option is granted (ITEPA 2003 Sch 5 para 57A).	£500.
A social enterprise fraudulently or negligently issuing a compliance certificate or statement (ITA 2007 s 257PD).	Up to £3,000.
Failure by a qualifying company or partnership, or by the head of a UK group of companies or by the head of a UK sub-group of a foreign group of companies to publish the company's, partnership's, group's or sub-group's tax strategy or to make it freely available after publication. Applies to financial years beginning on or after 15 September 2016 (FA 2016 Sch 19).	(*a*) Initial penalty of up to £7,500. (*b*) further penalty of £7,500 if failure continues for 6 months; and (*c*) further penalty of £7,500 for every subsequent month that failure continues.
Enablers of defeated tax avoidance. Penalty applies to persons who enable the use of abusive tax avoidance arrangements which are later defeated (F(No 2)A 2017 Sch 16).	The amount of consideration received or receivable by enabler for enabling the tax avoidance arrangements.
Failure to correct on or by 30 September 2018 irregularities in relation to undeclared past UK IT, CGT and IHT liabilities involving offshore interests which exist at 5 April 2017 (F(No 2)A 2017 Sch 18).	200% of the offshore potential lost revenue (PLR). Reductions apply for disclosure but minimum penalty will be 100% of PLR.
Failure to provide loan charge information for income provided through third parties (F(No 2) A 2017 Schs 11 and 12).	(*a*) an initial penalty of £300. (*b*) if failure continues, a further penalty up to £60 per day up to a maximum of 90 days.
Inaccuracy in information or document relating to loan charge for income provided through third parties (F(No 2)A 2017 Schs 11 and 12).	Up to £3,000 per inaccuracy.
Failure to amend a company tax return in relation to corporate interest restriction (TIOPA 2010 Sch 7A).	£500.
Failure by the lead trustee to register a trust before the trust deadline, or to tell HMRC about any changes to the registration.	(*a*) £100 if registered within up to 3 months of deadline[2]. (*b*) £200 if registered between 3 to 6 months of deadline. (*c*) higher of £300 or 5% of total tax liability in relevant year if registered more than 6 months after deadline.

Offence	Penalty
Repealed provisions	
Assisting in the delivery of incorrect returns, accounts or information (TMA 1970 s 99; SI 2013/279).	*Penalty up to £3,000.* ***Repealed with effect from 1 April 2013. See now tax agent dishonest conduct penalties under FA 2012 Sch 38 on p 18.***

1 Before 26 March 2015 the penalties were fixed amounts of £100, £500, and £1,000 respectively.

2 Penalties not issued automatically and to be reviewed on a case by case basis. Penalties relating to notification of changes will only apply once facility to notify has been set up.

Mitigation of penalties

HMRC have discretion to mitigate or entirely remit any penalty or to stay or compound any penalty proceedings (TMA 1970 s 102).

Interest on penalties

Penalties under TMA 1970 Parts II (ss 7–12B), IV (ss 28A–43B), VA (ss 59A–59D) and X (ss 93–107), and FA 1998 Sch 18 carry interest at the prescribed rate (see p 5): TMA 1970 s 103A. This applies to penalties in relation to promoters of tax avoidance schemes from 17 July 2014. For interest which applies to penalties under the **harmonised interest regime** see p 4.

Publishing details of deliberate tax defaulters

From 1 April 2010 HMRC have the power to publish the names and details of taxpayers who are penalised for deliberate defaults leading to a loss of tax of more than £25,000. From 1 April 2017 the power applies to certain individuals who control a body corporate or a partnership, or who are trustees of a settlement, which is penalised for such deliberate defaults relating to an offshore matter or transfer, but only where the individual would obtain a tax advantage from the default. From the same date, only taxpayers who make full unprompted disclosures are protected (FA 2009 s 94; SI 2017/261).

Publishing details of deliberate enablers of offshore evasion or non-compliance

From 1 January 2017 HMRC have the power to publish the names and details of enablers of offshore tax evasion or non-compliance who are found liable for a penalty and the potential lost revenue involved exceeds £25,000. They may also publish information about a person who has been found to have incurred 5 or more penalties in any 5-year period (FA 2016 Sch 20; SI 2016/1249).

Publishing details of serial tax avoiders

Broadly from 15 September 2016 HMRC have the power to publish the names and details of serial tax avoiders if they are given three warning notices in respect of schemes used while in a warning period and which are defeated (FA 2016 Sch 18).

Publishing details of persistently uncooperative large businesses

HMRC have the power to publish the names and details of a large company, partnership, UK group of companies, or UK sub-group of a foreign group of companies which is subject to a confirmed special measures notice. The provisions apply in relation to the body or entity's first financial year and subsequent years following 15 September 2016 (FA 2016 Sch 19).

Publishing details of enablers of defeated abusive tax avoidance arrangements

HMRC have the power to publish the names and details of persons who have been assessed to a penalty which has become final in relation to enabling defeated tax avoidance arrangements, provided they have incurred at least 50 other such penalties, or total penalties incurred including the current one will exceed £25,000 (F(No 2)A 2017 Sch 16).

Criminal offence for offshore matters

From 7 October 2017 a criminal offence which does not require the need to prove intent will apply for failing to accurately declare taxable offshore income and gains. The specific offences are failure to notify, failure to deliver a return and making an inaccurate return. It will apply where the loss of tax exceeds £25,000 (TMA 1970 ss 106B–106H; SI 2017/970; SI 2017/988).

Corporate offence of failure to prevent criminal facilitation of tax evasion

From 30 September 2017 an offence will be committed where a body corporate or partnership fails to prevent an associated person (broadly an employee, agent or other person who performs services for them) criminally facilitating the evasion of a tax in the UK or abroad (Criminal Finances Act 2017 ss 44–52; SI 2017/739).

Tax agent dishonest conduct

From 1 April 2013, in addition to the penalties listed above, HMRC have the power to publish names and details of tax agents who incur penalties for dishonest conduct over £5,000 (FA 2012 Sch 38; SI 2013/279).

Failure to provide security

A person who fails to comply with a requirement imposed under the PAYE regulations to give security or further security is liable on summary conviction to a fine not exceeding level 5 on the standard scale (£5,000) (ITEPA 2003 s 684(4A)).

Time limits for claims and elections

Whenever possible, a claim or election must be made on the tax return or by an amendment to the return (TMA 1970 s 42 and FA 1998 Sch 18 paras 9, 10, 67 and 79). Exceptions to this general rule are dealt with in TMA 1970 Sch 1A. Except where another period is expressly prescribed, a claim for relief in respect of income tax and capital gains tax must be made within four years after the end of the tax year. (TMA 1970 s 43(1); FA 2008 Sch 39 para 12.) The time limit for claims by companies is four years from the end of the accounting period to which it relates (FA 1998 Sch 18 para 55; FA 2008 Sch 39 para 45). The tables below set out some of the main exceptions to the general limits.

Income tax

Claim	*Time limit*
Trading losses: Loss sustained in a trade, profession or vocation to be set against other income of the year or the last preceding year. Extended to certain pre-trading expenditure by ITTOIA 2005 s 57 (ITA 2007 s 64). SEE TOLLEY'S TAX COMPUTATIONS **26.2**.	One year after 31 January next following tax year in which loss arose.
Unrelieved trading losses to be set against capital gains (TCGA 1992 ss 261B, 261C). SEE TOLLEY'S TAX COMPUTATIONS **15.2**.	One year after 31 January next following tax year in which loss arose.
Losses of new trade etc: Loss sustained in the first four years of a new trade, profession or vocation to be offset against other income arising in the three years immediately preceding the year of loss. Extended to certain pre-trading expenditure by ITTOIA 2005 s 57 (ITA 2007 s 72). SEE TOLLEY'S TAX COMPUTATIONS **15.3**.	One year after 31 January next following tax year in which loss arose.
Property business losses: Claim for relief against total income (ITA 2007 s 124).	One year after 31 January next following tax year specified in claim.
Simplified cash basis for unincorporated property businesses: Cash basis *not* to apply (ITTOIA 2005 s 271A).	One year after 31 January next following tax year specified in claim.
Loss on disposal of unlisted shares: Loss on disposal of shares in an EIS company or a qualifying trading company to be offset against other income of the year of loss or the last preceding year (ITA 2007 s 132). SEE TOLLEY'S TAX COMPUTATIONS **15.5**.	One year after 31 January next following tax year in which loss arose.
Gift aid: Election to treat donations to charity under gift aid made after 5 April 2003 as made in the previous tax year (ITA 2007 s 426).	On or before date on which donor delivers tax return for the previous tax year and not later than 31 January after that year.
Enterprise investment scheme relief: Income tax relief of 30% on amount invested within specified limits (ITA 2007 s 202).	5 years after 31 January next following tax year in which shares are issued.
Seed enterprise investment scheme relief: Income tax relief of 50% on amount invested within specified limits (ITA 2007 s 257EA). SEE TOLLEY'S TAX COMPUTATIONS **227.3**.	5 years after 31 January next following tax year in which shares are issued.
Social investment tax relief: Income tax relief of 30% on amount invested within specified limits (ITA 2007 s 257P).	5 years after 31 January next following tax year in which investment is made.
Rent-a-room relief: Relief not to apply; to apply to gross income in excess of limit; withdrawal of claim (ITTOIA 2005 ss 799, 800).	One year after 31 January next following tax year specified in claim.
Trading or property allowance: Full relief not to apply; partial relief to apply (ITTOIA 2005 ss 783AL, 783AM, 783BJ, 783BK).	One year after 31 January next following tax year specified in claim.

Capital gains

Claim	*Time limit*
Assets of negligible value: Loss to be allowed where the value of an asset has become negligible (TCGA 1992 s 24(2)). SEE TOLLEY'S TAX COMPUTATIONS **217.1**.	Two years after end of chargeable period of deemed sale (and reacquisition).
Assets held on 31 March 1982 for corporation tax purposes only: Events occurring prior to 31 March 1982 to be ignored in computing gains arising after 5 April 1988 (TCGA 1992 s 35(5), (6) as amended). SEE TOLLEY'S TAX COMPUTATIONS **205.2, 214.1** ONWARDS.	Two years after end of accounting period in which first relevant disposal made after 31.3.88; or such further time as HMRC may allow.

Claim	*Time limit*
Main residence: Determination of main residence for principal private residence exemption (TCGA 1992 s 222(5)(*a*)). SEE TOLLEY'S TAX COMPUTATIONS **223.2**.	Two years after acquisition of second residence.
Relief for loans to traders: Losses on certain loans to traders to be allowed as capital losses at the time of claim or 'earlier time' (TCGA 1992 s 253(3A)).	Two years after the end of the tax year or accounting period of loss.
Relief for loans to traders (payments by guarantor): Losses arising from payments by guarantor of certain irrecoverable loans to traders to be allowed as capital losses at time of claim or 'earlier time' (TCGA 1992 s 253(4), (4A)).	Four years after the end of the tax year or accounting period in which payment made (for claims before 1 April 2010, five years after 31 January following tax year in which payment made (capital gains tax); six years after end of accounting period in which payment made (corporation tax)).
Election for valuation at 6 April 1965 for corporation tax purposes only: Gain on a disposal of an asset held at 6 April 1965 to be computed as if the asset had been acquired on that date. An election once made is irrevocable (TCGA 1992 Sch 2 para 17).	Two years after end of accounting period in which disposal made; or such further time as HMRC may allow.
Entrepreneurs' relief: Gain to be taxed at reduced rate of 10% (TCGA 1992 s 169M). SEE TOLLEY'S TAX COMPUTATIONS **211.1**.	One year after 31 January next following tax year of qualifying business disposal.

Corporation tax

Claim	*Time limit*
Trading losses: Loss sustained by a company in a trade in an accounting period to be offset against profits of that accounting period and profits of the preceding year. Extended to certain pre-trading expenditure by CTA 2009 s 61 (CTA 2010 s 37(7)).	Two years after end of loss-making period; or such further period as HMRC may allow.
Trading losses: Post-1 April 2017 loss to be offset against *total* profits of a later accounting period (CTA 2010 s 45A(7)).	Two years after end of loss-making period; or such further period as HMRC may allow.
Trading losses: Post-1 April 2017 loss *not* to be carried forward against *trade* profits of next accounting period (CTA 2010 s 45B(6)).	Two years after end of loss-making period; or such further period as HMRC may allow.
Property losses: Carry forward of post-1 April 2017 losses (CTA 2010 s 62(5C)).	Two years after end of loss-making period; or such further period as HMRC may allow.
Group relief and Group relief for carried forward losses: Group relief to be given for accounting periods ending after 30 June 1999. The surrendering company must consent to the claim (FA 1998 Sch 18 paras 66–77A).	The last of: (*a*) one year from filing date of claimant company's return for accounting period for which claim is made; (*b*) 30 days after end of an enquiry into return; (*c*) if HMRC amend return after an enquiry, 30 days after issue of notice of amendment; (*d*) if an appeal is made against amendment, 30 days after determination of appeal; (or such later time as HMRC may allow).
Non-trading deficit on loan relationship: Claim for non-trading deficits on loan relationships (including non-trading debits on derivative contracts) in an accounting period to be: SEE TOLLEY'S TAX COMPUTATIONS **113.1** ONWARDS.	
(*a*) offset against profits of same period or carried back (CTA 2009 s 460);	Two years after end of accounting period in which deficit arose (or such later time as HMRC may allow).
(*b*) not treated as non-trading deficit of subsequent accounting period but to be carried forward to succeeding accounting periods (CTA 2009 ss 458, 463B).	Two years after end of that subsequent accounting period.
(*c*) for post-1 April 2017 deficits only, carried forward against *total* profits of succeeding accounting periods (CTA 2009 s 463G).	Two years after end of that subsequent accounting period.
Intangible assets: Election to replace accounts depreciation with fixed writing-down allowance of 4% (CTA 2009 s 730). SEE TOLLEY'S TAX COMPUTATIONS **108.1**.	Two years after end of the accounting period in which asset was created or acquired.
Research and development: Claim for tax relief to be made, amended or withdrawn in company tax return (or amended return) (FA 1998 Sch 18 para 83E).	One year from the filing date for return or such later time as HMRC may allow.

Capital allowances

Claim	*Time limit*
Corporation tax claims: Claims, amended claims and withdrawals of claims in respect of corporation tax capital allowances (CAA 2001 s 3(2), (3)(*b*); FA 1998 Sch 18 para 82).	The last of: (*a*) one year after filing date of claimant company's return for accounting period for which claim is made; (*b*) 30 days after end of enquiry into return; (*c*) if HMRC amend the return after an enquiry, 30 days after issue of notice of amendment; (*d*) if appeal is made against amendment, 30 days after determination of appeal; (or such later time as HMRC may allow).
Short life assets: Plant or machinery to be treated as a short life asset (CAA 2001 s 85(2)). **SEE TOLLEY'S TAX COMPUTATIONS 4.4**. ***continued on next page***	One year after 31 January after tax year in which chargeable period ends (income tax); two years after end of chargeable period (corporation tax).
Connected persons: Succession to a trade between connected persons to be ignored in computing capital allowances (CAA 2001 s 266). **SEE TOLLEY'S TAX COMPUTATIONS 4.2**.	Two years after date of the succession.
Sales between persons under common control treated as made at the lower of open market value and tax written down value (CAA 2001 s 570(5)).	Two years after date of the disposal.

Exchanges

Recognised stock exchanges

The following is a list of countries with exchanges which have been designated as recognised stock exchanges under ITA 2007 s 1005; CTA 2010 s 1137. Unless otherwise specified, any stock exchange (or options exchange) in a country listed below is a recognised stock exchange provided it is recognised under the law of the country concerned relating to stock exchanges.

HMRC may make an order designating a market in the UK as a recognised stock exchange.

Country	*Date of recognition*
Australian Stock Exchange and its stock exchange subsidiaries	22 September 1988
National Stock Exchange of Australia	19 June 2014
Austria[3]	22 October 1970
Bahamas	
Bahamas International Securities Exchange	19 April 2010
Belgium[3]	22 October 1970
Bermuda	4 December 2007
Brazil	
Rio De Janeiro Stock Exchange	17 August 1995
São Paulo Stock Exchange	11 December 1995
Canada	
Any stock exchange prescribed for the purposes of the Canadian Income Tax Act	22 October 1970
Caribbean	
Dutch Caribbean Securities Exchange	8 December 2014
Cayman Islands Stock Exchange	4 March 2004
Channel Islands Securities Exchange Authority[3]	20 December 2013
China	
Hong Kong – Any stock exchange recognised under Section 2A(1) of the Hong Kong Companies Ordinance[3]	26 February 1971
Cyprus	
Cyprus Stock Exchange	22 June 2009
Denmark	
Copenhagen Stock Exchange	22 October 1970
Estonia	
NASDAQ OMX Tallinn	5 May 2010
European Wholesale Securities Market	17 January 2013
Finland	
Helsinki Stock Exchange	22 October 1970
France[3]	22 October 1970
Germany[3]	5 August 1971
Gibraltar	16 August 2016
Global Board of Trade	30 July 2013
Greece	
Athens Stock Exchange	14 June 1993
Guernsey[3]	10 December 2002

Country	*Date of recognition*
GXG Main Quote	23 September 2013
GXG Official List	16 May 2013
Iceland	31 March 2006
Irish Republic[3]	22 October 1970
Italy[3]	3 May 1972
Japan[3]	22 October 1970
Korea	10 October 1994
Lithuania	
NASDAQ OMX Vilnius	12 March 2012
Luxembourg[3]	21 February 1972
Malaysia	
Kuala Lumpur Stock Exchange	10 October 1994
Malta Stock Exchange	29 December 2005
Mauritius Stock Exchange	31 January 2011
Mexico	10 October 1994
Netherlands[3]	22 October 1970
New Zealand	22 September 1988
Norway[3]	22 October 1970
Poland	
Warsaw Stock Exchange	25 February 2010
Portugal[3]	21 February 1972
Russia	
MICEX Stock Exchange	5 January 2011
Singapore	30 June 1977
Singapore Exchange Securities Trading Limited (SGX-ST)[4]	7 October 2014
Singapore Exchange Derivatives Trading Limited (SGX-DT)[4]	7 October 2014
South Africa	
Bond Exchange of South Africa	16 April 2008
Johannesburg Stock Exchange	22 October 1970
Spain[3]	5 August 1971
Sri Lanka	
Colombo Stock Exchange	21 February 1972
Sweden	
Stockholm Stock Exchange	16 July 1985
Swiss Stock Exchange	12 May 1997
Thailand	10 October 1994
United Kingdom	
London Stock Exchange	19 July 2007
PLUS-listed Market	19 July 2007
ICAP Securities & Derivatives Exchange Ltd	25 April 2013
LIFFE Administration and Management	26 September 2011
Euronext London	4 February 2015
United States	
Any stock exchange registered with the SEC as a national securities exchange[1]	22 October 1970
Nasdaq Stock Market[2]	10 March 1992

1 'National securities exchange' does not include any local exchanges registered with Securities and Exchange Commission.

2 As maintained through the facilities of the National Association of Securities Dealers Inc and its subsidiaries.

3 i.e., a stock exchange according to the law of the country concerned relating to stock exchanges.

4 The original Singapore Stock Exchange merged with two other exchanges and is now known as SGX. The SGX-ST market was identified as representing the originally designated exchange.

Recognised futures exchanges

The following is a list of exchanges which have been designated as recognised futures exchanges under TCGA 1992 s 288(6). By concession, those exchanges were recognised futures exchanges for the tax year of recognition onwards.

Recognised futures exchanges	*Date of recognition*
International Petroleum Exchange of London	6 August 1985
London Metal Exchange	6 August 1985
London Gold Market	12 December 1985
London Silver Market	12 December 1985
CME Group (formerly Chicago Mercantile Exchange and Chicago Board of Trade)	19 December 1986
New York Mercantile Exchange	19 December 1986
Philadelphia Board of Trade	19 December 1986

Recognised futures exchanges	*Date of recognition*
Mid America Commodity Exchange	29 July 1987
Montreal Exchange	29 July 1987
Hong Kong Futures Exchange	15 December 1987
Commodity Exchange (Comex)	25 August 1988
Sydney Futures Exchange	13 October 1988
Euronext (London International Financial Futures and Options Exchange)	22 March 1992
OM Stockholm	18 March 1992
OMLX (formerly OM London)	18 March 1992
New York Board of Trade	10 June 2004
Eurex Deutschland	13 March 2015

Recognised investment exchanges and clearing houses

The following is a list of investment exchanges and clearing houses recognised as investment exchanges under the Financial Services and Markets Act 2000 and able to carry out investment business in the UK.

Recognised investment exchanges	*Date of recognition*
London Stock Exchange plc	22 November 2001
LIFFE Administration and Management[1]	22 November 2001
The London Metal Exchange Ltd	22 November 2001
ICE Futures Europe	22 November 2001
NEX Exchange Ltd (formerly ICAP Securities & Derivatives Exchange Ltd)	19 July 2007
Cboe Europe Ltd (formerly BATS Trading Ltd)	20 May 2013
CME Europe Ltd[2]	*10 March 2014*
Euronext UK Markets Ltd	2 June 2014

1 Taken over by ICE Futures Europe in December 2013.
2 De-recognised with effect from 12 October 2017.

Recognised clearing houses[2]	*Date of recognition*
LCH Ltd[1]	22 November 2001
Euroclear UK & Ireland Ltd	23 November 2001
ICE Clear Europe Ltd[1]	15 May 2008
CME Clearing Europe Ltd[2]	*15 December 2010*
LME Clear Ltd[1]	3 September 2014

1 These clearing houses are recognised central counterparties. LCH Ltd was recognised as such on 12 June 2014. CME Clearing Europe Ltd was recognised as such on 4 August 2014. LME Clear Ltd was recognised as such on 3 September 2014. ICE Clear Europe Ltd was recognised as such on 19 September 2016.
2 De-recognised with effect from 12 October 2017.
3 List as at 11 April 2018 on Bank of England website.

Recognised overseas investment exchanges and clearing houses

The following is a list of overseas investment exchanges and clearing houses recognised under the Financial Services and Markets Act 2000 and able to conduct investment business in the UK.

Recognised overseas investment exchange	*Date of recognition*
National Association of Securities Dealers Automated Quotations (NASDAQ)	23 November 2001
Australian Securities Exchange Ltd	30 January 2002
The Chicago Mercantile Exchange (CME)	23 November 2001
Chicago Board of Trade (CBOT)	23 November 2001
New York Mercantile Exchange Inc (NYMEX Inc)	23 November 2001
SIX Swiss Exchange AG	23 November 2001
EUREX (Zurich)	23 November 2001
ICE Futures US Inc	17 May 2007

Recognised clearing house[1]	*Date of recognition*
None	

1 List as at 11 April 2018 on Bank of England website.

Alternative finance investment bonds

List of recognised stock exchanges designated solely for the purposes of ITA 2007 s 564G, TCGA 1992 s 151N, CTA 2009 s 507.

Recognised stock exchanges	*Date of recognition*
Abu Dhabi Securities Market	1 April 2007
Bahrain Stock Exchange	1 April 2007
Dubai Financial Market	1 April 2007
NASDAQ Dubai (formerly Dubai International Financial Exchange)	1 April 2007
Labuan International Financial Exchange	1 April 2007
Saudi Stock Exchange (Tadawul)	1 April 2007
Surabaya Stock Exchange	1 April 2007

Applications for clearances and approvals

Statutory clearance applications and approvals	*Address*
Demergers (CTA 2010 s 1091); Company purchase of own shares (CTA 2010 s 1044); Transactions in securities (CTA 2010 s 748; ITA 2007 s 701); Enterprise Investment Scheme – acquisition of shares by new company (ITA 2007 s 247(1)(f)); Share exchanges (TCGA 1992 s 138); Reconstruction regarding transfer of a business (TCGA 1992 s 139); Transfer of a UK trade between EU member states (TCGA 1992 ss 140B, 140D); Intangible fixed assets (CTA 2009 s 831); Loan relationships transfers/mergers (CTA 2009 ss 426, 427, 438); Derivative contracts transfers/mergers (CTA 2009 ss 677, 686); Schemes converting income to capital (TCGA 1992 ss 184G–H); Assignment of lease granted at undervalue (CTA 2009 s 237; ITTOIA 2005 s 300); Transactions in land (CTA 2010 s 831; ITA 2007 s 770); Collective investment schemes (TCGA 1992 s 103K)	HM Revenue & Customs, CTIS Clearance S0483, Newcastle NE98 1ZZ (Applications should be marked "market sensitive" or "non-market sensitive" as appropriate.)[1]
Employee share schemes (ITEPA 2003 Schs 2, 3, 4)	Self-certification applies and can be made through HMRC Online services; see www.gov.uk/guidance/self-certify-your-tax-advantaged-employment-related-securities
Pensions	Registration of a pension scheme from 6 April 2006 must be done online, but HMRC can be contacted at Pension Schemes Services, HM Revenue & Customs, BX9 1GH, United Kingdom
Qualifying life assurance policies (TA 1988 Sch 15)	HM Revenue & Customs, CTISA Corporation Tax and Business Income Tax, Financial Services Team, 3rd Floor, 100 Parliament Street, London SW1A 2BQ
Transactions in shares or debentures (TA 1988 ss 765 and 765A)	The recommendation is that businesses should address the reports directly to the customer relationship manager dealing with their affairs

Non-statutory clearance applications	*Address*
Controlled foreign companies (TIOPA 2010 Part 9A; TA 1988 ss 747–756, Schs 24–26)	HM Revenue & Customs, Business, Assets and International, Foreign Profits Team Registry (CFC clearances), Room 3C/21, 100 Parliament Street, London SW1A 2BQ
Company migration (TMA 1970 s 109B–F, formerly FA 1988 s 130)	HM Revenue & Customs, Business, Assets and International, Foreign Profits Team, Room 3C/21, 100 Parliament Street, London SW1A 2BQ
Inward investment (in Statement of Practice 02/07)	Inward Investment Support, HM Revenue & Customs, CTIAA Business International, 100 Parliament Street, London SW1A 2BQ
Creative industries (CTA 2009 Pts 15, 15A, 15B)	Creative Industries Unit (Film, Television/Animation and Video Games Tax Reliefs), Local Compliance S0717, PO Box 3900, Glasgow G70 6AA
Enterprise Investment Scheme (EIS), Seed Enterprise Investment Scheme (SEIS) and Venture Capital Trust (VCT) scheme (ITA 2007 Pts 5, 5A, 6)	Local Compliance, Small Company Enterprise Centre Admin Team, HM Revenue & Customs, SO777, PO Box 3900, Glasgow G70 6AA
Business investment relief (ITA 2007 s 809VC)	Wealthy and Mid-sized Business Compliance, HM Revenue & Customs, BX9 1BN
IHT business property relief (IHTA 1984 Pt 5 Ch 1)	Inheritance Tax, HM Revenue & Customs, BX9 1HT, United Kingdom
Social investment tax relief (ITA 2007 Pt 5B)	Small Company Enterprise Centre (Admin team), Mid-size Business S0777, PO Box 3900, Glasgow G70 6AA

Non-statutory clearance applications	*Address*
Other non-statutory clearances including VAT	Large businesses should contact their client relationship manager. All other businesses and their agents should send applications to HM Revenue & Customs Non-statutory Clearances Team, 5th Floor Alexander House, 21 Victoria Avenue, Southend-on-Sea, Essex SS99 1AA[2] or email hmrc.southendteam@hmrc.gsi.gov.uk. Regarding emails see[1]

Confirmation or pre-transaction or general advice	*Address*
General enquiries on IR35	HM Revenue & Customs, IR35 Customer Service Unit, S0733, Newcastle Upon Tyne, NE98 1ZZ Telephone 0300 123 2326
Advance thin capitalisation agreements (Statement of Practice 1/12)	The first contact for information about advance thin capitalisation agreements under the Statement of Practice should be the Customer Relationship Manager (CRM) or Customer Contact (CC) of the business concerned, and they will engage the assistance of a transfer pricing specialist. If there is no known CRM or CC, the application may be sent to the local Transfer Pricing team leader
CGT post-transaction value checks	Completed form CG34 which must be received by HMRC at least two months before the relevant filing deadline
Professional bodies (relief for subscriptions) (ITEPA 2003 s 343)	A list of approved professional bodies and learned societies is available on the HMRC website (at www.gov.uk/government/publications/professional-bodies-approved-for-tax-relief-list-3)
General advice on specialist technical issues	See www.gov.uk/contact-hmrc
SDLT transactions	See www.gov.uk/stamp-duty-land-tax
Post-transaction clearances connected to an offshore disclosure	HM Revenue & Customs, WDF Clearance Team, Individual & Small Business Compliance, Compliance Centres, Digital Disclosure Service Room BP3002, Benton Park View, S1250 Newcastle upon Tyne, NE98 1YX Email isbc.disclosureposttransactionclearance@hmrc.gsi.gov.uk

1 Where clearance is sought under any one or more of the sections handled by the Clearance and Counteraction Team, clearance applications may be sent in a single letter to the above Newcastle address for clearances under those sections. The letter should make clear what clearance(s) is required. HMRC acknowledge only those applications that request acknowledgement. An email acknowledgement may be requested. E-mail applications can be sent to reconstructions@hmrc.gsi.gov.uk. Attachments to emails should be no larger than 2MB. Self-extracting zip files should not be sent as HMRC software will block them. Security of emails is not guaranteed. Information about market or price sensitive matters, or well known individuals, should not be sent by email.

2 Non-statutory clearances: Taxpayers may apply for a non-statutory clearance where they require clarification on guidance or legislation for other circumstances after having checked that the transaction is not covered by a more appropriate clearance or approval route. Taxpayers must provide all the necessary information requested in the relevant checklist. HMRC will not give clearances or advice in respect of the application of the 'settlements legislation' in ITTOIA 2005 Pt 5 Ch 5 or the tax consequences of executing non-charitable trust deeds or settlements. See www.gov.uk/non-statutory-clearance-service-guidance.

Capital allowances

Rates of capital allowances

Dredging

SEE TOLLEY'S TAX COMPUTATIONS 3.2.

	Expenditure incurred after	% Rate
Writing-down allowance	**5 November 1962**	**4**

Flat conversions *for periods before April 2013*

Initial allowance	*Expenditure incurred*	*% Rate*
	10 May 2001 to 1 or 6 April 2013	100

Applies to expenditure on renovating or converting certain space above commercial properties into flats for rent. Annual 25% writing-down allowance (on a straight-line basis). (CAA 2001 ss 393A–393W; FA 2001 s 67, Sch 19.)

Relief is withdrawn for expenditure on or after 1 April 2013 (corporation tax) or 6 April 2013 (income tax). The entitlement to a writing down allowance also ceased with effect from the same dates (FA 2012 Sch 39).

Know-how

Expenditure incurred after 31 March 1986: **annual 25% writing-down allowance** (reducing balance basis).

Mineral extraction

SEE TOLLEY'S TAX COMPUTATIONS 3.3.

First-year allowance: **100% FYA** is available for certain expenditure incurred after 16 April 2002 wholly for the purposes of a North Sea Oil ring-fence trade or on plant and machinery used in such a trade.

Writing-down allowance: for expenditure incurred after 31 March 1986, **10%** for expenditure on the acquisition of a mineral asset and certain pre-trading expenditure, otherwise **25%** (on reducing balance basis). (CAA 2001 s 418.)

Motor cars other than low-emission cars

SEE TOLLEY'S TAX COMPUTATIONS 4.3.

Expenditure *on or after* 1 April 2009 (corporation tax) or 6 April 2009 (income tax) on cars is allocated to the special rate (**currently 8%**) plant and machinery pool if the car's CO_2 emissions exceed 110g/km for expenditure incurred on or after 1 April 2018 (130g/km for expenditure incurred before 1 April 2018, 160g/km for expenditure incurred before 1 April 2013 (corporation tax) or 6 April 2013 (income tax)) and otherwise to the (**currently 18%**) main pool. Cars with non-business use are allocated to a single asset pool, but rate of WDA depends on emissions. (CAA 2001 ss 104AA, 104F, 208A, 268A–268D; SI 2016/984.)

The position for expenditure *before* 1 April 2009 (corporation tax) or 6 April 2009 (income tax) is as follows. Transitional rules applied — see note 2.

		% Rate[1, 2]
Writing-down allowance (WDA)	Chargeable period ending before 1 or 6 April 2012	20%
	Chargeable period straddling 1 or 6 April 2012	hybrid rate
	Chargeable period beginning on or after 1 or 6 April 2012	18%

1 Restricted to £3,000 for cars costing more than £12,000 and bought outright, on hire purchase or by way of a lease with an option to purchase (CAA 2001 ss 74, 75).

2 Expenditure still in a single asset pool for cars costing more than £12,000 on the last day of the first chargeable period ending on or after 31 March 2014 (corporation tax) or 5 April 2014 (income tax) was carried forward to the main pool (FA 2009 Sch 11 para 31).

3 See also Low-emission cars, note 5, p 31 and Car hire, p 82.

Patent rights

SEE TOLLEY'S TAX COMPUTATIONS 3.4.

Writing-down allowance

Expenditure incurred after 31 March 1986: **annual 25% writing-down allowance** (reducing balance basis). (CAA 2001 s 472.)

Plant and machinery

	Expenditure incurred after	Expenditure incurred before	Up to pa
Annual investment allowance[1]			
for income tax purposes	**31 December 2015**		**£200,000**
	5 April 2014	1 January 2016	£500,000
	31 December 2012	6 April 2014	£250,000
	5 April 2012	1 January 2013	£25,000
	5 April 2010	6 April 2012	£100,000
	5 April 2008	6 April 2010	£50,000
for corporation tax purposes	**31 December 2015**		**£200,000**
	31 March 2014	1 January 2016	£500,000
	31 December 2012	1 April 2014	£250,000
	31 March 2012	1 January 2013	£25,000
	31 March 2010	1 April 2012	£100,000
	31 March 2008	1 April 2010	£50,000
First-year allowance (FYA)[13]			
General[12]			***% Rate***
for income tax purposes	5 April 2009	6 April 2010	40
for corporation tax purposes	31 March 2009	1 April 2010	40
Small and medium-sized businesses[2]			
for income tax purposes	1 July 1998	6 April 2008	40
for corporation tax purposes	1 July 1998	1 April 2008	40
	1 July 1997	2 July 1998	50
in Northern Ireland *only*	11 May 1998	12 May 2002	100
Small businesses[3]			
for income tax purposes	5 April 2006	6 April 2008	50
	5 April 2004	6 April 2005	50
for corporation tax purposes	31 March 2006	1 April 2008	50
	31 March 2004	1 April 2005	50
ICT	31 March 2000	1 April 2004	100
Energy-saving plant or machinery[4]	**31 March 2001**		100
New low-emission cars[5]	**16 April 2002**	**1 April 2021**[5]	100
Certain refuelling equipment[5]	**16 April 2002**	**1 April 2021**[5]	100
Environmentally beneficial plant or machinery[6]	**31 March 2003**		100
Zero-emission goods vehicles[7]			
for income tax purposes	**5 April 2010**	**6 April 2021**[7]	**100**
for corporation tax purposes	**31 March 2010**	**1 April 2021**[7]	**100**
Enterprise zones[18]	**31 March 2012**		**100**
Electric charge-point equipment[19]			
for income tax purposes	**22 November 2016**	**6 April 2019**	**100**
for corporation tax purposes	**22 November 2016**	**1 April 2019**	**100**
Writing-down allowance (WDA)[8]			
Foreign leased assets[11]	9 March 1982	1 April 2006	10
	Chargeable period beginning on or after		
Long-life assets[8, 9]			
for income tax purposes	**6 April 2012**		**8**
for corporation tax purposes	**1 April 2012**		**8**
	Chargeable period ending before		
for income tax purposes	6 April 2012		10
for corporation tax purposes	1 April 2012		10
for income tax purposes	6 April 2008		6
for corporation tax purposes	1 April 2008		6
Integral features[8, 10]	**Chargeable period beginning on or after**		
for income tax purposes	**6 April 2012**		**8**
for corporation tax purposes	**1 April 2012**		**8**
	Chargeable period ending before		
for income tax purposes	6 April 2012		10
for corporation tax purposes	1 April 2012		10
Thermal insulation[8, 15]	**Chargeable period beginning on or after**		
for income tax purposes	**6 April 2012**		**8**
for corporation tax purposes	**1 April 2012**		**8**

	Chargeable period ending before	
for income tax purposes	6 April 2012	10
for corporation tax purposes	1 April 2012	10
Certain cars[8, 14]	**Chargeable period beginning on or after**	
for income tax purposes	**6 April 2012**	**8**
for corporation tax purposes	**1 April 2012**	**8**
	Chargeable period ending before	
for income tax purposes	6 April 2012	10
for corporation tax purposes	1 April 2012	10
Solar panels[8, 17]	**Chargeable period beginning on or after**	
for income tax purposes	**6 April 2012**	**8**
for corporation tax purposes	**1 April 2012**	**8**
Cushion gas[8, 16]	**Chargeable period beginning on or after**	
for income tax purposes	**6 April 2012**	**8**
for corporation tax purposes	**1 April 2012**	**8**
	Chargeable period ending before	
for income tax purposes	6 April 2012	10
for corporation tax purposes	1 April 2012	10
Generally	**Chargeable periods beginning on or after**	
for income tax purposes	**6 April 2012**	**18**
for corporation tax purposes	**1 April 2012**	**18**
	Chargeable period ending before	
for income tax purposes	6 April 2012	20
for corporation tax purposes	1 April 2012	20
	Chargeable periods straddling	
for income tax purposes	6 April 2012	Hybrid rate[8, 9]
for corporation tax purposes	1 April 2012	Hybrid rate[8, 9]

1 **Annual investment allowance:** The first £200,000 (for expenditure on or after 1 January 2016; see table for earlier amounts) of qualifying expenditure incurred in a chargeable period qualifies for the annual investment allowance at 100%. Where a chargeable period spans the date of an increase or decrease, transitional rules apply. The limit is proportionately increased or decreased where the chargeable period is longer or shorter than a year. A group of companies (defined as for company law purposes) can only receive a single allowance. This restriction also applies to certain related businesses or companies. Expenditure on cars does not qualify (CAA 2001 ss 38A, 38B, 51A–51N; FA 2011 s 11; FA 2013 Sch 1; FA 2014 s 10, Sch 2, F(No 2)A 2015 s 8).
SEE TOLLEY'S TAX COMPUTATIONS 4.6.

2 **Small and medium-sized businesses:** The allowance did not apply to certain expenditure including that on plant and machinery for leasing, motor cars, ships, railway assets or long-life assets. After the first year, allowances revert to the normal WDA. The rate of 50% applied only for expenditure incurred during the year ended 1 July 1998 when a 12% FYA applied to long-life assets. (See note 9 below.) Small and medium-sized businesses are, broadly, those satisfying any two of the following conditions: (*a*) turnover £22,800,000 or less (*b*) assets £11,400,000 or less (*c*) not more than 250 employees (CAA 1990 ss 22(3C), (6B), 22A, 44, 46–49). For accounting periods ending before 30 January 2004, the thresholds were: (*a*) turnover £11,200,000 or less (*b*) assets £5,600,000 or less.

3 **Small businesses:** See note 2 above for conditions for relief. Small businesses are, broadly, those satisfying any two of the following conditions: (*a*) turnover £5,600,000 or less (*b*) assets £2,800,000 or less (*c*) not more than 50 employees. For accounting periods ending before 30 January 2004, the thresholds were: (*a*) turnover £2,800,000 or less (*b*) assets £1,400,000 or less (FA 2004 s 142).

4 **Energy-saving plant or machinery:** The allowances are available for investment by *any* business in designated energy-saving plant and machinery in accordance with the Government's Energy Technology Product List. 100% first-year allowances are not available for expenditure incurred on or after 1 April 2012 (corporation tax) or 6 April 2012 (income tax) on plant or machinery to generate renewable electricity or heat where tariff payments are received under either of the renewable energy schemes introduced by the Department of Energy and Climate Change. The restriction applies from April 2014 for combined heat and power equipment (CAA 2001 ss 45A–45C, 46; FA 2001 s 65, Sch 17; SI 2005/1114; SI 2018/268). The product lists are available at www.gov.uk/energy-technology-list.

5 **Low-emission cars:** The allowance is given on (*a*) new cars which are either electrically propelled or emit not more than 50g/km of CO_2 for expenditure incurred on or after 1 April 2018 (75g/km for expenditure incurred before 1 April 2018, 95g/km for expenditure incurred before 1 April 2015, 110g/km for expenditure incurred before 1 April 2013, 120g/km for expenditure incurred before 1 April 2008), registered after 16 April 2002 and (*b*) new plant and machinery to refuel vehicles in a gas refuelling station with natural gas, hydrogen fuels, or (for expenditure on or after 1 April 2008) biogas. For expenditure incurred after 31 March 2013 cars provided for leasing no longer qualify for the FYA (CAA 2001 ss 45D, 45E, 46; SI 2016/984; SI 2017/1304).
SEE TOLLEY'S TAX COMPUTATIONS 4.3.

6 **Environmentally beneficial plant or machinery:** Allowances are available for expenditure by *any* business on new and unused designated technologies and products which satisfy the relevant environmental criteria in accordance with the Government's technologies or products lists (CAA 2001 ss 45H–45J, 46; FA 2003 s 167, Sch 30; SI 2003/2076). The product lists are available at www.gov.uk/government/publications/water-efficient-enhanced-capital-allowances.

7 **Zero-emission goods vehicles:** The allowance is given on new (and not second hand) vehicles which cannot under any circumstances produce CO_2 emissions when driven and which are of a design primarily suited to the conveyance of goods or burden. The expenditure must be incurred before 1 April 2021 (corporation tax) or 6 April 2021 (income tax) and is limited to expenditure of € 85 million per undertaking (as defined) over the period for which the provisions apply. The allowance is not available where another State aid has been or will be received towards the qualifying expenditure. Other exclusions apply (CAA 2001 ss 45DA–45DB, 212T; FA 2015 s 45; SI 2017/1304).

8 **WDAs** are calculated on a reducing balance basis. For chargeable periods beginning before 6 April 2012 and ending on or after that date (income tax) or, beginning before 1 April 2012 and ending on or after that date (corporation tax) a hybrid rate of WDAs applies, calculated by time apportionment of the 20% and 18% rates, or, for the special rate expenditure, the 10% and 8% rates. For chargeable periods beginning on or after 6 April 2008 (income tax) or 1 April 2008 (corporation tax), a WDA of up to £1,000 can be claimed in respect of the main pool and/or the special rate pool where the unrelieved expenditure in the pool concerned is £1,000 or less.

9 **Long-life assets:** Applies to plant or machinery with an expected working life, when new, of 25 years or more. Applies where expenditure on long-life assets in a year is £100,000 or more (in the case of companies the de minimis limit is £100,000 divided by one plus the number of associated companies). Transitional provisions apply to maintain a 25% allowance for expenditure incurred before 1 January 2001 under a contract entered into before 26 November 1996 and to expenditure on second-hand plant or machinery if old rules applied to vendor. It does not apply to plant or machinery in a building used wholly or mainly as, or for purposes ancillary to, a dwelling-house, retail shop, showroom, hotel or office; cars; or sea-going ships and railway assets acquired before 1 January 2011. Expenditure on or after 1 April 2008 (corporation tax) or 6 April 2008 (income tax) qualifies, as special rate expenditure, for a writing down allowance of 8% (10% for periods before 1 or 6 April 2012, see note 8 above) reducing balance. The balance of the long-life asset pool at 1 or 6 April 2008 was also transferred into the special rate pool. The rate applying for chargeable periods beginning before 1 or 6 April 2008 was 6% and a hybrid rate applied for chargeable periods spanning those dates calculated by a time apportionment of the 6% and 10% rates (CAA 2001 ss 90–104, Sch 3 para 20).

SEE TOLLEY'S TAX COMPUTATIONS 4.5.

10 **Integral features** of a building are electrical systems (including lighting systems); cold water systems; space or water heating systems, powered ventilation systems, air cooling or purification and any floor or ceiling comprised in such systems; lifts, escalators and moving walkways and external solar shading. Applies to expenditure incurred on or after 1 April 2008 (corporation tax) and 6 April 2008 (income tax). They all fall into the special rate pool and qualify for a 8% (10% for periods before 1 or 6 April 2012, see note 8 above) writing down allowance (CAA 2001 ss 33A, 104A).

SEE TOLLEY'S TAX COMPUTATIONS 4.5.

11 **Foreign leased assets:** The relief applies only to leases finalised before 1 April 2006 (CAA 2001 s 109; FA 2006 Sch 9 para 13).

12 **First-year tax credits:** For expenditure incurred on or after 1 April 2008 and before 1 April 2023, a company can surrender a tax loss attributable to first-year allowances for energy-saving or environmentally beneficial equipment in exchange for a cash payment from the Government. The cash payment is equal to a percentage of the loss surrendered, subject to an upper limit of the greater of £250,000 and the company's PAYE and NIC liability for the period concerned. For chargeable periods beginning before 1 April 2018 the percentage was fixed at 19%. For chargeable periods beginning on or after 1 April 2018 the percentage is 2/3 of the corporation tax rate chargeable (CAA 2001 Sch A1; SI 2013/464; FA 2018 s 29).

13 **First year allowances**, where applicable, are available on expenditure over the annual investment allowance level or on which annual investment allowance has not been claimed, which would otherwise qualify for writing down allowance at 18% in the general plant and machinery pool.

14 **Cars:** For expenditure on and after 1 April 2009 (corporation tax), 6 April 2009 (income tax), cars with CO_2 emissions exceeding 110g/km for expenditure incurred on or after 1 April 2018 (130g/km for expenditure incurred before 1 April 2018, 160g/km for expenditure incurred before 1 April 2013 (corporation tax) or 6 April 2013 (income tax)) will be allocated to the special rate pool. All other cars will go into the general pool (CAA 2001 ss 104A, 104AA; SI 2016/984).

SEE TOLLEY'S TAX COMPUTATIONS 4.3.

15 **Thermal insulation**: Expenditure on thermal insulation incurred on or after 1 April 2008 (corporation tax) and 6 April 2008 (income tax) falls into the special rate pool and qualifies for a 8% (10% for periods before 1 or 6 April 2012, see note 8 above) writing down allowance (CAA 2001 ss 28, 104A).

16 **Cushion gas:** Expenditure on cushion gas incurred on or after 1 April 2010 falls into the special rate pool and qualifies for a 8% (10% for periods before 1 or 6 April 2012, see note 8 above) writing down allowance (CAA 2001 ss 70J, 104A).

17 **Solar panels**: Expenditure on solar panels incurred on or after 1 April 2012 (corporation tax) and 6 April 2012 (income tax) falls into the special rate pool and qualifies for a 8% writing down allowance (CAA 2001 s 104A).

18 **Enterprise zones:** For expenditure incurred for the purpose of a qualifying activity in the eight-year period from the date the area is (or is treated as) designated, 100% first-year allowances are available for companies chargeable to corporation tax which invest in unused (not second hand) plant or machinery for use primarily in designated assisted areas within certain enterprise zones. Expenditure must be incurred for the purposes of broadly a new or expanding business carried on by the company, must not be replacement expenditure and is limited to €125 million per single investment project (as

defined) over the eight years. Exclusions apply. See SI 2014/3183, SI 2015/2047, SI 2016/751 and SI 2018/485 for details of the current enterprise zones. The Northern Ireland Executive proposes to establish a pilot enterprise zone in Northern Ireland which, if implemented, will benefit from the enhanced capital allowances (CAA 2001 ss 45K–N, 212U).

19 **Electric charge-point equipment**. 100% first-year allowance is available for expenditure incurred in the period from 23 November 2016 to 31 March 2019 (corporation tax) and 23 November 2016 to 5 April 2019 (income tax) on new (not second hand), unused electric vehicle charging point equipment installed solely for the purpose of charging electric vehicles (CAA 2001 s 45EA).

Cars: Car hire p 82.

Renovation of business premises *for periods before April 2017*

SEE TOLLEY'S TAX COMPUTATIONS 3.1.

	Expenditure incurred between	% Rate
First-year allowance	11 April 2007 and 1 or 6 April 2017	100

The expenditure must be incurred on renovating or converting vacant business properties in Northern Ireland or the designated disadvantaged areas in the UK that have been vacant for at least a year, to bring the property back into business use. From April 2014 the type of qualifying expenditure has been specifically clarified. Premises refurbished by or used by businesses in the following trades are excluded from the scheme: fisheries and aquaculture, shipbuilding, the coal or steel industries, synthetic fibres, primary production of certain agricultural products and the manufacture of products which imitate or substitute for milk or milk products. For qualifying expenditure incurred on or after 1 April 2014 (corporation tax) and on or after 6 April 2014 (income tax), allowances are not available if another form of State aid has been, or will be, received. A writing-down allowance is given at 25% (on a straight-line basis) on unrelieved expenditure. (FA 2005 s 92, Sch 6; SI 2012/868)

The relief is withdrawn for expenditure incurred on or after 1 April 2017 (corporation tax) and 6 April 2017 (income tax). (SI 2012/868)

Research and development (formerly scientific research)

SEE TOLLEY'S TAX COMPUTATIONS 3.5.

	Expenditure incurred after	% Rate
Allowance in year 1	**5 November 1962**	**100**

Note: Land and houses are excluded from 1 April 1985.

Capital gains

Annual exemption

(TCGA 1992 s 3; SI 2018/244)

Individuals[a], personal representatives[b] and certain trusts[c]

SEE TOLLEY'S TAX COMPUTATIONS 225.1.

[a] For 2008–09 onwards, an individual who claims to use the remittance basis for a tax year is not entitled to the capital gains tax annual exemption for that year. This does not apply if the individual's unremitted foreign income and gains for the year are less than £2,000 (TCGA 1992 s 3(1A); ITA 2007 s 809D).

[b] Year of death and following two years (maximum) (TCGA 1992 s 3(7)).

[c] Trusts for disabled persons as defined. Exemption divided by number of qualifying settlements created (after 9 March 1981) by one settlor, subject to a minimum of one-tenth (TCGA 1992 Sch para 1(1); FA 2005 Sch 1A).

Exempt amount of net gains	***2013–14***	***2014–15***	***2015–16***	***2016–17***	***2017–18***	***2018–19***
	£10,900	£11,000	£11,100	£11,100	£11,300	**£11,700**

Trusts[a] generally

SEE TOLLEY'S TAX COMPUTATIONS 228.1.

Exempt amount of net gains	***2013–14***	***2014–15***	***2015–16***	***2016–17***	***2017–18***	***2018–19***
	£5,450	£5,500	£5,550	£5,550	£5,650	**£5,850**

[a] Exemption divided by number of qualifying settlements created (after 6 June 1978) by one settlor, subject to a minimum of one-fifth (TCGA 1992 Sch 1 para 1(4)).

Chattel exemption

SEE TOLLEY'S TAX COMPUTATIONS 212.1.

(TCGA 1992 s 262)

	Disposals exemption	*Marginal relief: Maximum chargeable gain*
From 1989–90 onwards	£6,000	5/3 excess over £6,000

Rates of tax

SEE TOLLEY'S TAX COMPUTATIONS **201.1**.
(TCGA 1992 s 4)

2018–19*	**Gains accruing on the disposal of interests in residential properties (where not exempt), and gains arising in respect of carried interest**			
	Individuals	•	to income tax basic rate limit £34,500 (see note)	**18%**
		•	above income tax basic rate limit £34,500	**28%**
	Trusts and personal representatives			**28%**
	Other gains			
	Individuals	•	to income tax basic rate limit £34,500	**10%**
		•	above income tax basic rate limit £34,500	**20%**
	Trusts and personal representatives			**20%**
2017–18*	**Gains accruing on the disposal of interests in residential properties (where not exempt), and gains arising in respect of carried interest**			
	Individuals	•	to income tax basic rate limit £33,500 (see note)	18%
		•	above income tax basic rate limit £33,500	28%
	Trusts and personal representatives			28%
	Other gains			
	Individuals	•	to income tax basic rate limit £33,500	10%
		•	above income tax basic rate limit £33,500	20%
	Trusts and personal representatives			20%
2016–17*	**Gains accruing on the disposal of interests in residential properties (where not exempt), and gains arising in respect of carried interest**			
	Individuals	•	to income tax basic rate limit £32,000	18%
		•	above income tax basic rate limit £32,000	28%
	Trusts and personal representatives			28%
	Other gains			
	Individuals	•	to income tax basic rate limit £32,000	10%
		•	above income tax basic rate limit £32,000	20%
	Trusts and personal representatives			20%
2015–16*	*Individuals*	•	to income tax basic rate limit £31,785	18%
		•	above income tax basic rate limit £31,785	28%
	Trusts and personal representatives			28%
2014–15*	*Individuals*	•	to income tax basic rate limit £31,865	18%
		•	above income tax basic rate limit £31,865	28%
	Trusts and personal representatives			28%
2013–14*	*Individuals*	•	to income tax basic rate limit £32,010	18%
		•	above income tax basic rate limit £32,010	28%
	Trusts and personal representatives			28%

* A rate of **10% applies where entrepreneurs' relief is claimed** — see p 37.
For gains arising on or after 23 June 2010, the rate of tax for an individual is determined by treating gains as the top slice of income.
Scottish taxpayers: The Scottish basic rate limit (see p 75) does not apply to determine the rate of capital gains tax payable.
Disposals of high value UK residential property by certain non-natural persons: A rate of 28% applies to gains arising on disposals on or after 6 April 2013 of high value UK residential property by certain non-natural persons — see p 65.
Non-resident CGT gains on disposal of UK residential property by certain companies: A rate of 20% applies to NRCGT gains arising on disposals on or after 6 April 2015 of UK residential property interests at a time when the company is not resident in the UK. The normal rates above apply to individuals subject to the charge.
Trusts for vulnerable persons: From 2004–05 onwards, gains taxed at beneficiary's rates (on beneficiary if UK resident or on trustees if beneficiary not UK-resident) (FA 2005 ss 30–32).
SEE TOLLEY'S TAX COMPUTATIONS **228.2**.

Share identification rules

SEE TOLLEY'S TAX COMPUTATIONS 230.1, 230.2.

(TCGA 1992 ss 104–106A)

For disposals on or after 6 April 2008 by individuals, trustees or personal representatives, shares and securities of the same class in the same company are identified with acquisitions in the following order[2]:

- acquisitions on the same day as the disposal;
- acquisitions within 30 days after the day of disposal on a first in/first out basis[1];
- shares comprised in a single pool incorporating all other shares of the same class, whenever acquired.

For the purposes of corporation tax on chargeable gains, disposals of shares etc are identified with acquisitions in the following order:

- same day acquisitions;
- acquisitions within the previous nine days on a first in/first out basis;
- the pool of shares acquired after 31 March 1982;
- any shares held at 31 March 1982;
- any shares acquired on or before 6 April 1965 on a last in/first out basis;
- (if shares disposed of still not fully matched) subsequent acquisitions.

1 The 30-day matching rule does not apply in relation to acquisitions after 21 March 2006 where the individual making the disposal is not (or is not treated as) resident (or before 6 April 2013, ordinarily resident) in the UK at the time of the acquisition.

2 Different rules apply for SIP shares, exempt employee shareholder shares, BES shares, community investment tax relief shares, relevant EMI shares, EIS shares, VCT shares, SEIS shares, EOT exempt shares and social investment tax relief shares.

Entrepreneurs' relief

SEE TOLLEY'S TAX COMPUTATIONS 211.1.

(TCGA 1992 ss 169H–169V)

Entrepreneurs' relief applies to disposals by an individual on or after 6 April 2008 of:

- all or part of a trade carried on alone or in partnership;
- assets of such a trade following cessation; or
- shares or securities in the individual's 'personal trading company' (as defined).

Where a disposal of shares or of an interest in the assets of a partnership qualifies for relief, an associated disposal of assets owned by the individual and used by the company or partnership also qualifies for relief. However, for disposals on or after 18 March 2015, in order to qualify for this relief the claimant must generally reduce his participation in the business by also disposing of a minimum 5% of the shares of the company carrying on the business, or (where the business is carried on in partnership) of a minimum 5% share in the assets of the partnership carrying on the business. However, the disposal may be of less than a 5% share in the assets of the partnership providing the claimant disposes of the whole of his interest and owned 5% or more of the assets for a continuous period of three years in the eight years preceding the disposal. In addition, for assets acquired on or after 13 June 2016, the asset must have been held for three years before disposal.

Where a qualifying disposal is not of shares or securities in the individual's 'personal trading company', entrepreneurs' relief is given only in respect of the disposal of 'relevant business assets' comprised in the qualifying business disposal (assets used for purpose of the business but excluding shares and securities and assets, other than shares or securities, which are held as investments). Relief is not available for disposals of goodwill on or after 3 December 2014 to a close company to which the seller is related (this type of goodwill is excluded from the definition of relevant business assets) unless the business is transferred to a company controlled by 5 or fewer persons or by its directors and the claimant holds less than 5% of the shares, and less than 5% of the voting power, in the acquiring company. Relief will still also be due where the claimant does hold 5% or more of the shares or voting power provided the transfer of the business to the company is part of arrangements for the company to be sold to a new, independent owner.

Trustees can claim relief where a qualifying beneficiary has an interest in the business concerned.

Relief is extended to a disposal by an employee or officer of a trading company (or one or more companies in same trading group) of relevant EMI shares (as defined). Relief applies from 6 April 2013 where the shares were acquired on or after 6 April 2012.

The relief is available where the relevant conditions are met throughout a period of one year. The relief operates by charging qualifying net gains to CGT at 10% and is subject to a lifetime limit of gains of £10 million (£5 million for disposals before 6 April 2011; £2 million for disposals before 23 June 2010; £1 million for disposals before 6 April 2010), but disposals before 6 April 2008 do not count towards the limit. Relief given to trustees counts towards the limit of the qualifying beneficiary.

Transitional rules apply to allow relief to be claimed in certain circumstances where a gain made before 6 April 2008 is deferred and becomes chargeable on or after that date. In addition, gains which would have originally accrued on or after 3 December 2014 but which are deferred into the Enterprise Investment Scheme (see p 38) or Social Investment Tax Relief (see p 39) remain eligible for relief when the deferred gain becomes chargeable.

Investors' relief

SEE TOLLEY'S TAX COMPUTATIONS **215.1**.

(TCGA 1992 ss 169VA–169VY, Sch 7ZB)

Relief is available for gains accruing on the disposal of ordinary shares in an unlisted trading company, held for a period of at least three years starting on or after 6 April 2016, which are newly issued to the claimant and acquired for new consideration on or after 17 March 2016. Generally neither the investor nor a person connected to them can be an employee or officer of the company or a connected company, though some exceptions apply. The relief operates by charging relevant gains to CGT at 10% and is subject to a lifetime limit of £10 million. Relief can be claimed by trustees where an eligible beneficiary has an interest in settled property which includes the qualifying shares.

Other reliefs

The following is a summary of the other main capital gains tax reliefs and exemptions.

Charities

Gains accruing to charities which are both applicable and applied for charitable purposes are exempt. The exemption also applies from 1 April 2002 to Community Amateur Sports Clubs (CASCs).

Individuals

Companies owned by employee-ownership trusts	From 6 April 2014 relief from capital gains tax is available for disposals by a person other than a company of shares in either a trading company which is not a member of a group, or a parent company of a trading group, where the disposal is to a trust with specified characteristics. The disposal is treated as being made at no gain/no loss if the settlement is for the benefit of all eligible employees of the company or group and the settlement acquires a controlling interest in the company during the tax year in which the disposal is made. Further conditions apply.
Compensation (injury to person, profession or vocation)	Exempt.
Decorations for valour (acquired otherwise than for money or money's worth)	Gain exempt.
Employee shareholder shares (see p 98) SEE TOLLEY'S TAX COMPUTATIONS **218.2**.	Gains on or after 1 September 2013 on disposals of shares which were worth up to £50,000 on acquisition are exempt, provided the Employee Shareholder Agreement was entered into before 1 December 2016 (or 2 December 2016 where professional advice was given in relation to the share offer on 23 November 2016 before 1.30pm). A lifetime limit of £100,000 applies to exempt gains on disposal of shares acquired under Employee Shareholder Agreements entered into after 16 March 2016.
Enterprise Investment Scheme (see p 96) SEE TOLLEY'S TAX COMPUTATIONS **210.1** ONWARDS.	Gain on disposal after relevant three-year period exempt to extent full relief given on shares. Deferral relief is available on gains on assets where the disposal proceeds are reinvested in EIS shares within one year before and three years after the disposal.
Entrepreneurs' relief (see p 37) SEE TOLLEY'S TAX COMPUTATIONS **211.1** ONWARDS.	Gains on specified assets chargeable at 10% rate up to lifetime limit.
Foreign currency acquired for personal expenditure	Gain exempt.
Gifts for public benefit, works of art, historic buildings etc	No chargeable gain/allowable loss.
Gifts of pre-eminent objects	Donors who gift pre-eminent objects to the nation will receive a reduction in their UK tax liability of 30% of the value of the object they are donating. The tax reduction can be against income or capital gains tax and can be spread forward across a period of up to five years starting with the tax year in which the object is offered. The legislation has effect in relation to liabilities for tax years and accounting periods beginning on or after 1 April 2012. The gift must be accepted as pre-eminent by the Arts Council under the Cultural Gifts Scheme. See p 64 for relief applying to companies.
Gilt-edged stock	No chargeable gain/allowable loss.
Hold-over relief for gifts SEE TOLLEY'S TAX COMPUTATIONS **213.1** ONWARDS.	Restricted to: (1) gifts of business assets (including unquoted shares in trading companies and holding companies of trading groups). Relief is not available on the transfer of shares or securities to a company made after 8 November 1999 (other than transfers between 6 April 2003 and 20 October 2003); (2) gifts of heritage property; (3) gifts to heritage maintenance funds;

	(4) gifts to political parties; and (5) gifts which are chargeable transfers for inheritance tax. Where available, transferee's acquisition cost treated as reduced by held-over gain.
Investors' relief (see p 37) **SEE TOLLEY'S TAX COMPUTATIONS 215.1 ONWARDS.**	Gains on qualifying ordinary shares in an unlisted trading company chargeable at 10% rate up to lifetime limit.
Married persons or civil partners living together **SEE TOLLEY'S TAX COMPUTATIONS 218.1 ONWARDS.**	No chargeable gain/allowable loss on transfers between spouses or civil partners.
Motor vehicles	Gain exempt.
Principal private residence **SEE TOLLEY'S TAX COMPUTATIONS 223.1 ONWARDS.**	Gain exempt if property is main residence throughout period of ownership, or throughout the period of ownership except for all or any part of the last 18 months of that period (36 months for disposals before 6 April 2014). The 36-month period continues to apply where property is disposed of by an individual who is, or whose spouse or civil partner is, a disabled person or long-term resident of a care home, provided that neither holds an interest in any other dwelling on which private residence relief can be claimed. For disposals after 5 April 2015 property is treated as not being occupied as a residence for tax years when neither the taxpayer nor their spouse or civil partner is tax-resident in the territory in which the property is situated, and they do not stay overnight at the property at least 90 times during the year (pro-rated for part tax years). Period of ownership does not include any period before 31 March 1982. Certain other periods of absence qualify for exemption.
If residence is partly let, exemption for the let part is limited to the smaller of–	(1) exemption on owner-occupied part; and (2) £40,000.
Qualifying corporate bonds **SEE TOLLEY'S TAX COMPUTATIONS 224.1 ONWARDS.**	No chargeable gain (for loans made before 17 March 1998, allowable loss in certain cases if all or part of loss is irrecoverable).
Seed enterprise investment scheme (see p 96) **SEE TOLLEY'S TAX COMPUTATIONS 227.1 ONWARDS.**	From 2012–13 reinvestment relief may be claimed where an individual realises capital gains on disposals of assets in a tax year and in the same year makes investments that qualify for, and he claims, the main seed enterprise investment scheme (SEIS) relief from income tax. For disposals of assets in 2012–13 the relief applies to the full qualifying re-invested amount. From 2013–14 the relief applies to half the qualifying re-invested amount. SEIS shares can be treated as issued in the previous tax year as a result of a SEIS income tax relief carry-back claim. SEIS re-investment relief then also has effect as if those shares had been issued on a day in the previous tax year. The maximum exemption is £100,000 of gains for 2012–13 and £50,000 thereafter. A disposal of shares on which SEIS income tax relief has been given and not withdrawn is exempt.
Social investment tax relief (see p 97) **SEE TOLLEY'S TAX COMPUTATIONS 231.1 ONWARDS.**	Deferral relief is available for gains arising on assets in the period 6 April 2014 to 5 April 2019 where the disposal proceeds are reinvested in shares or debt investments which qualify for the social investment tax relief (SITR) income tax relief and investor is UK-resident. The qualifying investment must be made in the period from one year before to three years after the disposal. Limit of £1 million of gains which can be relieved in a tax year. A gain on a disposal of shares on which SITR income tax relief has been given and not withdrawn is exempt from capital gains tax where shares held for at least 3 years.
Venture capital trusts (see p 97) **SEE TOLLEY'S TAX COMPUTATIONS 32.3.**	Gain on disposal of shares by original investor exempt if company still a venture capital trust. Exemption applies only to shares acquired up to the permitted maximum of £200,000 per year of assessment. Deferral relief was available on gains on assets where the disposal proceeds were reinvested in VCT shares issued before 6 April 2004 and within one year before or after the disposal. This relief is withdrawn for shares issued after that date.

Businesses

Roll-over relief for replacement of business assets

SEE TOLLEY'S TAX COMPUTATIONS 103.3, 226.1 ONWARDS.

(TCGA 1992 s 155)

Qualifying assets:
Buildings and land both occupied and used for the purposes of the trade.
Fixed plant and machinery.
Ships, aircraft and hovercraft.
Satellites, space stations and spacecraft.
Goodwill[1].
continued on next page

Milk and potato quotas[1]. Ewe and suckler cow premium quotas[1]. Fish quotas[1]. Payment entitlement under farmers' single payment scheme. Payment entitlement under farmers' basic payment scheme (from 20 December 2013). Lloyd's syndicate rights.

1 From 1 April 2002 onwards, subject to transitional rules, these items are removed from the list for companies only (as they fall within the intangible assets regime from that date (FA 2002 Sch 29 para 132(5)).

2 The 'replacement' assets must be acquired within 12 months before or three years after the disposal of the old asset. Both assets must be within any of the above classes. Holdover relief is available where the new asset is a depreciating asset (having a predictable useful life not exceeding 60 years).

Roll-over relief on the transfer of a business ('incorporation relief')

SEE TOLLEY'S TAX COMPUTATIONS 213.3.

(TCGA 1992 s 162)

On incorporation of a business, the assets of the business are transferred to a company which then carries on the business in succession to the former proprietor. Gains realised on the transfer can be rolled over where the transfer is wholly or partly in consideration for the issue of shares. Relief is automatic (no claim is required).

See p 64 for disincorporation relief for companies. See p 39 for gifts of business assets.

Personal representatives

Allowable expenses

(SP 2/04)

Expenses allowable for the costs of establishing title in computing chargeable gains on disposal of assets in a deceased person's estate: deaths occurring after 5 April 2004. (HMRC accepts computations based either on the scale or on the actual allowable expenditure incurred.)

Gross value of estate	*Allowable expenditure*
Up to £50,000	1.8% of the probate value of the assets sold by the personal representatives.
Between £50,001 and £90,000	£900, to be divided between all the assets of the estate in proportion to the probate values and allowed in those proportions on assets sold by the personal representatives.
Between £90,001 and £400,000	1% of the probate value of the assets sold.
Between £400,001 and £500,000	£4,000, to be divided between all the assets of the estate in proportion to the probate values and allowed in those proportions on assets sold by the personal representatives.
Between £500,001 and £1,000,000	0.8% of the probate value of the assets sold.
Between £1,000,001 and £5,000,000	£8,000 to be divided between all the assets of the estate in proportion to the probate values and allowed in those proportions on assets sold by the personal representatives.
Exceeding £5,000,000	0.16% of the probate value of the assets sold subject to a maximum of £10,000.

Trustees

Allowable expenses

(SP 2/04)

Expenses allowable in computing chargeable gains of corporate trustees in the administration of trusts and estates: acquisition, disposals and deemed disposals after 5 April 2004. (HMRC accepts computations based either on the scale or on the actual allowable expenditure incurred.)

Transfers of assets to beneficiaries etc	
(*a*) Quoted stocks and shares	
(i) One beneficiary	£25 per holding.
(ii) More than one beneficiary	£25 per holding, divided equally between the beneficiaries.
(*b*) Unquoted shares	As (*a*) above, plus any exceptional expenditure.
(*c*) Other assets	As (*a*) above, plus any exceptional expenditure.
Actual disposals and acquisitions	
(*a*) Quoted stocks and shares	Investment fee as charged by the trustees (where a comprehensive annual management fee is charged, the investment fee is taken to be £0.25 per £100 of the sale or purchase moneys).
(*b*) Unquoted shares	As (*a*) above, plus actual valuation costs.

Transfers of assets to beneficiaries etc	
(*c*) Other assets	Investment fee (as (*a*) above), subject to a maximum of £75, plus actual valuation costs.
Deemed disposals by trustees	
(*a*) Quoted stocks and shares	£8 per holding.
(*b*) Unquoted shares	Actual valuation costs.
(*c*) Other assets	Actual valuation costs.

Indexation allowance – corporation tax on chargeable gains

SEE TOLLEY'S TAX COMPUTATIONS 214.1.

(TCGA 1992 ss 53–57, 109; FA 2018 s 26)

For corporation tax purposes, an indexation allowance is given as a deduction in calculating gains on disposals from the amount realised (or deemed to be realised) on disposal. Indexation allowance is 'frozen' from 1 January 2018, so for disposals on or after this date the allowance is calculated up to December 2017. Indexation allowance is calculated by multiplying each item of allowable expenditure by:

$$\frac{RD - RI}{RI}$$

Where:

RD is the retail prices index figure for month of disposal (or December 2017 if earlier);
RI is the retail prices index for month of expenditure (or March 1982 if later).

Indexation allowance can only be used to reduce or extinguish a gain. It cannot be used to create or increase a capital loss. It is not available to individuals, trustees and personal representatives. See p 60 for RPI values. The factors below can be used to calculate the indexation allowance for corporation tax purposes.

MONTH OF DISPOSAL

	2015						*2016*								
1982	July	Aug	Sep	Oct	Nov	Dec	Jan	Feb	Mar	Apr	May	June	July	Aug	Sep
Mar	2.255	2.270	2.268	2.267	2.270	2.280	2.258	2.273	2.287	2.290	2.299	2.312	2.316	2.328	2.334
Apr	2.191	2.206	2.203	2.202	2.206	2.216	2.194	2.208	2.222	2.226	2.234	2.247	2.250	2.263	2.269
May	2.168	2.183	2.181	2.179	2.183	2.193	2.171	2.185	2.199	2.203	2.211	2.223	2.227	2.239	2.245
June	2.159	2.174	2.172	2.170	2.174	2.184	2.162	2.177	2.190	2.194	2.202	2.214	2.218	2.230	2.236
July	2.158	2.173	2.171	2.169	2.173	2.183	2.161	2.176	2.189	2.193	2.201	2.213	2.217	2.229	2.235
Aug	2.157	2.172	2.170	2.168	2.172	2.182	2.160	2.175	2.188	2.192	2.200	2.212	2.216	2.228	2.234
Sept	2.159	2.174	2.172	2.170	2.174	2.184	2.162	2.177	2.190	2.194	2.202	2.214	2.218	2.230	2.236
Oct	2.144	2.158	2.156	2.155	2.158	2.168	2.146	2.161	2.174	2.178	2.186	2.199	2.202	2.214	2.220
Nov	2.128	2.143	2.141	2.139	2.143	2.153	2.131	2.145	2.159	2.162	2.171	2.183	2.186	2.199	2.205
Dec	2.134	2.149	2.146	2.145	2.149	2.158	2.137	2.151	2.164	2.168	2.177	2.189	2.192	2.204	2.211
1983	July	Aug	Sep	Oct	Nov	Dec	Jan	Feb	Mar	Apr	May	June	July	Aug	Sep
Jan	2.130	2.145	2.142	2.141	2.145	2.155	2.133	2.147	2.161	2.164	2.173	2.185	2.188	2.201	2.207
Feb	2.117	2.131	2.129	2.128	2.131	2.141	2.119	2.134	2.147	2.151	2.159	2.171	2.175	2.187	2.193
Mar	2.111	2.126	2.123	2.122	2.126	2.135	2.114	2.128	2.141	2.145	2.153	2.165	2.169	2.181	2.187
Apr	2.068	2.082	2.080	2.079	2.082	2.092	2.071	2.085	2.098	2.101	2.110	2.122	2.125	2.137	2.143
May	2.055	2.070	2.067	2.066	2.070	2.079	2.058	2.072	2.085	2.088	2.097	2.109	2.112	2.124	2.130
June	2.048	2.062	2.060	2.059	2.062	2.072	2.050	2.065	2.078	2.081	2.089	2.101	2.105	2.116	2.122
July	2.032	2.046	2.043	2.042	2.046	2.055	2.034	2.048	2.061	2.065	2.073	2.084	2.088	2.100	2.106
Aug	2.018	2.032	2.030	2.029	2.032	2.042	2.021	2.035	2.047	2.051	2.059	2.071	2.074	2.086	2.092
Sept	2.005	2.019	2.017	2.015	2.019	2.028	2.007	2.021	2.034	2.037	2.046	2.057	2.061	2.072	2.078
Oct	1.994	2.008	2.006	2.005	2.008	2.018	1.997	2.011	2.023	2.027	2.035	2.046	2.050	2.062	2.067
Nov	1.984	1.998	1.995	1.994	1.998	2.007	1.986	2.000	2.013	2.016	2.024	2.036	2.039	2.051	2.057
Dec	1.976	1.990	1.988	1.986	1.990	1.999	1.978	1.992	2.005	2.008	2.016	2.028	2.031	2.043	2.049
1984	July	Aug	Sep	Oct	Nov	Dec	Jan	Feb	Mar	Apr	May	June	July	Aug	Sep
Jan	1.978	1.992	1.989	1.988	1.992	2.001	1.980	1.994	2.007	2.010	2.018	2.030	2.033	2.045	2.050
Feb	1.968	1.979	1.977	1.976	1.979	1.989	1.968	1.982	1.994	1.998	2.006	2.017	2.021	2.032	2.038
Mar	1.956	1.970	1.968	1.966	1.970	1.979	1.958	1.972	1.985	1.988	1.996	2.008	2.011	2.022	2.028
Apr	1.917	1.931	1.929	1.927	1.931	1.940	1.920	1.933	1.945	1.949	1.957	1.968	1.971	1.983	1.988
May	1.906	1.920	1.918	1.917	1.920	1.929	1.909	1.922	1.935	1.938	1.946	1.957	1.960	1.972	1.977
June	1.899	1.913	1.910	1.909	1.913	1.921	1.901	1.915	1.927	1.930	1.938	1.950	1.953	1.964	1.970
July	1.902	1.916	1.914	1.912	1.916	1.925	1.905	1.918	1.930	1.934	1.942	1.953	1.956	1.967	1.973
Aug	1.875	1.889	1.886	1.885	1.889	1.898	1.878	1.891	1.903	1.906	1.914	1.925	1.929	1.940	1.945
Sept	1.870	1.883	1.881	1.880	1.883	1.892	1.872	1.885	1.897	1.901	1.909	1.920	1.923	1.934	1.940
Oct	1.852	1.865	1.863	1.862	1.865	1.874	1.854	1.867	1.880	1.883	1.891	1.902	1.905	1.916	1.922
Nov	1.843	1.856	1.854	1.853	1.856	1.865	1.846	1.859	1.871	1.874	1.882	1.893	1.896	1.907	1.913
Dec	1.846	1.859	1.857	1.856	1.859	1.868	1.848	1.861	1.873	1.876	1.884	1.895	1.899	1.910	1.915
1985	July	Aug	Sep	Oct	Nov	Dec	Jan	Feb	Mar	Apr	May	June	July	Aug	Sep
Jan	1.835	1.849	1.846	1.845	1.849	1.857	1.838	1.851	1.863	1.866	1.874	1.885	1.888	1.899	1.904
Feb	1.813	1.826	1.824	1.823	1.826	1.834	1.815	1.828	1.840	1.843	1.851	1.862	1.865	1.876	1.881
Mar	1.787	1.800	1.797	1.796	1.800	1.808	1.789	1.802	1.814	1.817	1.824	1.835	1.838	1.849	1.854
Apr	1.728	1.741	1.739	1.738	1.741	1.750	1.731	1.743	1.755	1.758	1.765	1.776	1.779	1.790	1.795
May	1.716	1.729	1.727	1.726	1.729	1.737	1.718	1.731	1.742	1.746	1.753	1.763	1.767	1.777	1.782
June	1.710	1.723	1.721	1.720	1.723	1.731	1.712	1.725	1.737	1.740	1.747	1.758	1.761	1.771	1.776
July	1.715	1.728	1.726	1.725	1.728	1.736	1.718	1.730	1.742	1.745	1.752	1.763	1.766	1.776	1.782
Aug	1.708	1.721	1.719	1.718	1.721	1.729	1.710	1.723	1.734	1.738	1.745	1.755	1.758	1.769	1.774
Sept	1.710	1.722	1.720	1.719	1.722	1.731	1.712	1.724	1.736	1.739	1.746	1.757	1.760	1.770	1.776
Oct	1.705	1.718	1.716	1.715	1.718	1.726	1.707	1.720	1.731	1.735	1.742	1.752	1.756	1.766	1.771
Nov	1.696	1.709	1.706	1.705	1.709	1.717	1.698	1.711	1.722	1.725	1.733	1.743	1.746	1.756	1.762
Dec	1.692	1.705	1.703	1.702	1.705	1.713	1.695	1.707	1.718	1.722	1.729	1.739	1.742	1.753	1.758

MONTH OF DISPOSAL

	2016			***2017***											
1982	Oct	Nov	Dec	Jan	Feb	Mar	Apr	May	June	July	Aug	Sep	Oct	Nov	Dec
Mar	2.333	2.342	2.362	2.342	2.379	2.390	2.406	2.420	2.428	2.435	2.458	2.463	2.465	2.472	2.501
Apr	2.268	2.276	2.296	2.276	2.312	2.323	2.339	2.353	2.360	2.368	2.390	2.395	2.397	2.403	2.432
May	2.244	2.253	2.272	2.253	2.288	2.299	2.315	2.329	2.336	2.343	2.366	2.370	2.373	2.379	2.407
June	2.235	2.244	2.263	2.244	2.279	2.290	2.306	2.319	2.327	2.334	2.356	2.361	2.363	2.370	2.398
July	2.234	2.243	2.262	2.243	2.278	2.289	2.305	2.318	2.326	2.333	2.355	2.360	2.362	2.369	2.397
Aug	2.233	2.242	2.261	2.242	2.277	2.288	2.304	2.317	2.325	2.332	2.354	2.359	2.361	2.367	2.396
Sept	2.235	2.244	2.263	2.244	2.279	2.290	2.306	2.319	2.327	2.334	2.356	2.361	2.363	2.370	2.398
Oct	2.219	2.228	2.247	2.228	2.263	2.274	2.290	2.303	2.310	2.318	2.340	2.344	2.347	2.353	2.381
Nov	2.203	2.212	2.231	2.212	2.247	2.258	2.274	2.287	2.294	2.301	2.323	2.328	2.330	2.336	2.364
Dec	2.209	2.218	2.237	2.218	2.253	2.264	2.280	2.293	2.300	2.307	2.329	2.334	2.337	2.343	2.371
1983	Oct	Nov	Dec	Jan	Feb	Mar	Apr	May	June	July	Aug	Sep	Oct	Nov	Dec
Jan	2.205	2.214	2.233	2.214	2.249	2.260	2.276	2.289	2.296	2.303	2.325	2.330	2.332	2.339	2.366
Feb	2.192	2.200	2.219	2.200	2.235	2.246	2.262	2.275	2.282	2.289	2.311	2.316	2.318	2.324	2.352
Mar	2.186	2.194	2.214	2.194	2.229	2.240	2.256	2.269	2.276	2.283	2.305	2.310	2.312	2.318	2.346
Apr	2.142	2.150	2.169	2.150	2.184	2.195	2.211	2.224	2.231	2.238	2.259	2.264	2.266	2.272	2.300
May	2.129	2.137	2.156	2.137	2.171	2.182	2.197	2.210	2.217	2.224	2.246	2.250	2.253	2.259	2.286
June	2.121	2.129	2.148	2.129	2.164	2.174	2.189	2.202	2.210	2.217	2.238	2.243	2.245	2.251	2.278
July	2.104	2.113	2.131	2.113	2.147	2.157	2.172	2.185	2.192	2.199	2.220	2.225	2.228	2.233	2.260
Aug	2.091	2.099	2.117	2.099	2.133	2.143	2.158	2.171	2.178	2.185	2.206	2.211	2.213	2.219	2.246
Sept	2.077	2.085	2.104	2.085	2.119	2.129	2.144	2.157	2.164	2.171	2.192	2.197	2.199	2.205	2.232
Oct	2.066	2.074	2.093	2.074	2.108	2.118	2.133	2.146	2.153	2.160	2.181	2.185	2.188	2.194	2.220
Nov	2.055	2.063	2.082	2.063	2.097	2.107	2.122	2.135	2.142	2.149	2.170	2.174	2.177	2.182	2.209
Dec	2.047	2.055	2.074	2.055	2.089	2.099	2.114	2.127	2.134	2.141	2.161	2.166	2.168	2.174	2.200
1984	Oct	Nov	Dec	Jan	Feb	Mar	Apr	May	June	July	Aug	Sep	Oct	Nov	Dec
Jan	2.049	2.057	2.076	2.057	2.091	2.101	2.116	2.129	2.136	2.142	2.163	2.168	2.170	2.176	2.202
Feb	2.037	2.045	2.063	2.045	2.078	2.088	2.103	2.116	2.123	2.130	2.150	2.155	2.157	2.163	2.189
Mar	2.027	2.035	2.053	2.035	2.068	2.078	2.093	2.106	2.113	2.120	2.140	2.145	2.147	2.153	2.179
Apr	1.987	1.995	2.013	1.995	2.028	2.038	2.053	2.065	2.072	2.079	2.099	2.103	2.106	2.111	2.137
May	1.976	1.984	2.002	1.984	2.017	2.027	2.041	2.054	2.060	2.067	2.087	2.092	2.094	2.100	2.126
June	1.969	1.976	1.994	1.976	2.009	2.019	2.034	2.046	2.053	2.059	2.080	2.084	2.086	2.092	2.118
July	1.972	1.980	1.998	1.980	2.012	2.022	2.037	2.049	2.056	2.063	2.083	2.088	2.090	2.095	2.121
Aug	1.944	1.952	1.970	1.952	1.984	1.994	2.009	2.021	2.028	2.034	2.054	2.059	2.061	2.067	2.092
Sept	1.938	1.946	1.964	1.946	1.978	1.988	2.003	2.015	2.022	2.028	2.048	2.053	2.055	2.061	2.086
Oct	1.920	1.928	1.946	1.928	1.960	1.970	1.984	1.997	2.003	2.010	2.030	2.034	2.036	2.042	2.067
Nov	1.911	1.919	1.937	1.919	1.951	1.961	1.975	1.987	1.994	2.001	2.020	2.025	2.027	2.032	2.058
Dec	1.914	1.922	1.939	1.922	1.954	1.963	1.978	1.990	1.996	2.003	2.023	2.027	2.029	2.035	2.060
1985	Oct	Nov	Dec	Jan	Feb	Mar	Apr	May	June	July	Aug	Sep	Oct	Nov	Dec
Jan	1.903	1.911	1.929	1.911	1.943	1.953	1.967	1.979	1.986	1.992	2.012	2.016	2.019	2.024	2.049
Feb	1.880	1.888	1.905	1.888	1.919	1.929	1.943	1.955	1.962	1.968	1.988	1.992	1.994	2.000	2.025
Mar	1.853	1.861	1.878	1.861	1.892	1.902	1.916	1.928	1.934	1.941	1.960	1.964	1.967	1.972	1.997
Apr	1.794	1.801	1.818	1.801	1.832	1.841	1.855	1.867	1.873	1.879	1.898	1.903	1.905	1.910	1.934
May	1.781	1.789	1.805	1.789	1.819	1.829	1.842	1.854	1.860	1.866	1.885	1.889	1.892	1.897	1.921
June	1.775	1.783	1.799	1.783	1.813	1.822	1.836	1.848	1.854	1.860	1.879	1.883	1.885	1.891	1.915
July	1.781	1.788	1.805	1.788	1.818	1.828	1.841	1.853	1.859	1.866	1.884	1.889	1.891	1.896	1.920
Aug	1.773	1.780	1.797	1.780	1.811	1.820	1.834	1.845	1.852	1.858	1.877	1.881	1.883	1.888	1.912
Sept	1.775	1.782	1.799	1.782	1.812	1.822	1.835	1.847	1.853	1.859	1.878	1.883	1.885	1.890	1.914
Oct	1.770	1.778	1.794	1.778	1.808	1.817	1.831	1.842	1.849	1.855	1.874	1.878	1.880	1.885	1.909
Nov	1.761	1.768	1.785	1.768	1.798	1.808	1.821	1.833	1.839	1.845	1.864	1.868	1.870	1.875	1.899
Dec	1.757	1.764	1.781	1.764	1.795	1.804	1.817	1.829	1.835	1.841	1.860	1.864	1.866	1.872	1.895

MONTH OF DISPOSAL

	2015						***2016***								
1986	July	Aug	Sep	Oct	Nov	Dec	Jan	Feb	Mar	Apr	May	June	July	Aug	Sep
Jan	1.687	1.699	1.697	1.696	1.699	1.708	1.689	1.701	1.713	1.716	1.723	1.734	1.737	1.747	1.752
Feb	1.677	1.689	1.687	1.686	1.689	1.698	1.679	1.691	1.703	1.706	1.713	1.724	1.727	1.737	1.742
Mar	1.673	1.686	1.684	1.683	1.686	1.694	1.675	1.688	1.699	1.702	1.710	1.720	1.723	1.733	1.739
Apr	1.648	1.660	1.658	1.657	1.660	1.668	1.650	1.662	1.673	1.676	1.684	1.694	1.697	1.707	1.712
May	1.643	1.655	1.653	1.652	1.655	1.663	1.645	1.657	1.668	1.672	1.679	1.689	1.692	1.702	1.707
June	1.644	1.657	1.655	1.654	1.657	1.665	1.646	1.659	1.670	1.673	1.680	1.690	1.693	1.704	1.709
July	1.652	1.664	1.662	1.661	1.664	1.672	1.654	1.666	1.678	1.681	1.688	1.698	1.701	1.711	1.716
Aug	1.644	1.656	1.654	1.653	1.656	1.664	1.646	1.658	1.669	1.672	1.679	1.690	1.693	1.703	1.708
Sept	1.631	1.643	1.641	1.640	1.643	1.651	1.633	1.645	1.656	1.659	1.666	1.676	1.680	1.690	1.695
Oct	1.627	1.639	1.637	1.636	1.639	1.647	1.629	1.641	1.652	1.655	1.662	1.672	1.675	1.686	1.691
Nov	1.604	1.617	1.615	1.614	1.617	1.625	1.606	1.619	1.630	1.633	1.640	1.650	1.653	1.663	1.668
Dec	1.596	1.608	1.606	1.605	1.608	1.616	1.598	1.610	1.621	1.624	1.631	1.641	1.644	1.654	1.659
1987	July	Aug	Sep	Oct	Nov	Dec	Jan	Feb	Mar	Apr	May	June	July	Aug	Sep
Jan	1.586	1.598	1.596	1.595	1.598	1.606	1.588	1.600	1.611	1.614	1.621	1.631	1.634	1.644	1.649
Feb	1.576	1.588	1.586	1.585	1.588	1.596	1.578	1.590	1.601	1.604	1.611	1.621	1.624	1.633	1.638
Mar	1.571	1.583	1.581	1.580	1.583	1.590	1.573	1.584	1.595	1.598	1.605	1.615	1.618	1.628	1.633
Apr	1.540	1.552	1.550	1.549	1.552	1.560	1.542	1.554	1.565	1.568	1.575	1.584	1.587	1.597	1.602
May	1.538	1.550	1.548	1.547	1.550	1.557	1.540	1.552	1.562	1.565	1.572	1.582	1.585	1.595	1.600
June	1.538	1.550	1.548	1.547	1.550	1.557	1.540	1.552	1.562	1.565	1.572	1.582	1.585	1.595	1.600
July	1.540	1.552	1.550	1.549	1.552	1.560	1.542	1.554	1.565	1.568	1.575	1.584	1.587	1.597	1.602
Aug	1.533	1.545	1.543	1.542	1.545	1.552	1.535	1.547	1.557	1.560	1.567	1.577	1.580	1.590	1.595
Sept	1.525	1.537	1.535	1.534	1.537	1.545	1.527	1.539	1.550	1.553	1.560	1.569	1.572	1.582	1.587
Oct	1.513	1.525	1.523	1.522	1.525	1.533	1.515	1.527	1.537	1.540	1.547	1.557	1.560	1.569	1.574
Nov	1.501	1.513	1.511	1.510	1.513	1.520	1.503	1.515	1.525	1.528	1.535	1.544	1.547	1.557	1.562
Dec	1.503	1.515	1.513	1.512	1.515	1.523	1.505	1.517	1.528	1.530	1.537	1.547	1.550	1.560	1.564
1988	July	Aug	Sep	Oct	Nov	Dec	Jan	Feb	Mar	Apr	May	June	July	Aug	Sep
Jan	1.503	1.515	1.513	1.512	1.515	1.523	1.505	1.517	1.528	1.530	1.537	1.547	1.550	1.560	1.564
Feb	1.494	1.505	1.503	1.502	1.505	1.513	1.496	1.507	1.518	1.521	1.527	1.537	1.540	1.550	1.554
Mar	1.484	1.496	1.494	1.493	1.496	1.503	1.486	1.498	1.508	1.511	1.518	1.527	1.530	1.540	1.545
Apr	1.444	1.456	1.454	1.453	1.456	1.463	1.446	1.457	1.468	1.471	1.477	1.487	1.490	1.499	1.504
May	1.435	1.446	1.444	1.444	1.446	1.454	1.437	1.448	1.459	1.461	1.468	1.477	1.480	1.490	1.494
June	1.426	1.437	1.435	1.434	1.437	1.445	1.428	1.439	1.449	1.452	1.459	1.468	1.471	1.480	1.485
July	1.424	1.435	1.433	1.432	1.435	1.442	1.425	1.437	1.447	1.450	1.456	1.466	1.469	1.478	1.483
Aug	1.397	1.408	1.406	1.405	1.408	1.415	1.399	1.410	1.420	1.423	1.429	1.438	1.441	1.450	1.455
Sept	1.386	1.397	1.395	1.394	1.397	1.404	1.387	1.399	1.409	1.411	1.418	1.427	1.430	1.439	1.444
Oct	1.362	1.373	1.371	1.370	1.373	1.380	1.363	1.374	1.384	1.387	1.394	1.403	1.405	1.415	1.419
Nov	1.351	1.362	1.360	1.359	1.362	1.369	1.353	1.364	1.374	1.376	1.383	1.392	1.395	1.404	1.408
Dec	1.345	1.355	1.354	1.353	1.355	1.363	1.346	1.357	1.367	1.370	1.376	1.385	1.388	1.397	1.402
1989	July	Aug	Sep	Oct	Nov	Dec	Jan	Feb	Mar	Apr	May	June	July	Aug	Sep
Jan	1.330	1.341	1.339	1.338	1.341	1.348	1.332	1.342	1.352	1.355	1.361	1.370	1.373	1.382	1.386
Feb	1.313	1.324	1.322	1.321	1.324	1.331	1.315	1.326	1.335	1.338	1.344	1.353	1.356	1.365	1.369
Mar	1.303	1.313	1.312	1.311	1.313	1.321	1.305	1.315	1.325	1.328	1.334	1.343	1.346	1.354	1.359
Apr	1.262	1.273	1.271	1.270	1.273	1.280	1.264	1.275	1.284	1.287	1.293	1.302	1.304	1.313	1.318
May	1.249	1.259	1.257	1.257	1.259	1.266	1.250	1.261	1.270	1.273	1.279	1.288	1.290	1.299	1.303
June	1.241	1.251	1.250	1.249	1.251	1.258	1.243	1.253	1.263	1.265	1.271	1.280	1.282	1.291	1.295
July	1.239	1.249	1.248	1.247	1.249	1.256	1.241	1.251	1.261	1.263	1.269	1.278	1.281	1.289	1.294
Aug	1.233	1.244	1.242	1.241	1.244	1.250	1.235	1.245	1.255	1.257	1.263	1.272	1.275	1.283	1.288
Sept	1.218	1.228	1.226	1.226	1.228	1.235	1.220	1.230	1.239	1.242	1.248	1.256	1.259	1.268	1.272
Oct	1.201	1.211	1.209	1.209	1.211	1.218	1.203	1.213	1.222	1.225	1.231	1.239	1.242	1.250	1.254
Nov	1.182	1.192	1.191	1.190	1.192	1.199	1.184	1.194	1.203	1.206	1.212	1.220	1.223	1.231	1.235
Dec	1.177	1.187	1.185	1.184	1.187	1.194	1.178	1.189	1.198	1.200	1.206	1.215	1.217	1.226	1.230

MONTH OF DISPOSAL

	2016			*2017*											
1986	Oct	Nov	Dec	Jan	Feb	Mar	Apr	May	June	July	Aug	Sep	Oct	Nov	Dec
Jan	1.751	1.758	1.775	1.758	1.789	1.798	1.811	1.823	1.829	1.835	1.854	1.858	1.860	1.866	1.889
Feb	1.741	1.748	1.765	1.748	1.778	1.788	1.801	1.813	1.819	1.825	1.844	1.848	1.850	1.855	1.879
Mar	1.738	1.745	1.761	1.745	1.775	1.784	1.797	1.809	1.815	1.821	1.840	1.844	1.846	1.851	1.875
Apr	1.711	1.718	1.735	1.718	1.748	1.757	1.771	1.782	1.788	1.794	1.813	1.817	1.819	1.824	1.847
May	1.706	1.713	1.730	1.713	1.743	1.752	1.766	1.777	1.783	1.789	1.807	1.812	1.814	1.819	1.842
June	1.708	1.715	1.731	1.715	1.745	1.754	1.767	1.778	1.784	1.791	1.809	1.813	1.815	1.820	1.844
July	1.715	1.723	1.739	1.723	1.752	1.762	1.775	1.786	1.792	1.799	1.817	1.821	1.823	1.828	1.852
Aug	1.707	1.714	1.731	1.714	1.744	1.753	1.766	1.778	1.784	1.790	1.808	1.812	1.814	1.819	1.843
Sept	1.694	1.701	1.717	1.701	1.730	1.740	1.753	1.764	1.770	1.776	1.794	1.799	1.801	1.806	1.829
Oct	1.690	1.697	1.713	1.697	1.726	1.735	1.748	1.760	1.766	1.772	1.790	1.794	1.796	1.801	1.825
Nov	1.667	1.674	1.690	1.674	1.703	1.712	1.725	1.736	1.742	1.749	1.767	1.771	1.773	1.778	1.801
Dec	1.658	1.665	1.681	1.665	1.694	1.703	1.716	1.727	1.733	1.739	1.757	1.762	1.764	1.769	1.792
1987	Oct	Nov	Dec	Jan	Feb	Mar	Apr	May	June	July	Aug	Sep	Oct	Nov	Dec
Jan	1.648	1.655	1.671	1.655	1.684	1.693	1.706	1.717	1.723	1.729	1.747	1.751	1.753	1.758	1.781
Feb	1.637	1.644	1.660	1.644	1.673	1.682	1.695	1.706	1.712	1.718	1.736	1.740	1.742	1.747	1.770
Mar	1.632	1.639	1.655	1.639	1.668	1.677	1.690	1.701	1.707	1.713	1.731	1.735	1.737	1.742	1.764
Apr	1.601	1.608	1.624	1.608	1.637	1.645	1.658	1.669	1.675	1.681	1.698	1.702	1.704	1.709	1.732
May	1.599	1.605	1.621	1.605	1.634	1.643	1.656	1.666	1.672	1.678	1.696	1.700	1.702	1.707	1.729
June	1.599	1.605	1.621	1.605	1.634	1.643	1.656	1.666	1.672	1.678	1.696	1.700	1.702	1.707	1.729
July	1.601	1.608	1.624	1.608	1.637	1.645	1.658	1.669	1.675	1.681	1.698	1.702	1.704	1.709	1.732
Aug	1.594	1.600	1.616	1.600	1.629	1.638	1.650	1.661	1.667	1.673	1.690	1.694	1.696	1.701	1.724
Sept	1.586	1.593	1.608	1.593	1.621	1.630	1.643	1.653	1.659	1.665	1.683	1.687	1.688	1.693	1.716
Oct	1.573	1.580	1.596	1.580	1.608	1.617	1.630	1.640	1.646	1.652	1.670	1.673	1.675	1.680	1.703
Nov	1.561	1.568	1.583	1.568	1.596	1.604	1.617	1.628	1.633	1.639	1.657	1.661	1.662	1.667	1.690
Dec	1.563	1.570	1.586	1.570	1.598	1.607	1.620	1.630	1.636	1.642	1.659	1.663	1.665	1.670	1.692
1988	Oct	Nov	Dec	Jan	Feb	Mar	Apr	May	June	July	Aug	Sep	Oct	Nov	Dec
Jan	1.563	1.570	1.586	1.570	1.598	1.607	1.620	1.630	1.636	1.642	1.659	1.663	1.665	1.670	1.692
Feb	1.554	1.560	1.576	1.560	1.588	1.597	1.609	1.620	1.626	1.632	1.649	1.653	1.655	1.660	1.682
Mar	1.544	1.550	1.566	1.550	1.578	1.587	1.599	1.610	1.616	1.622	1.639	1.643	1.645	1.649	1.671
Apr	1.503	1.509	1.525	1.509	1.537	1.545	1.558	1.568	1.574	1.579	1.596	1.600	1.602	1.607	1.629
May	1.493	1.500	1.515	1.500	1.527	1.536	1.548	1.558	1.564	1.570	1.587	1.590	1.592	1.597	1.619
June	1.484	1.491	1.506	1.491	1.518	1.526	1.538	1.549	1.554	1.560	1.577	1.581	1.583	1.587	1.609
July	1.482	1.488	1.503	1.488	1.515	1.524	1.536	1.546	1.552	1.558	1.575	1.578	1.580	1.585	1.606
Aug	1.454	1.461	1.475	1.461	1.487	1.496	1.508	1.518	1.524	1.529	1.546	1.550	1.551	1.556	1.577
Sept	1.443	1.449	1.464	1.449	1.476	1.484	1.496	1.506	1.512	1.518	1.534	1.538	1.540	1.544	1.565
Oct	1.418	1.425	1.439	1.425	1.451	1.459	1.471	1.481	1.487	1.492	1.509	1.512	1.514	1.519	1.540
Nov	1.407	1.414	1.428	1.414	1.440	1.448	1.460	1.470	1.475	1.481	1.497	1.501	1.503	1.507	1.528
Dec	1.401	1.407	1.422	1.407	1.433	1.442	1.453	1.463	1.469	1.474	1.490	1.494	1.496	1.500	1.521
1989	Oct	Nov	Dec	Jan	Feb	Mar	Apr	May	June	July	Aug	Sep	Oct	Nov	Dec
Jan	1.386	1.392	1.406	1.392	1.418	1.426	1.438	1.448	1.453	1.459	1.475	1.478	1.480	1.485	1.505
Feb	1.369	1.375	1.389	1.375	1.401	1.409	1.420	1.430	1.436	1.441	1.457	1.461	1.462	1.467	1.487
Mar	1.358	1.364	1.378	1.364	1.390	1.398	1.410	1.419	1.425	1.430	1.446	1.450	1.451	1.456	1.476
Apr	1.317	1.323	1.337	1.323	1.348	1.356	1.367	1.377	1.382	1.388	1.403	1.407	1.409	1.413	1.433
May	1.303	1.309	1.323	1.309	1.334	1.342	1.353	1.363	1.368	1.373	1.389	1.392	1.394	1.398	1.418
June	1.295	1.301	1.315	1.301	1.326	1.334	1.345	1.354	1.360	1.365	1.380	1.384	1.386	1.390	1.410
July	1.293	1.299	1.313	1.299	1.324	1.332	1.343	1.352	1.358	1.363	1.378	1.382	1.384	1.388	1.408
Aug	1.287	1.293	1.307	1.293	1.318	1.326	1.337	1.346	1.351	1.357	1.372	1.376	1.377	1.382	1.402
Sept	1.271	1.277	1.291	1.277	1.302	1.310	1.321	1.330	1.335	1.340	1.356	1.359	1.361	1.365	1.385
Oct	1.254	1.260	1.273	1.260	1.284	1.292	1.303	1.312	1.317	1.323	1.338	1.341	1.343	1.347	1.367
Nov	1.235	1.241	1.254	1.241	1.265	1.273	1.284	1.293	1.298	1.303	1.318	1.322	1.323	1.327	1.347
Dec	1.229	1.235	1.248	1.235	1.259	1.267	1.278	1.287	1.292	1.297	1.312	1.316	1.317	1.322	1.341

MONTH OF DISPOSAL

	2015						*2016*								
1990	July	Aug	Sep	Oct	Nov	Dec	Jan	Feb	Mar	Apr	May	June	July	Aug	Sep
Jan	1.164	1.174	1.172	1.172	1.174	1.181	1.166	1.176	1.185	1.187	1.193	1.202	1.204	1.213	1.217
Feb	1.151	1.161	1.160	1.159	1.161	1.168	1.153	1.163	1.172	1.175	1.181	1.189	1.191	1.200	1.204
Mar	1.130	1.140	1.138	1.138	1.140	1.147	1.132	1.142	1.151	1.153	1.159	1.167	1.170	1.178	1.182
Apr	1.067	1.077	1.075	1.074	1.077	1.083	1.069	1.078	1.087	1.090	1.095	1.103	1.106	1.114	1.118
May	1.049	1.059	1.057	1.056	1.059	1.065	1.051	1.060	1.069	1.071	1.077	1.085	1.087	1.095	1.099
June	1.041	1.051	1.049	1.048	1.051	1.057	1.043	1.052	1.061	1.063	1.069	1.077	1.079	1.087	1.091
July	1.039	1.049	1.047	1.047	1.049	1.055	1.041	1.050	1.059	1.062	1.067	1.075	1.077	1.085	1.089
Aug	1.019	1.028	1.027	1.026	1.028	1.034	1.020	1.030	1.038	1.041	1.046	1.054	1.056	1.064	1.068
Sept	1.000	1.009	1.008	1.007	1.009	1.015	1.002	1.011	1.019	1.022	1.027	1.035	1.037	1.045	1.049
Oct	.985	.994	.992	.992	.994	1.000	.986	.995	1.004	1.006	1.012	1.019	1.021	1.029	1.033
Nov	.989	.998	.997	.996	.998	1.005	.991	1.000	1.008	1.011	1.016	1.024	1.026	1.034	1.038
Dec	.991	1.000	.998	.998	1.000	1.006	.992	1.002	1.010	1.012	1.018	1.025	1.028	1.035	1.039
1991	July	Aug	Sep	Oct	Nov	Dec	Jan	Feb	Mar	Apr	May	June	July	Aug	Sep
Jan	.986	.995	.994	.993	.995	1.002	.988	.997	1.005	1.008	1.013	1.021	1.023	1.031	1.035
Feb	.976	.985	.983	.982	.985	.991	.977	.986	.995	.997	1.002	1.010	1.012	1.020	1.024
Mar	.968	.977	.976	.975	.977	.983	.970	.979	.987	.989	.995	1.002	1.005	1.012	1.016
Apr	.943	.952	.950	.950	.952	.958	.944	.953	.962	.964	.969	.977	.979	.986	.990
May	.937	.946	.945	.944	.946	.952	.939	.948	.956	.958	.963	.971	.973	.981	.984
June	.928	.937	.936	.935	.937	.943	.930	.939	.947	.949	.955	.962	.964	.972	.975
July	.933	.942	.940	.939	.942	.948	.934	.943	.951	.954	.959	.966	.969	.976	.980
Aug	.928	.937	.936	.935	.937	.943	.930	.939	.947	.949	.955	.962	.964	.972	.975
Sept	.921	.930	.929	.928	.930	.936	.923	.932	.940	.942	.947	.955	.957	.964	.968
Oct	.914	.923	.922	.921	.923	.929	.916	.925	.933	.935	.940	.947	.950	.957	.961
Nov	.907	.916	.914	.914	.916	.922	.909	.917	.926	.928	.933	.940	.942	.950	.954
Dec	.906	.915	.913	.912	.915	.920	.907	.916	.924	.926	.931	.939	.941	.948	.952
1992	July	Aug	Sep	Oct	Nov	Dec	Jan	Feb	Mar	Apr	May	June	July	Aug	Sep
Jan	.907	.916	.914	.914	.916	.922	.909	.917	.926	.928	.933	.940	.942	.950	.954
Feb	.897	.906	.905	.904	.906	.912	.899	.908	.916	.918	.923	.930	.933	.940	.944
Mar	.892	.901	.899	.898	.901	.906	.893	.902	.910	.912	.917	.925	.927	.934	.938
Apr	.863	.872	.870	.870	.872	.878	.865	.873	.881	.883	.888	.896	.898	.905	.909
May	.856	.865	.864	.863	.865	.871	.858	.866	.874	.877	.882	.889	.891	.898	.902
June	.856	.865	.864	.863	.865	.871	.858	.866	.874	.877	.882	.889	.891	.898	.902
July	.863	.872	.870	.870	.872	.878	.865	.873	.881	.883	.888	.896	.898	.905	.909
Aug	.862	.870	.869	.868	.870	.876	.863	.872	.880	.882	.887	.894	.896	.904	.907
Sept	.855	.864	.862	.862	.864	.869	.857	.865	.873	.875	.880	.887	.890	.897	.900
Oct	.848	.857	.856	.855	.857	.863	.850	.858	.866	.868	.873	.881	.883	.890	.893
Nov	.851	.860	.858	.858	.860	.865	.853	.861	.869	.871	.876	.883	.885	.893	.896
Dec	.858	.866	.865	.864	.866	.872	.859	.868	.876	.878	.883	.890	.892	.899	.903
1993	July	Aug	Sep	Oct	Nov	Dec	Jan	Feb	Mar	Apr	May	June	July	Aug	Sep
Jan	.875	.884	.883	.882	.884	.890	.877	.885	.893	.896	.901	.908	.910	.917	.921
Feb	.863	.872	.870	.870	.872	.878	.865	.873	.881	.883	.888	.896	.898	.905	.909
Mar	.856	.865	.864	.863	.865	.871	.858	.866	.874	.877	.882	.889	.891	.898	.902
Apr	.839	.848	.846	.846	.848	.853	.841	.849	.857	.859	.864	.871	.873	.881	.884
May	.833	.841	.840	.839	.841	.847	.834	.843	.850	.853	.858	.865	.867	.874	.877
June	.834	.843	.841	.840	.843	.848	.835	.844	.852	.854	.859	.866	.868	.875	.879
July	.838	.846	.845	.844	.846	.852	.839	.848	.856	.858	.863	.870	.872	.879	.883
Aug	.830	.839	.837	.837	.839	.844	.832	.840	.848	.850	.855	.862	.864	.871	.875
Sept	.822	.831	.829	.829	.831	.837	.824	.832	.840	.842	.847	.854	.856	.863	.867
Oct	.824	.832	.831	.830	.832	.838	.825	.834	.841	.843	.848	.855	.858	.865	.868
Nov	.826	.835	.833	.833	.835	.840	.828	.836	.844	.846	.851	.858	.860	.867	.871
Dec	.822	.831	.829	.829	.831	.837	.824	.832	.840	.842	.847	.854	.856	.863	.867

MONTH OF DISPOSAL

	2016			***2017***											
1990	Oct	Nov	Dec	Jan	Feb	Mar	Apr	May	June	July	Aug	Sep	Oct	Nov	Dec
Jan	1.216	1.222	1.235	1.222	1.246	1.254	1.264	1.274	1.279	1.284	1.299	1.302	1.304	1.308	1.327
Feb	1.203	1.209	1.222	1.209	1.233	1.240	1.251	1.260	1.265	1.270	1.285	1.289	1.290	1.295	1.314
Mar	1.181	1.187	1.200	1.187	1.211	1.218	1.229	1.238	1.243	1.248	1.263	1.266	1.268	1.272	1.291
Apr	1.117	1.122	1.135	1.122	1.145	1.153	1.163	1.172	1.177	1.181	1.196	1.199	1.201	1.205	1.223
May	1.098	1.104	1.116	1.104	1.127	1.134	1.144	1.153	1.158	1.162	1.177	1.180	1.181	1.185	1.204
June	1.090	1.096	1.108	1.096	1.118	1.125	1.136	1.144	1.149	1.154	1.168	1.171	1.173	1.177	1.195
July	1.088	1.094	1.106	1.094	1.117	1.124	1.134	1.143	1.147	1.152	1.166	1.170	1.171	1.175	1.193
Aug	1.067	1.073	1.085	1.073	1.095	1.102	1.112	1.121	1.126	1.130	1.144	1.148	1.149	1.153	1.171
Sept	1.048	1.053	1.066	1.053	1.076	1.083	1.093	1.101	1.106	1.111	1.125	1.128	1.129	1.133	1.151
Oct	1.032	1.038	1.050	1.038	1.060	1.067	1.077	1.085	1.090	1.094	1.108	1.111	1.113	1.117	1.134
Nov	1.037	1.042	1.055	1.042	1.065	1.072	1.082	1.090	1.095	1.099	1.113	1.116	1.118	1.122	1.139
Dec	1.038	1.044	1.056	1.044	1.066	1.073	1.083	1.092	1.096	1.101	1.115	1.118	1.119	1.123	1.141
1991	Oct	Nov	Dec	Jan	Feb	Mar	Apr	May	June	July	Aug	Sep	Oct	Nov	Dec
Jan	1.034	1.039	1.051	1.039	1.061	1.068	1.078	1.087	1.091	1.096	1.110	1.113	1.114	1.118	1.136
Feb	1.023	1.028	1.040	1.028	1.050	1.057	1.067	1.076	1.080	1.085	1.099	1.102	1.103	1.107	1.125
Mar	1.015	1.021	1.033	1.021	1.043	1.049	1.059	1.068	1.072	1.077	1.091	1.094	1.095	1.099	1.116
Apr	.989	.995	1.007	.995	1.017	1.023	1.033	1.041	1.046	1.050	1.064	1.067	1.068	1.072	1.089
May	.984	.989	1.001	.989	1.010	1.017	1.027	1.035	1.040	1.044	1.058	1.061	1.062	1.066	1.083
June	.975	.980	.992	.980	1.001	1.008	1.018	1.026	1.031	1.035	1.048	1.051	1.053	1.057	1.074
July	.979	.984	.996	.984	1.006	1.013	1.022	1.031	1.035	1.040	1.053	1.056	1.058	1.061	1.078
Aug	.975	.980	.992	.980	1.001	1.008	1.018	1.026	1.031	1.035	1.048	1.051	1.053	1.057	1.074
Sept	.967	.973	.984	.973	.994	1.001	1.010	1.019	1.023	1.027	1.041	1.044	1.045	1.049	1.066
Oct	.960	.965	.977	.965	.987	.993	1.003	1.011	1.016	1.020	1.033	1.036	1.038	1.041	1.058
Nov	.953	.958	.970	.958	.979	.986	.996	1.004	1.008	1.013	1.026	1.029	1.030	1.034	1.051
Dec	.951	.957	.968	.957	.978	.985	.994	1.002	1.007	1.011	1.024	1.027	1.029	1.032	1.049
1992	Oct	Nov	Dec	Jan	Feb	Mar	Apr	May	June	July	Aug	Sep	Oct	Nov	Dec
Jan	.953	.958	.970	.958	.979	.986	.996	1.004	1.008	1.013	1.026	1.029	1.030	1.034	1.051
Feb	.943	.948	.960	.948	.969	.976	.985	.993	.998	1.002	1.015	1.018	1.020	1.023	1.040
Mar	.937	.942	.954	.942	.963	.970	.980	.988	.992	.996	1.010	1.012	1.014	1.018	1.034
Apr	.908	.913	.924	.913	.934	.940	.950	.957	.962	.966	.979	.982	.983	.987	1.004
May	.901	.906	.917	.906	.927	.933	.943	.950	.955	.959	.972	.975	.976	.980	.996
June	.901	.906	.917	.906	.927	.933	.943	.950	.955	.959	.972	.975	.976	.980	.996
July	.908	.913	.924	.913	.934	.940	.950	.957	.962	.966	.979	.982	.983	.987	1.004
Aug	.906	.911	.923	.911	.932	.939	.948	.956	.960	.965	.978	.981	.982	.986	1.002
Sept	.900	.905	.916	.905	.925	.932	.941	.949	.953	.958	.971	.973	.975	.978	.995
Oct	.893	.898	.909	.898	.919	.925	.934	.942	.946	.951	.964	.966	.968	.971	.988
Nov	.895	.901	.912	.901	.921	.928	.937	.945	.949	.953	.966	.969	.971	.974	.991
Dec	.902	.907	.919	.907	.928	.935	.944	.952	.956	.960	.973	.976	.978	.981	.998
1993	Oct	Nov	Dec	Jan	Feb	Mar	Apr	May	June	July	Aug	Sep	Oct	Nov	Dec
Jan	.920	.925	.937	.925	.946	.953	.962	.970	.975	.979	.992	.995	.996	1.000	1.017
Feb	.908	.913	.924	.913	.934	.940	.950	.957	.962	.966	.979	.982	.983	.987	1.004
Mar	.901	.906	.917	.906	.927	.933	.943	.950	.955	.959	.972	.975	.976	.980	.996
Apr	.883	.888	.900	.888	.909	.915	.925	.932	.937	.941	.954	.957	.958	.962	.978
May	.877	.882	.893	.882	.902	.909	.918	.926	.930	.934	.947	.950	.951	.955	.971
June	.878	.883	.894	.883	.904	.910	.919	.927	.931	.935	.948	.951	.952	.956	.972
July	.882	.887	.898	.887	.908	.914	.923	.931	.935	.940	.952	.955	.957	.960	.977
Aug	.874	.879	.890	.879	.900	.906	.915	.923	.927	.931	.944	.947	.948	.952	.968
Sept	.866	.871	.882	.871	.891	.898	.907	.915	.919	.923	.936	.939	.940	.944	.960
Oct	.867	.872	.884	.872	.893	.899	.908	.916	.920	.925	.937	.940	.941	.945	.961
Nov	.870	.875	.886	.875	.895	.902	.911	.919	.923	.927	.940	.943	.944	.948	.964
Dec	.866	.871	.882	.871	.891	.898	.907	.915	.919	.923	.936	.939	.940	.944	.960

MONTH OF DISPOSAL

	2015						***2016***								
1994	July	Aug	Sep	Oct	Nov	Dec	Jan	Feb	Mar	Apr	May	June	July	Aug	Sep
Jan	.830	.839	.837	.837	.839	.844	.832	.840	.848	.850	.855	.862	.864	.871	.875
Feb	.820	.828	.827	.826	.828	.834	.821	.830	.837	.840	.844	.852	.854	.861	.864
Mar	.815	.823	.822	.821	.823	.829	.816	.825	.832	.834	.839	.846	.848	.855	.859
Apr	.793	.802	.800	.800	.802	.807	.795	.803	.811	.813	.818	.825	.827	.834	.837
May	.787	.795	.794	.793	.795	.801	.789	.797	.804	.806	.811	.818	.820	.827	.831
June	.787	.795	.794	.793	.795	.801	.789	.797	.804	.806	.811	.818	.820	.827	.831
July	.796	.804	.803	.802	.804	.810	.797	.806	.813	.815	.820	.827	.829	.836	.840
Aug	.787	.795	.794	.793	.795	.801	.789	.797	.804	.806	.811	.818	.820	.827	.831
Sept	.783	.792	.790	.790	.792	.797	.785	.793	.801	.803	.808	.814	.817	.823	.827
Oct	.781	.789	.788	.787	.789	.795	.782	.791	.798	.800	.805	.812	.814	.821	.824
Nov	.780	.788	.787	.786	.788	.794	.781	.789	.797	.799	.804	.811	.813	.820	.823
Dec	.771	.779	.778	.777	.779	.785	.773	.781	.788	.790	.795	.802	.804	.811	.814
1995	July	Aug	Sep	Oct	Nov	Dec	Jan	Feb	Mar	Apr	May	June	July	Aug	Sep
Jan	.771	.779	.778	.777	.779	.785	.773	.781	.788	.790	.795	.802	.804	.811	.814
Feb	.760	.769	.767	.767	.769	.774	.762	.770	.777	.779	.784	.791	.793	.800	.803
Mar	.753	.761	.760	.759	.761	.767	.755	.763	.770	.772	.777	.784	.786	.793	.796
Apr	.736	.744	.742	.742	.744	.749	.737	.745	.752	.754	.759	.766	.768	.774	.778
May	.729	.737	.735	.735	.737	.742	.730	.738	.745	.747	.752	.759	.761	.767	.771
June	.726	.734	.733	.732	.734	.740	.728	.736	.743	.745	.750	.756	.758	.765	.768
July	.734	.742	.741	.740	.742	.748	.736	.744	.751	.753	.758	.765	.767	.773	.777
Aug	.725	.733	.732	.731	.733	.738	.726	.734	.742	.744	.748	.755	.757	.764	.767
Sept	.717	.725	.724	.723	.725	.730	.718	.726	.734	.736	.740	.747	.749	.756	.759
Oct	.726	.734	.733	.732	.734	.740	.728	.736	.743	.745	.750	.756	.758	.765	.768
Nov	.726	.734	.733	.732	.734	.740	.728	.736	.743	.745	.750	.756	.758	.765	.768
Dec	.716	.724	.723	.722	.724	.729	.717	.725	.733	.735	.739	.746	.748	.754	.758
1996	July	Aug	Sep	Oct	Nov	Dec	Jan	Feb	Mar	Apr	May	June	July	Aug	Sep
Jan	.722	.730	.728	.728	.730	.735	.723	.731	.738	.740	.745	.752	.754	.760	.764
Feb	.714	.722	.720	.720	.722	.727	.715	.723	.730	.732	.737	.744	.746	.752	.755
Mar	.707	.715	.714	.713	.715	.720	.708	.716	.723	.725	.730	.737	.739	.745	.749
Apr	.695	.702	.701	.701	.702	.708	.696	.704	.711	.713	.718	.724	.726	.733	.736
May	.691	.699	.698	.697	.699	.704	.693	.700	.708	.710	.714	.721	.723	.729	.733
June	.690	.698	.697	.696	.698	.703	.692	.699	.707	.708	.713	.720	.722	.728	.731
July	.697	.705	.703	.703	.705	.710	.698	.706	.713	.715	.720	.726	.728	.735	.738
Aug	.689	.697	.696	.695	.697	.702	.690	.698	.705	.707	.712	.718	.720	.727	.730
Sept	.681	.689	.688	.687	.689	.694	.683	.691	.698	.700	.704	.711	.713	.719	.722
Oct	.681	.689	.688	.687	.689	.694	.683	.691	.698	.700	.704	.711	.713	.719	.722
Nov	.680	.688	.687	.686	.688	.693	.682	.689	.697	.699	.703	.710	.712	.718	.721
Dec	.675	.683	.681	.681	.683	.688	.676	.684	.691	.693	.698	.704	.706	.712	.716
1997	July	Aug	Sep	Oct	Nov	Dec	Jan	Feb	Mar	Apr	May	June	July	Aug	Sep
Jan	.675	.683	.681	.681	.683	.688	.676	.684	.691	.693	.698	.704	.706	.712	.716
Feb	.668	.676	.675	.674	.676	.681	.670	.677	.685	.686	.691	.697	.699	.706	.709
Mar	.664	.672	.671	.670	.672	.677	.665	.673	.680	.682	.687	.693	.695	.701	.705
Apr	.655	.662	.661	.660	.662	.667	.656	.663	.671	.672	.677	.683	.685	.692	.695
May	.648	.656	.655	.654	.656	.661	.649	.657	.664	.666	.670	.677	.679	.685	.688
June	.642	.650	.648	.648	.650	.655	.643	.651	.658	.660	.664	.670	.672	.679	.682
July	.642	.650	.648	.648	.650	.655	.643	.651	.658	.660	.664	.670	.672	.679	.682
Aug	.632	.639	.638	.637	.639	.644	.633	.640	.647	.649	.654	.660	.662	.668	.671
Sept	.623	.631	.630	.629	.631	.636	.625	.632	.639	.641	.645	.652	.653	.660	.663
Oct	.621	.629	.628	.627	.629	.634	.623	.630	.637	.639	.643	.650	.651	.658	.661
Nov	.620	.628	.627	.626	.628	.633	.622	.629	.636	.638	.642	.648	.650	.657	.660
Dec	.616	.624	.623	.622	.624	.629	.618	.625	.632	.634	.638	.644	.646	.653	.656

MONTH OF DISPOSAL

	2016			***2017***											
1994	Oct	Nov	Dec	Jan	Feb	Mar	Apr	May	June	July	Aug	Sep	Oct	Nov	Dec
Jan	.874	.879	.890	.879	.900	.906	.915	.923	.927	.931	.944	.947	.948	.952	.968
Feb	.863	.868	.880	.868	.889	.895	.904	.912	.916	.920	.933	.936	.937	.941	.957
Mar	.858	.863	.874	.863	.884	.890	.899	.907	.911	.915	.928	.931	.932	.935	.952
Apr	.836	.841	.852	.841	.861	.868	.877	.884	.888	.893	.905	.908	.909	.913	.929
May	.830	.835	.846	.835	.855	.861	.870	.878	.882	.886	.898	.901	.903	.906	.922
June	.830	.835	.846	.835	.855	.861	.870	.878	.882	.886	.898	.901	.903	.906	.922
July	.839	.844	.855	.844	.864	.870	.879	.887	.891	.895	.908	.910	.912	.915	.931
Aug	.830	.835	.846	.835	.855	.861	.870	.878	.882	.886	.898	.901	.903	.906	.922
Sept	.826	.831	.842	.831	.851	.857	.866	.874	.878	.882	.894	.897	.899	.902	.918
Oct	.824	.829	.840	.829	.848	.855	.864	.871	.875	.879	.892	.895	.896	.899	.915
Nov	.822	.827	.838	.827	.847	.853	.862	.870	.874	.878	.891	.893	.895	.898	.914
Dec	.814	.818	.829	.818	.838	.845	.853	.861	.865	.869	.882	.884	.886	.889	.905
1995	Oct	Nov	Dec	Jan	Feb	Mar	Apr	May	June	July	Aug	Sep	Oct	Nov	Dec
Jan	.814	.818	.829	.818	.838	.845	.853	.861	,865	.869	.882	.884	.886	.889	.905
Feb	.803	.807	.818	.807	.827	.833	.842	.850	.854	.858	.870	.873	.874	.877	.893
Mar	.795	.800	.811	.800	.820	.826	.835	.842	.846	.850	.862	.865	.866	.870	.885
Apr	.777	.782	.793	.782	.801	.807	.816	.823	.828	.832	.844	.846	.848	.851	.866
May	.770	.775	.785	.775	.794	.800	.809	.816	.820	.824	.836	.839	.840	.844	.859
June	.768	.772	.783	.772	.792	.798	.806	.814	.818	.822	.834	.836	.838	.841	.856
July	.776	.781	.791	.781	.800	.806	.815	.822	.826	.830	.842	.845	.846	.850	.865
Aug	.767	.771	.782	.771	.791	.797	.805	.813	.817	.821	.833	.835	.837	.840	.855
Sept	.758	.763	.774	.763	.782	.788	.797	.804	.808	.812	.824	.827	.828	.831	.847
Oct	.768	.772	.783	.772	.792	.798	.806	.814	.818	.822	.834	.836	.838	.841	.856
Nov	.768	.772	.783	.772	.792	.798	.806	.814	.818	.822	.834	.836	.838	.841	.856
Dec	.757	.762	.772	.762	.781	.787	.796	.803	.807	.811	.823	.825	.827	.830	.845
1996	Oct	Nov	Dec	Jan	Feb	Mar	Apr	May	June	July	Aug	Sep	Oct	Nov	Dec
Jan	.763	.768	.778	.768	.787	.793	.802	.809	.813	.817	.829	.832	.833	.836	.852
Feb	.755	.759	.770	.759	.779	.785	.793	.801	.805	.808	.820	.823	.824	.828	.843
Mar	.748	.752	.763	.752	.772	.778	.786	.793	.797	.801	.813	.816	.817	.820	.836
Apr	.735	.740	.750	.740	.759	.765	.773	.780	.784	.788	.800	.803	.804	.807	.822
May	.732	.736	.747	.736	.755	.761	.770	.777	.781	.785	.797	.799	.801	.804	.819
June	.731	.735	.746	.735	.754	.760	.769	.776	.780	.784	.795	.798	.799	.803	.818
July	.738	.742	.753	.742	.761	.767	.776	.783	.787	.791	.802	.805	.806	.810	.825
Aug	.730	.734	.745	.734	.753	.759	.767	.775	.779	.782	.794	.797	.798	.801	.816
Sept	.722	.726	.737	.726	.745	.751	.759	.767	.770	.774	.786	.789	.790	.793	.808
Oct	.722	.726	.737	.726	.745	.751	.759	.767	.770	.774	.786	.789	.790	.793	.808
Nov	.721	.725	.736	.725	.744	.750	.758	.765	.769	.773	.785	.788	.789	.792	.807
Dec	.715	.720	.730	.720	.738	.744	.753	.760	.764	.767	.779	.782	.783	.786	.801
1997	Oct	Nov	Dec	Jan	Feb	Mar	Apr	May	June	July	Aug	Sep	Oct	Nov	Dec
Jan	.715	.720	.730	.720	.738	.744	.753	.760	.764	.767	.779	.782	.783	.786	.801
Feb	.708	.713	.723	.713	.732	.737	.746	.753	.757	.761	.772	.775	.776	.779	.794
Mar	.704	.708	.719	.708	.727	.733	.741	.748	.752	.756	.768	.770	.772	.775	.790
Apr	.694	.699	.709	.699	.717	.723	.731	.738	.742	.746	.758	.760	.761	.765	.779
May	.688	.692	.702	.692	.711	.716	.725	.732	.736	.739	.751	.753	.755	.758	.772
June	.681	.686	.696	.686	.704	.710	.718	.725	.729	.733	.744	.747	.748	.751	.766
July	.681	.686	.696	.686	.704	.710	.718	.725	.729	.733	.744	.747	.748	.751	.766
Aug	.671	.675	.685	.675	.693	.699	.707	.714	.718	.722	.733	.736	.737	.740	.755
Sept	.662	.667	.677	.667	.685	.691	.699	.706	.709	.713	.724	.727	.728	.731	.746
Oct	.660	.665	.675	.665	.683	.688	.697	.703	.707	.711	.722	.725	.726	.729	.744
Nov	.659	.664	.674	.664	.682	.687	.695	.702	.706	.710	.721	.724	.725	.728	.742
Dec	.655	.659	.669	.659	.678	.683	.691	.698	.702	.706	.717	.719	.721	.724	.738

MONTH OF DISPOSAL

	2015						**2016**								
1998	July	Aug	Sep	Oct	Nov	Dec	Jan	Feb	Mar	Apr	May	June	July	Aug	Sep
Jan	.621	.629	.628	.627	.629	.634	.623	.630	.637	.639	.643	.650	.651	.658	.661
Feb	.613	.621	.619	.619	.621	.626	.614	.622	.629	.631	.635	.641	.643	.649	.653
Mar	.608	.616	.614	.614	.616	.621	.609	.617	.624	.626	.630	.636	.638	.644	.647
Apr	.590	.598	.597	.596	.598	.603	.592	.599	.606	.608	.612	.618	.620	.626	.629
May	.582	.589	.588	.587	.589	.594	.583	.590	.597	.599	.603	.609	.611	.617	.620
June	.583	.590	.589	.588	.590	.595	.584	.591	.598	.600	.604	.610	.612	.618	.621
July	.587	.594	.593	.592	.594	.599	.588	.595	.602	.604	.608	.614	.616	.622	.625
Aug	.580	.587	.586	.585	.587	.592	.581	.588	.595	.597	.601	.607	.609	.615	.618
Sept	.573	.580	.579	.578	.580	.585	.574	.582	.588	.590	.594	.600	.602	.608	.611
Oct	.572	.579	.578	.578	.579	.584	.573	.581	.587	.589	.593	.599	.601	.607	.610
Nov	.573	.580	.579	.578	.580	.585	.574	.582	.588	.590	.594	.600	.602	.608	.611
Dec	.573	.580	.579	.578	.580	.585	.574	.582	.588	.590	.594	.600	.602	.608	.611
1999	July	Aug	Sep	Oct	Nov	Dec	Jan	Feb	Mar	Apr	May	June	July	Aug	Sep
Jan	.583	.590	.589	.588	.590	.595	.584	.591	.598	.600	.604	.610	.612	.618	.621
Feb	.580	.587	.586	.585	.587	.592	.581	.588	.595	.597	.601	.607	.609	.615	.618
Mar	.576	.583	.582	.581	.583	.588	.577	.584	.591	.593	.597	.603	.605	.611	.614
Apr	.565	.573	.571	.571	.573	.577	.567	.574	.581	.582	.587	.593	.594	.600	.604
May	.562	.569	.568	.567	.569	.574	.563	.570	.577	.579	.583	.589	.591	.597	.600
June	.562	.569	.568	.567	.569	.574	.563	.570	.577	.579	.583	.589	.591	.597	.600
July	.566	.574	.572	.572	.574	.578	.568	.575	.581	.583	.588	.594	.595	.601	.604
Aug	.563	.570	.569	.568	.570	.575	.564	.571	.578	.579	.584	.590	.592	.598	.601
Sept	.556	.563	.562	.561	.563	.568	.557	.564	.571	.573	.577	.583	.585	.591	.594
Oct	.553	.560	.559	.559	.560	.565	.554	.562	.568	.570	.574	.580	.582	.588	.591
Nov	.551	.558	.557	.557	.558	.563	.552	.560	.566	.568	.572	.578	.580	.586	.589
Dec	.546	.553	.552	.551	.553	.558	.547	.554	.561	.562	.567	.573	.574	.580	.583
2000	July	Aug	Sep	Oct	Nov	Dec	Jan	Feb	Mar	Apr	May	June	July	Aug	Sep
Jan	.552	.559	.558	.558	.559	.564	.553	.561	.567	.569	.573	.579	.581	.587	.590
Feb	.544	.551	.550	.549	.551	.556	.545	.552	.559	.561	.565	.571	.573	.579	.581
Mar	.536	.543	.542	.541	.543	.548	.537	.544	.550	.552	.556	.562	.564	.570	.573
Apr	.520	.527	.526	.526	.527	.532	.521	.529	.535	.537	.541	.547	.549	.554	.557
May	.515	.522	.521	.520	.522	.527	.516	.523	.530	.531	.535	.541	.543	.549	.552
June	.511	.518	.517	.517	.518	.523	.513	.520	.526	.528	.532	.538	.539	.545	.548
July	.517	.524	.523	.522	.524	.528	.518	.525	.531	.533	.537	.543	.545	.551	.554
Aug	.517	.524	.523	.522	.524	.528	.518	.525	.531	.533	.537	.543	.545	.551	.554
Sept	.506	.513	.512	.511	.513	.518	.507	.514	.521	.522	.526	.532	.534	.540	.543
Oct	.507	.514	.513	.512	.514	.519	.508	.515	.522	.523	.527	.533	.535	.541	.544
Nov	.503	.510	.508	.508	.510	.514	.504	.511	.517	.519	.523	.529	.531	.536	.539
Dec	.502	.509	.508	.507	.509	.513	.503	.510	.516	.518	.522	.528	.530	.535	.538
2001	July	Aug	Sep	Oct	Nov	Dec	Jan	Feb	Mar	Apr	May	June	July	Aug	Sep
Jan	.511	.518	.517	.517	.518	.523	.513	.520	.526	.528	.532	.538	.539	.545	.548
Feb	.503	.510	.509	.509	.510	.515	.505	.512	.518	.520	.524	.530	.531	.537	.540
Mar	.502	.509	.508	.507	.509	.513	.503	.510	.516	.518	.522	.528	.530	.535	.538
Apr	.494	.501	.500	.499	.501	.505	.495	.502	.508	.510	.514	.520	.522	.527	.530
May	.485	.491	.490	.490	.491	.496	.486	.493	.499	.501	.505	.510	.512	.518	.521
June	.483	.490	.489	.488	.490	.494	.484	.491	.497	.499	.503	.509	.510	.516	.519
July	.492	.499	.498	.497	.499	.504	.493	.500	.507	.508	.512	.518	.520	.526	.529
Aug	.486	.493	.492	.491	.493	.498	.487	.494	.501	.502	.506	.512	.514	.520	.522
Sept	.481	.488	.487	.486	.488	.493	.482	.489	.495	.497	.501	.507	.509	.514	.517
Oct	.484	.491	.489	.489	.491	.495	.485	.492	.498	.500	.504	.509	.511	.517	.520
Nov	.490	.497	.495	.495	.497	.501	.491	.498	.504	.506	.510	.516	.517	.523	.526
Dec	.491	.498	.497	.497	.498	.503	.493	.499	.506	.507	.512	.517	.519	.525	.528

MONTH OF DISPOSAL

	2016			*2017*											
1998	Oct	Nov	Dec	Jan	Feb	Mar	Apr	May	June	July	Aug	Sep	Oct	Nov	Dec
Jan	.660	.665	.675	.665	.683	.688	.697	.703	.707	.711	.722	.725	.726	.729	.744
Feb	.652	.656	.666	.656	.674	.680	.688	.695	.699	.702	.714	.716	.717	.721	.735
Mar	.647	.651	.661	.651	.669	.675	.683	.690	.693	.697	.708	.711	.712	.715	.729
Apr	.629	.633	.643	.633	.651	.656	.664	.671	.675	.678	.689	.692	.693	.696	.710
May	.620	.624	.634	.624	.642	.647	.655	.662	.665	.669	.680	.683	.684	.687	.701
June	.621	.625	.635	.625	.643	.648	.656	.663	.666	.670	.681	.684	.685	.688	.702
July	.625	.629	.639	.629	.647	.652	.660	.667	.671	.674	.685	.688	.689	.692	.706
Aug	.618	.622	.632	.622	.640	.645	.653	.660	.663	.667	.678	.681	.682	.685	.699
Sept	.611	.615	.625	.615	.633	.638	.646	.653	.656	.660	.671	.673	.675	.678	.692
Oct	.610	.614	.624	.614	.632	.637	.645	.652	.655	.659	.670	.672	.674	.677	.691
Nov	.611	.615	.625	.615	.633	.638	.646	.653	.656	.660	.671	.673	.675	.678	.692
Dec	.611	.615	.625	.615	.633	.638	.646	.653	.656	.660	.671	.673	.675	.678	.692
1999	Oct	Nov	Dec	Jan	Feb	Mar	Apr	May	June	July	Aug	Sep	Oct	Nov	Dec
Jan	.621	.625	.635	.625	.643	.648	.656	.663	.666	.670	.681	.684	.685	.688	.702
Feb	.618	.622	.632	.622	.640	.645	.653	.660	.663	.667	.678	.681	.682	.685	.699
Mar	.614	.618	.628	.618	.636	.641	.649	.656	.659	.663	.674	.676	.678	.681	.695
Apr	.603	.607	.617	.607	.625	.630	.638	.645	.648	.652	.663	.665	.666	.669	.683
May	.599	.603	.613	.603	.621	.626	.634	.641	.644	.648	.659	.661	.662	.665	.679
June	.599	.603	.613	.603	.621	.626	.634	.641	.644	.648	.659	.661	.662	.665	.679
July	.604	.608	.618	.608	.626	.631	.639	.646	.649	.653	.664	.666	.667	.671	.684
Aug	.600	.604	.614	.604	.622	.627	.635	.642	.645	.649	.660	.662	.663	.666	.680
Sept	.593	.597	.607	.597	.615	.620	.628	.635	.638	.642	.653	.655	.656	.659	.673
Oct	.590	.595	.604	.595	.612	.617	.625	.632	.635	.639	.650	.652	.653	.656	.670
Nov	.588	.593	.602	.593	.610	.615	.623	.630	.633	.637	.648	.650	.651	.654	.668
Dec	.583	.587	.597	.587	.604	.610	.617	.624	.628	.631	.642	.644	.646	.649	.662
2000	Oct	Nov	Dec	Jan	Feb	Mar	Apr	May	June	July	Aug	Sep	Oct	Nov	Dec
Jan	.589	.594	.603	.594	.611	.616	.624	.631	.634	.638	.649	.651	.652	.655	.669
Feb	.581	.585	.595	.585	.602	.608	.616	.622	.626	.629	.640	.642	.644	.647	.660
Mar	.572	.577	.586	.577	.594	.599	.607	.613	.617	.621	.631	.634	.635	.638	.651
Apr	.557	.561	.570	.561	.578	.583	.591	.597	.601	.604	.615	.617	.618	.621	.635
May	.551	.555	.565	.555	.572	.578	.585	.592	.595	.599	.609	.612	.613	.616	.629
June	.548	.552	.561	.552	.569	.574	.582	.588	.591	.595	.605	.608	.609	.612	.625
July	.553	.557	.567	.557	.574	.579	.587	.594	.597	.601	.611	.613	.615	.618	.631
Aug	.553	.557	.567	.557	.574	.579	.587	.594	.597	.601	.611	.613	.615	.618	.631
Sept	.542	.546	.556	.546	.563	.568	.576	.582	.586	.589	.600	.602	.603	.606	.620
Oct	.543	.547	.557	.547	.564	.569	.577	.583	.587	.590	.601	.603	.604	.607	.621
Nov	.539	.543	.552	.543	.560	.565	.572	.579	.582	.586	.596	.598	.600	.603	.616
Dec	.538	.542	.551	.542	.559	.564	.571	.578	.581	.585	.595	.598	.599	.602	.615
2001	Oct	Nov	Dec	Jan	Feb	Mar	Apr	May	June	July	Aug	Sep	Oct	Nov	Dec
Jan	.548	.552	.561	.552	.569	.574	.582	.588	.591	.595	.605	.608	.609	.612	.625
Feb	.540	.544	.553	.544	.560	.566	.573	.580	.583	.587	.597	.599	.601	.603	.617
Mar	.538	.542	.551	.542	.559	.564	.571	.578	.581	.585	.595	.598	.599	.602	.615
Apr	.530	.534	.543	.534	.551	.556	.563	.570	.573	.577	.587	.589	.590	.593	.607
May	.520	.524	.533	.524	.541	.546	.553	.560	.563	.567	.577	.579	.580	.583	.596
June	.518	.522	.532	.522	.539	.544	.552	.558	.561	.565	.575	.577	.579	.581	.595
July	.528	.532	.541	.532	.549	.554	.561	.568	.571	.575	.585	.587	.589	.591	.605
Aug	.522	.526	.535	.526	.543	.548	.555	.561	.565	.568	.579	.581	.582	.585	.598
Sept	.517	.521	.530	.521	.537	.542	.550	.556	.560	.563	.573	.576	.577	.580	.593
Oct	.519	.523	.532	.523	.540	.545	.552	.559	.562	.566	.576	.578	.579	.582	.596
Nov	.525	.529	.539	.529	.546	.551	.559	.565	.569	.572	.582	.585	.586	.589	.602
Dec	.527	.531	.540	.531	.548	.553	.561	.567	.570	.574	.584	.587	.588	.591	.604

MONTH OF DISPOSAL

	2015						***2016***								
2002	July	Aug	Sep	Oct	Nov	Dec	Jan	Feb	Mar	Apr	May	June	July	Aug	Sep
Jan	.492	.499	.498	.497	.499	.504	.493	.500	.507	.508	.512	.518	.520	.526	.529
Feb	.488	.495	.494	.493	.495	.499	.489	.496	.502	.504	.508	.514	.516	.521	.524
Mar	.482	.489	.488	.487	.489	.493	.483	.490	.496	.498	.502	.508	.509	.515	.518
Apr	.472	.479	.478	.477	.479	.483	.473	.480	.486	.488	.492	.497	.499	.505	.508
May	.468	.474	.473	.473	.474	.479	.469	.476	.482	.484	.488	.493	.495	.501	.503
June	.468	.474	.473	.473	.474	.479	.469	.476	.482	.484	.488	.493	.495	.501	.503
July	.470	.477	.476	.475	.477	.482	.471	.478	.484	.486	.490	.496	.497	.503	.506
Aug	.466	.473	.472	.471	.473	.477	.467	.474	.480	.482	.486	.491	.493	.499	.502
Sept	.456	.463	.462	.461	.463	.467	.457	.464	.470	.472	.476	.481	.483	.489	.492
Oct	.454	.460	.459	.459	.460	.465	.455	.461	.468	.469	.473	.479	.481	.486	.489
Nov	.451	.458	.457	.456	.458	.462	.452	.459	.465	.467	.471	.476	.478	.484	.487
Dec	.449	.455	.454	.454	.455	.460	.450	.457	.463	.464	.468	.474	.476	.481	.484
2003	July	Aug	Sep	Oct	Nov	Dec	Jan	Feb	Mar	Apr	May	June	July	Aug	Sep
Jan	.450	.456	.455	.455	.456	.461	.451	.457	.464	.465	.469	.475	.476	.482	.485
Feb	.442	.449	.448	.447	.449	.453	.443	.450	.456	.458	.462	.467	.469	.475	.477
Mar	.437	.444	.443	.442	.444	.449	.439	.445	.451	.453	.457	.462	.464	.470	.472
Apr	.427	.434	.433	.432	.434	.438	.428	.435	.441	.443	.446	.452	.454	.459	.462
May	.425	.431	.430	.430	.431	.436	.426	.433	.439	.440	.444	.450	.451	.457	.460
June	.426	.433	.432	.431	.433	.437	.427	.434	.440	.442	.446	.451	.453	.458	.461
July	.426	.433	.432	.431	.433	.437	.427	.434	.440	.442	.446	.451	.453	.458	.461
Aug	.424	.431	.430	.429	.431	.435	.425	.432	.438	.439	.443	.449	.450	.456	.459
Sept	.416	.424	.422	.422	.424	.428	.418	.425	.431	.432	.436	.442	.443	.449	.452
Oct	.416	.423	.422	.421	.423	.427	.417	.424	.430	.432	.435	.441	.442	.448	.451
Nov	.415	.422	.421	.420	.422	.426	.417	.423	.429	.431	.435	.440	.442	.447	.450
Dec	.409	.416	.415	.414	.416	.420	.410	.417	.423	.425	.428	.434	.435	.441	.444
2004	July	Aug	Sep	Oct	Nov	Dec	Jan	Feb	Mar	Apr	May	June	July	Aug	Sep
Jan	.412	.419	.418	.417	.419	.423	.413	.420	.426	.428	.431	.437	.439	.444	.447
Feb	.407	.413	.412	.412	.413	.418	.408	.415	.421	.422	.426	.431	.433	.439	.441
Mar	.401	.407	.406	.406	.407	.412	.402	.408	.414	.416	.420	.425	.427	.432	.435
Apr	.393	.399	.398	.397	.399	.403	.394	.400	.406	.408	.411	.417	.418	.424	.426
May	.387	.393	.392	.391	.393	.397	.388	.394	.400	.402	.405	.411	.412	.418	.420
June	.384	.391	.390	.389	.391	.395	.385	.392	.398	.399	.403	.408	.410	.415	.418
July	.384	.391	.390	.389	.391	.395	.385	.392	.398	.399	.403	.408	.410	.415	.418
Aug	.380	.386	.385	.385	.386	.391	.381	.387	.393	.395	.399	.404	.406	.411	.414
Sept	.375	.381	.380	.380	.381	.385	.376	.382	.388	.390	.393	.399	.400	.406	.408
Oct	.371	.378	.376	.376	.378	.382	.372	.379	.384	.386	.390	.395	.397	.402	.405
Nov	.368	.375	.374	.373	.375	.379	.369	.376	.381	.383	.387	.392	.394	.399	.402
Dec	.362	.368	.367	.367	.368	.372	.363	.369	.375	.377	.380	.385	.387	.392	.395
2005	July	Aug	Sep	Oct	Nov	Dec	Jan	Feb	Mar	Apr	May	June	July	Aug	Sep
Jan	.369	.375	.374	.374	.375	.380	.370	.376	.382	.384	.388	.393	.394	.400	.402
Feb	.364	.370	.369	.369	.370	.374	.365	.371	.377	.379	.382	.388	.389	.395	.397
Mar	.357	.364	.363	.362	.364	.368	.359	.365	.371	.372	.376	.381	.383	.388	.391
Apr	.350	.356	.355	.354	.356	.360	.351	.357	.363	.364	.368	.373	.375	.380	.383
May	.347	.353	.352	.352	.353	.357	.348	.354	.360	.361	.365	.370	.372	.377	.380
June	.345	.352	.351	.350	.352	.356	.347	.353	.358	.360	.364	.369	.370	.376	.378
July	.345	.352	.351	.350	.352	.356	.347	.353	.358	.360	.364	.369	.370	.376	.378
Aug	.343	.349	.348	.347	.349	.353	.344	.350	.356	.357	.361	.366	.368	.373	.375
Sept	.339	.345	.344	.344	.345	.350	.340	.346	.352	.354	.357	.363	.364	.369	.372
Oct	.338	.344	.343	.342	.344	.348	.339	.345	.351	.352	.356	.361	.363	.368	.370
Nov	.336	.342	.341	.340	.342	.346	.337	.343	.349	.350	.354	.359	.361	.366	.368
Dec	.332	.338	.337	.337	.338	.343	.333	.340	.345	.347	.350	.355	.357	.362	.365

MONTH OF DISPOSAL

	2016			2017											
2002	Oct	Nov	Dec	Jan	Feb	Mar	Apr	May	June	July	Aug	Sep	Oct	Nov	Dec
Jan	.528	.532	.541	.532	.549	.554	.561	.568	.571	.575	.585	.587	.589	.591	.605
Feb	.524	.528	.537	.528	.544	.549	.557	.563	.567	.570	.581	.583	.584	.587	.600
Mar	.517	.521	.531	.521	.538	.543	.551	.557	.560	.564	.574	.577	.578	.581	.594
Apr	.507	.511	.520	.511	.528	.533	.540	.546	.550	.553	.563	.566	.567	.570	.583
May	.503	.507	.516	.507	.523	.528	.536	.542	.545	.549	.559	.561	.562	.565	.578
June	.503	.507	.516	.507	.523	.528	.536	.542	.545	.549	.559	.561	.562	.565	.578
July	.505	.509	.518	.509	.526	.531	.538	.545	.548	.551	.562	.564	.565	.568	.581
Aug	.501	.505	.514	.505	.522	.527	.534	.540	.544	.547	.557	.560	.561	.563	.577
Sept	.491	.495	.504	.495	.511	.516	.524	.530	.533	.537	.547	.549	.550	.553	.566
Oct	.488	.492	.501	.492	.509	.514	.521	.527	.531	.534	.544	.546	.547	.550	.563
Nov	.486	.490	.499	.490	.506	.511	.519	.525	.528	.531	.542	.544	.545	.548	.561
Dec	.483	.487	.496	.487	.504	.509	.516	.522	.525	.529	.539	.541	.542	.545	.558
2003	Oct	Nov	Dec	Jan	Feb	Mar	Apr	May	June	July	Aug	Sep	Oct	Nov	Dec
Jan	.484	.488	.497	.488	.504	.510	.517	.523	.526	.530	.540	.542	.543	.546	.559
Feb	.477	.481	.490	.481	.497	.502	.509	.515	.519	.522	.532	.534	.535	.538	.551
Mar	.472	.476	.485	.476	.492	.497	.504	.510	.514	.517	.527	.529	.530	.533	.546
Apr	.461	.465	.474	.465	.481	.486	.493	.499	.503	.506	.516	.518	.519	.522	.535
May	.459	.463	.472	.463	.479	.484	.491	.497	.500	.504	.513	.516	.517	.520	.532
June	.461	.464	.473	.464	.480	.485	.493	.499	.502	.505	.515	.517	.518	.521	.534
July	.461	.464	.473	.464	.480	.485	.493	.499	.502	.505	.515	.517	.518	.521	.534
Aug	.458	.462	.471	.462	.478	.483	.490	.496	.499	.503	.513	.515	.516	.519	.531
Sept	.451	.455	.464	.455	.471	.476	.483	.489	.492	.495	.505	.507	.508	.511	.524
Oct	.450	.454	.463	.454	.470	.475	.482	.488	.491	.495	.504	.507	.508	.510	.523
Nov	.449	.453	.462	.453	.469	.474	.481	.487	.490	.494	.504	.506	.507	.510	.522
Dec	.443	.447	.456	.447	.463	.468	.475	.481	.484	.487	.497	.499	.500	.503	.516
2004	Oct	Nov	Dec	Jan	Feb	Mar	Apr	May	June	July	Aug	Sep	Oct	Nov	Dec
Jan	.446	.450	.459	.450	.466	.471	.478	.484	.487	.490	.500	.502	.504	.506	.519
Feb	.441	.445	.453	.445	.460	.465	.472	.478	.482	.485	.495	.497	.498	.501	.513
Mar	.434	.438	.447	.438	.454	.459	.466	.472	.475	.478	.488	.490	.491	.494	.507
Apr	.426	.430	.438	.430	.445	.450	.457	.463	.466	.470	.479	.481	.482	.485	.498
May	.420	.424	.432	.424	.439	.444	.451	.457	.460	.463	.473	.475	.476	.479	.491
June	.418	.421	.430	.421	.437	.442	.449	.454	.458	.461	.471	.473	.474	.476	.489
July	.418	.421	.430	.421	.437	.442	.449	.454	.458	.461	.471	.473	.474	.476	.489
Aug	.413	.417	.425	.417	.432	.437	.444	.450	.453	.456	.466	.468	.469	.472	.484
Sept	.408	.411	.420	.411	.427	.432	.439	.444	.448	.451	.460	.463	.464	.466	.478
Oct	.404	.408	.416	.408	.423	.428	.435	.441	.444	.447	.457	.459	.460	.462	.475
Nov	.401	.405	.413	.405	.420	.425	.432	.438	.441	.444	.453	.456	.457	.459	.471
Dec	.394	.398	.407	.398	.413	. 418	.425	.431	.434	.437	.447	.449	.450	.452	.464
2005	Oct	Nov	Dec	Jan	Feb	Mar	Apr	May	June	July	Aug	Sep	Oct	Nov	Dec
Jan	.402	.406	.414	.406	.421	.426	.433	.438	.442	.445	.454	.456	.457	.460	.472
Feb	.397	.400	.409	.400	.416	.420	.427	.433	.436	.439	.449	.451	.452	.455	.467
Mar	.390	.394	.402	.394	.409	.414	.420	.426	.429	.433	.442	.444	.445	.448	.460
Apr	.382	.386	.394	.386	.401	.406	.412	.418	.421	.424	.434	.436	.437	.439	.451
May	.379	.383	.391	.383	.398	.403	.409	.415	.418	.421	.431	.433	.434	.436	.448
June	.378	.381	.390	.381	.396	.401	.408	.414	.417	.420	.429	.431	.432	.435	.447
July	.378	.381	.390	.381	.396	.401	.408	.414	.417	.420	.429	.431	.432	.435	.447
Aug	.375	.379	.387	.379	.394	.398	.405	.411	.414	.417	.426	.428	.429	.432	.444
Sept	.371	.375	.383	.375	.390	.395	.401	.407	.410	.413	.423	.425	.426	.428	.440
Oct	.370	.374	.382	.374	.389	.393	.400	.406	.409	.412	.421	.423	.424	.427	.439
Nov	.368	.371	.380	.371	.386	.391	.398	.403	.407	.410	.419	.421	.422	.425	.436
Dec	.364	.368	.376	.368	.383	.387	.394	.400	.403	.406	.415	.417	.418	.421	.433

MONTH OF DISPOSAL

	2015						**2016**								
2006	July	Aug	Sep	Oct	Nov	Dec	Jan	Feb	Mar	Apr	May	June	July	Aug	Sep
Jan	.337	.343	.342	.342	.343	.347	.338	.344	.350	.352	.355	.360	.362	.367	.370
Feb	.332	.338	.337	.336	.338	.342	.333	.339	.344	.346	.350	.355	.356	.361	.364
Mar	.326	.332	.331	.331	.332	.336	.327	.333	.339	.341	.344	.349	.351	.356	.358
Apr	.316	.322	.321	.321	.322	.326	.317	.323	.329	.330	.334	.339	.340	.346	.348
May	.308	.314	.313	.313	.314	.318	.309	.315	.321	.322	.326	.331	.332	.337	.340
June	.303	.309	.308	.307	.309	.313	.304	.310	.315	.317	.320	.325	.327	.332	.335
July	.303	.309	.308	.307	.309	.313	.304	.310	.315	.317	.320	.325	.327	.332	.335
Aug	.298	.304	.303	.303	.304	.308	.299	.305	.311	.312	.316	.321	.322	.327	.330
Sept	.292	.298	.297	.297	.298	.302	.293	.299	.305	.306	.310	.315	.316	.321	.324
Oct	.290	.296	.295	.295	.296	.300	.291	.297	.303	.304	.308	.313	.314	.319	.322
Nov	.286	.292	.291	.290	.292	.296	.287	.293	.298	.300	.303	.308	.310	.315	.317
Dec	.276	.282	.281	.280	.282	.286	.277	.283	.288	.290	.293	.298	.299	.304	.307
2007	July	Aug	Sep	Oct	Nov	Dec	Jan	Feb	Mar	Apr	May	June	July	Aug	Sep
Jan	.283	.289	.288	.287	.289	.293	.284	.290	.295	.297	.300	.305	.307	.312	.314
Feb	.273	.279	.278	.278	.279	.283	.274	.280	.286	.287	.290	.295	.297	.302	.304
Mar	.265	.271	.270	.270	.271	.275	.266	.272	.277	.279	.282	.287	.289	.294	.296
Apr	.259	.265	.264	.263	.265	.269	.260	.266	.271	.273	.276	.281	.282	.287	.290
May	.254	.260	.259	.258	.260	.264	.255	.261	.266	.268	.271	.276	.277	.282	.285
June	.247	.253	.252	.252	.253	.257	.248	.254	.260	.261	.264	.269	.271	.275	.278
July	.255	.261	.260	.259	.261	.264	.256	.262	.267	.268	.272	.277	.278	.283	.285
Aug	.247	.253	.252	.252	.253	.257	.248	.254	.260	.261	.264	.269	.271	.275	.278
Sept	.243	.249	.248	.248	.249	.253	.244	.250	.255	.257	.260	.265	.266	.271	.274
Oct	.238	.244	.243	.242	.244	.247	.239	.245	.250	.251	.255	.259	.261	.266	.268
Nov	.233	.239	.238	.237	.239	.243	.234	.240	.245	.247	.250	.255	.256	.261	.263
Dec	.226	.232	.231	.230	.232	.236	.227	.233	.238	.239	.243	.248	.249	.254	.256
2008	July	Aug	Sep	Oct	Nov	Dec	Jan	Feb	Mar	Apr	May	June	July	Aug	Sep
Jan	.233	.238	.237	.237	.238	.242	.234	.239	.245	.246	.249	.254	.255	.260	.263
Feb	.223	.229	.228	.228	.229	.233	.224	.230	.235	.237	.240	.245	.246	.251	.253
Mar	.219	.225	.224	.223	.225	.229	.220	.226	.231	.232	.236	.240	.242	.247	.249
Apr	.208	.214	.213	.213	.214	.218	.209	.215	.220	.221	.225	.229	.231	.236	.238
May	.202	.208	.207	.206	.208	.212	.203	.209	.214	.215	.219	.223	.225	.229	.232
June	.193	.198	.197	.197	.198	.202	.194	.199	.204	.206	.209	.214	.215	.220	.222
July	.194	.200	.199	.199	.200	.204	.195	.201	.206	.207	.211	.215	.217	.221	.224
Aug	.191	.196	.195	.195	.196	.200	.192	.197	.202	.203	.207	.211	.213	.217	.220
Sept	.184	.190	.189	.188	.190	.193	.185	.190	.196	.197	.200	.205	.206	.211	.213
Oct	.188	.193	.192	.192	.193	.197	.189	.194	.199	.201	.204	.209	.210	.215	.217
Nov	.197	.203	.202	.201	.203	.206	.198	.204	.209	.210	.213	.218	.219	.224	.226
Dec	.215	.220	.219	.219	.220	.224	.216	.221	.226	.228	.231	.236	.237	.242	.244
2009	July	Aug	Sep	Oct	Nov	Dec	Jan	Feb	Mar	Apr	May	June	July	Aug	Sep
Jan	.231	.237	.236	.235	.237	.240	.232	.238	.243	.244	.248	.252	.254	.258	.261
Feb	.223	.229	.228	.228	.229	.233	.224	.230	.235	.237	.240	.245	.246	.251	.253
Mar	.224	.230	.229	.228	.230	.233	.225	.230	.236	.237	.240	.245	.247	.251	.252
Apr	.223	.228	.227	.227	.228	.232	.224	.229	.235	.236	.239	.244	.245	.250	.252
May	.215	.221	.220	.219	.221	.225	.216	.222	.227	.228	.232	.236	.238	.242	.245
June	.212	.217	.216	.216	.217	.221	.213	.218	.224	.225	.228	.233	.234	.239	.241
July	.212	.217	.216	.216	.217	.221	.213	.218	.224	.225	.228	.233	.234	.239	.241
Aug	.206	.212	.211	.210	.212	.215	.207	.213	.218	.219	.222	.227	.229	.233	.236
Sept	.201	.207	.206	.205	.207	.210	.202	.208	.213	.214	.217	.222	.223	.228	.230
Oct	.197	.203	.202	.201	.203	.206	.198	.204	.209	.210	.213	.218	.219	.224	.226
Nov	.194	.199	.199	.198	.199	.203	.195	.200	.205	.207	.210	.215	.216	.221	.223
Dec	.186	.192	.191	.190	.192	.195	.187	.193	.198	.199	.202	.207	.208	.213	.215

MONTH OF DISPOSAL

	2016			***2017***											
2006	Oct	Nov	Dec	Jan	Feb	Mar	Apr	May	June	July	Aug	Sep	Oct	Nov	Dec
Jan	.369	.373	.381	.373	.388	.392	.399	.405	.408	.411	.420	.422	.423	.426	.438
Feb	.364	.367	.375	.367	.382	.387	.393	.399	.402	.405	.415	.417	.418	.420	.432
Mar	.358	.362	.370	.362	.376	.381	.388	.393	.396	.399	.409	.411	.412	.414	.426
Apr	.348	.351	.359	.351	.366	.370	.377	.383	.386	.389	.398	.400	.401	.404	.415
May	.339	.343	.351	.343	.358	.362	.369	.374	.377	.380	.389	.392	.393	.395	.407
June	.334	.338	.346	.338	.352	.357	.363	.369	.372	.375	.384	.386	.387	.389	.401
July	.334	.338	.346	.338	.352	.357	.363	.369	.372	.375	.384	.386	.387	.389	.401
Aug	.329	.333	.341	.333	.347	.352	.358	.364	.367	.370	.379	.381	.382	.385	.396
Sept	.323	.327	.335	.327	.341	.346	.352	.358	.361	.364	.373	.375	.376	.378	.390
Oct	.321	.325	.333	.325	.339	.344	.350	.356	.359	.362	.371	.373	.374	.376	.388
Nov	.317	.320	.328	.320	.335	.339	.346	.351	.354	.357	.366	.368	.369	.371	.383
Dec	.306	.310	.318	.310	.324	.329	.335	.340	.343	.346	.355	.357	.358	.361	.372
2007	Oct	Nov	Dec	Jan	Feb	Mar	Apr	May	June	July	Aug	Sep	Oct	Nov	Dec
Jan	.313	.317	.325	.317	.331	.336	.342	.348	.351	.354	.363	.365	.366	.368	.379
Feb	.304	.307	.315	.307	.322	.326	.332	.338	.341	.344	.353	.355	.355	.358	.369
Mar	.295	.299	.307	.299	.313	.318	.324	.329	.332	.335	.344	.346	.347	.349	.361
Apr	.289	.293	.300	.293	.307	.311	.317	.323	.326	.329	.337	.339	.340	.343	.354
May	.284	.288	.295	.288	.302	.306	.312	.318	.321	.323	.332	.334	.335	.338	.349
June	.277	.281	.288	.281	.295	.299	.305	.311	.314	.316	.325	.327	.328	.330	.342
July	.285	.288	.296	.288	.302	.307	.313	.318	.321	.324	.333	.335	.336	.338	.349
Aug	.277	.281	.288	.281	.295	.299	.305	.311	.314	.316	.325	.327	.328	.330	.342
Sept	.273	.276	.284	.276	.290	.295	.301	.306	.309	.312	.321	.323	.324	.326	.337
Oct	.268	.271	.279	.271	.285	.289	.295	.301	.303	.306	.315	.317	.318	.320	.331
Nov	.263	.266	.274	.266	.280	.284	.290	.296	.299	.301	.310	.312	.313	.315	.326
Dec	.256	.259	.266	.259	.273	.277	.283	.288	.291	.294	.303	.304	.305	.308	.319
2008	Oct	Nov	Dec	Jan	Feb	Mar	Apr	May	June	July	Aug	Sep	Oct	Nov	Dec
Jan	.262	.265	.273	.265	.279	.284	.290	.295	.298	.301	.309	.311	.312	.315	.326
Feb	.253	.256	.263	.256	.270	.274	.280	.285	.288	.291	.299	.301	.302	.305	.316
Mar	.248	.252	.259	.252	.265	.270	.276	.281	.284	.287	.295	.297	.298	.300	.311
Apr	.237	.241	.248	.241	.254	.258	.264	.270	.272	.275	.284	.286	.286	.289	.300
May	.231	.234	.242	.234	.248	.252	.258	.263	.266	.269	.277	.279	.280	.282	.293
June	.221	.225	.232	.225	.238	.242	.248	.253	.256	.259	.267	.269	.270	.272	.283
July	.223	.226	.234	.226	.240	.244	.250	.255	.258	.261	.269	.271	.272	.274	.285
Aug	.219	.222	.230	.222	.236	.240	.246	.251	.254	.256	.265	.267	.267	.270	.280
Sept	.212	.216	.223	.216	.229	.233	.239	.244	.247	.250	.258	.260	.261	.263	.273
Oct	.216	.220	.227	.220	.233	.237	.243	.248	.251	.254	.262	.264	.265	.267	.277
Nov	.226	.229	.237	.229	.243	.247	.253	.258	.261	.263	.272	.274	.275	.277	.288
Dec	.244	.247	.255	.247	.261	.265	.271	.276	.279	.282	.290	.292	.293	.295	.306
2009	Oct	Nov	Dec	Jan	Feb	Mar	Apr	May	June	July	Aug	Sep	Oct	Nov	Dec
Jan	.260	.264	.271	.264	.277	.282	.288	.293	.296	.299	.307	.309	.310	.313	.324
Feb	.253	.256	.263	.256	.270	.274	.280	.285	.288	.291	.299	.301	.302	.305	.316
Mar	.253	.257	.264	.257	.270	.274	.281	.286	.289	.292	.300	.302	.303	.305	.316
Apr	.252	.255	.263	.255	.269	.273	.279	.285	.287	.290	.299	.301	.302	.304	.315
May	.244	.248	.255	.248	.261	.266	.272	.277	.280	.282	.291	.293	.294	.296	.307
June	.241	.244	.252	.244	.258	.262	.268	.273	.276	.279	.287	.289	.290	.292	.303
July	.241	.244	.252	.244	.258	.262	.268	.273	.276	.279	.287	.289	.290	.292	.303
Aug	.235	.238	.246	.238	.252	.256	.262	.267	.270	.273	.281	.283	.284	.286	.297
Sept	.230	.233	.241	.233	.247	.251	257	.262	.265	.268	.276	.278	.279	.281	.292
Oct	.226	.229	.237	.229	.243	.247	.253	.258	.261	.263	.272	.274	.275	.277	.288
Nov	.223	.226	.233	.226	.239	.243	.249	.254	.257	.260	.268	.270	.271	.273	.284
Dec	.215	.218	.225	.218	.231	.235	.241	.246	.249	.252	.260	.262	.263	.265	.276

MONTH OF DISPOSAL

	2015						***2016***								
2010	July	Aug	Sep	Oct	Nov	Dec	Jan	Feb	Mar	Apr	May	June	July	Aug	Sep
Jan	.187	.192	.191	.191	.192	.196	.188	.193	.198	.200	.203	.207	.209	.213	.216
Feb	.180	.185	.184	.184	.185	.189	.181	.186	.191	.193	.196	.200	.202	.206	.208
Mar	.172	.177	.176	.176	.177	.181	.173	.178	.183	.184	.188	.192	.193	.198	.200
Apr	.161	.166	.165	.165	.166	.170	.162	.167	.172	.173	.176	.181	.182	.187	.189
May	.157	.162	.161	.161	.162	.165	.157	.163	.168	.169	.172	.177	.178	.182	.185
June	.154	.159	.158	.158	.159	.163	.155	.160	.165	.166	.170	.174	.175	.180	.182
July	.157	.162	.161	.161	.162	.165	.157	.163	.168	.169	.172	.177	.178	.182	.185
Aug	.152	.157	.156	.156	.157	.161	.153	.158	.163	.164	.167	.172	.173	.178	.180
Sept	.148	.153	.152	.152	.153	.157	.149	.154	.159	.160	.163	.168	.169	.174	.176
Oct	.145	.151	.150	.149	.151	.154	.146	.151	.156	.158	.161	.165	.167	.171	.173
Nov	.140	.146	.145	.144	.146	.149	.141	.146	.151	.153	.156	.160	.161	.166	.168
Dec	.132	.137	.137	.136	.137	.141	.133	.138	.143	.144	.148	.152	.153	.158	.160
2011	July	Aug	Sep	Oct	Nov	Dec	Jan	Feb	Mar	Apr	May	June	July	Aug	Sep
Jan	.129	.134	.134	.133	.134	.138	.130	.135	.140	.141	.145	.149	.150	.155	.157
Feb	.118	.123	.122	.122	.123	.127	.119	.124	.129	.130	.133	.137	.139	.143	.145
Mar	.112	.117	.117	.116	.117	.121	.113	.118	.123	.124	.127	.132	.133	.137	.139
Apr	.103	.108	.108	.107	.108	.112	.104	.109	.114	.115	.118	.122	.124	.128	.130
May	.099	.105	.104	.103	.105	.108	.100	.105	.110	.111	.114	.119	.120	.124	.126
Jun	.099	.105	.104	.103	.105	.108	.100	.105	.110	.111	.114	.119	.120	.124	.126
July	.102	.107	.106	.106	.107	.110	.103	.108	.112	.114	.117	.121	.122	.127	.129
Aug	.095	.100	.100	.099	.100	.104	.096	.101	.106	.107	.110	.114	.116	.120	.122
Sept	.087	.092	.091	.091	.092	.095	.088	.093	.098	.099	.102	.106	.107	.111	.113
Oct	.087	.092	.091	.090	.092	.095	.087	.092	.097	.098	.101	.105	.107	.111	.113
Nov	.084	.089	.088	.088	.089	.093	.085	.090	.095	.096	.099	.103	.104	.109	.111
Dec	.080	.085	.084	.084	.085	.089	.081	.086	.091	.092	.095	.099	.100	.104	.107
2012	July	Aug	Sep	Oct	Nov	Dec	Jan	Feb	Mar	Apr	May	June	July	Aug	Sep
Jan	.087	.092	.091	.090	.092	.095	.087	.092	.097	.098	.101	.105	.107	.111	.113
Feb	.078	.083	.082	.082	.083	.086	.079	.084	.088	.090	.093	.097	.098	.102	.104
Mar	.074	.079	.078	.078	.079	.082	.075	.080	.084	.086	.088	.093	.094	.098	.100
Apr	.066	.071	.071	.070	.071	.075	.067	.072	.077	.078	.081	.085	.086	.090	.092
May	.067	.072	.071	.071	.072	.075	.068	.073	.077	.078	.081	.085	.087	.091	.093
June	.069	.074	.074	.073	.074	.078	.070	.075	.080	.081	.084	.088	.089	.093	.096
July	.068	.073	.072	.072	.073	.076	.069	.074	.078	.080	.083	.087	.088	.092	.094
Aug	.064	.069	.068	.068	.069	.072	.065	.070	.074	.076	.079	.083	.084	.088	.090
Sept	.059	.064	.063	.063	.064	.067	.060	.065	.069	.070	.073	.077	.079	.083	.085
Oct	.053	.058	.057	.057	.058	.061	.054	.059	.063	.064	.067	.071	.072	.077	.079
Nov	.053	.058	.057	.057	.058	.061	.054	.059	.063	.064	.067	.071	.072	.077	.079
Dec	.048	.053	.052	.051	.053	.056	.049	.053	.058	.059	.062	.066	.067	.071	.073
2013	July	Aug	Sep	Oct	Nov	Dec	Jan	Feb	Mar	Apr	May	June	July	Aug	Sep
Jan	.052	.057	.056	.056	.057	.060	.053	.058	.062	.063	.066	.070	.072	.076	.078
Feb	.044	.049	.048	.048	.049	.053	.045	.050	.055	.056	.059	.063	.064	.068	.070
Mar	.040	.045	.044	.043	.045	.048	.041	.045	.050	.051	.054	.058	.059	.063	.065
Apr	.036	.041	.040	.040	.041	.044	.037	.042	.046	.048	.051	.055	.056	.060	.062
May	.034	.039	.038	.038	.039	.042	.035	.040	.044	.046	.048	.052	.054	.058	.060
June	.036	.040	.040	.039	.040	.044	.036	.041	.046	.047	.050	.054	.055	.059	.061
July	.036	.040	.040	.039	.040	.044	.036	.041	.046	.047	.050	.054	.055	.059	.061
Aug	.030	.035	.034	.034	.035	.038	.031	.036	.040	.041	.044	.048	.049	.053	.055
Sept	.027	.031	.031	.030	.031	.035	.027	.032	.037	.038	.040	.044	.046	.050	.052
Oct	.027	.031	.031	.030	.031	.035	.027	.032	.037	.038	.040	.044	.046	.050	.052
Nov	.026	.031	.030	.029	.031	.034	.027	.031	.036	.037	.040	.044	.045	.049	.051
Dec	.024	.029	.028	.027	.029	.032	.025	.029	.034	.035	.038	.042	.043	.047	.049

MONTH OF DISPOSAL

	2016			*2017*											
2010	Oct	Nov	Dec	Jan	Feb	Mar	Apr	May	June	July	Aug	Sep	Oct	Nov	Dec
Jan	.215	.218	.226	.218	.232	.236	.242	.247	.250	.252	.261	.263	.263	.266	.276
Feb	.208	.211	.219	.211	.224	.229	.234	.240	.242	.245	.253	.255	.256	.258	.269
Mar	.200	.203	.210	.203	.216	.220	.226	.231	.234	.237	.245	.246	.247	.250	.260
Apr	.189	.192	.199	.192	.205	.209	.215	.219	.222	.225	.233	.235	.236	.238	.248
May	.184	.187	.195	.187	.200	.204	.210	.215	.218	.220	.229	.230	.231	.233	.244
June	.182	.185	.192	.185	.198	.202	.207	.212	.215	.218	.226	.228	.228	.231	.241
July	.184	.187	.195	.187	.200	.204	.210	.215	.218	.220	.229	.230	.231	.233	.244
Aug	.180	.183	.190	.183	.196	.200	.205	.210	.213	.216	.224	.225	.226	.229	.239
Sept	.175	.178	.186	.178	.191	.195	.201	.206	.209	.211	.219	.221	.222	.224	.234
Oct	.173	.176	.183	.176	.189	.193	.198	.203	.206	.209	.217	.218	.219	.221	.232
Nov	.168	.171	.178	.171	.183	.187	.193	.198	.201	.203	.211	.213	.214	.216	.226
Dec	.159	.162	.169	.162	.175	.179	.185	.190	.192	.195	.203	.204	.205	.208	.218
2011	Oct	Nov	Dec	Jan	Feb	Mar	Apr	May	June	July	Aug	Sep	Oct	Nov	Dec
Jan	.156	.159	.166	.159	.172	.176	.182	.186	.189	.192	.200	.201	.202	.204	.214
Feb	.145	.148	.155	.148	.160	.164	.170	.175	.177	.180	.188	.189	.190	.192	.202
Mar	.139	.142	.149	.142	.154	.158	.164	.169	.171	.174	.182	.183	.184	.186	.196
Apr	.130	.133	.140	.133	.145	.149	.154	.159	.162	.164	.172	.174	.174	.177	.186
May	.126	.129	.136	.129	.141	.145	.151	.155	.158	.160	.168	.170	.170	.173	.182
June	.126	.129	.136	.129	.141	.145	.151	.155	.158	.160	.168	.170	.170	.173	.182
July	.128	.131	.138	.131	.144	.147	.153	.158	.160	.163	.170	.172	.173	.175	.185
Aug	.122	.125	.131	.125	.137	.141	.146	.151	.153	.156	.163	.165	.166	.168	.178
Sept	.113	.116	.123	.116	.128	.132	.137	.142	.145	.147	.155	.156	.157	.159	.169
Oct	.113	.116	.122	.116	.128	.132	.137	.142	.144	.147	.154	.156	.157	.159	.168
Nov	.110	.113	.120	.113	.125	.129	.135	.139	.142	.144	.152	.153	.154	.156	.166
Dec	.106	.109	.116	.109	.121	.125	.130	.135	.137	.140	.147	.149	.150	.152	.162
2012	Oct	Nov	Dec	Jan	Feb	Mar	Apr	May	June	July	Aug	Sep	Oct	Nov	Dec
Jan	.113	.116	.122	.116	.128	.132	.137	.142	.144	.147	.154	.156	.157	.159	.168
Feb	.104	.107	.113	.107	.119	.123	.128	.133	.135	.138	.145	.147	.148	.150	.159
Mar	.100	.103	.109	.103	.115	.118	.124	.128	.131	.133	.141	.142	.143	.145	.155
Apr	.092	.095	.101	.095	.107	.111	.116	.120	.123	.125	.133	.134	.135	.137	.147
May	.092	.095	.102	.095	.107	.111	.116	.121	.123	.126	.133	.135	.136	.138	.147
June	.095	.098	.105	.098	.110	.114	.119	.124	.126	.129	.136	.138	.139	.141	.150
July	.094	.097	.103	.097	.109	.112	.118	.122	.125	.127	.135	.136	.137	.139	.149
Aug	.090	.093	.099	.093	.105	.108	.114	.118	.121	.123	.130	.132	.133	.135	.144
Sept	.084	.087	.094	.087	.099	.103	.108	.113	.115	.118	.125	.127	.127	.129	.139
Oct	.078	.081	.088	.081	.093	.096	.102	.106	.109	.111	.118	.120	.121	.123	.132
Nov	.078	.081	.088	.081	.093	.096	.102	.106	.109	.111	.118	.120	.121	.123	.132
Dec	.073	.076	.082	.076	.088	.091	.096	.101	.103	.106	.113	.115	.115	.118	.127
2013	Oct	Nov	Dec	Jan	Feb	Mar	Apr	May	June	July	Aug	Sep	Oct	Nov	Dec
Jan	.077	.080	.087	.080	.092	.096	.101	.105	.108	.110	.118	.119	.120	.122	.131
Feb	.069	.072	.079	.072	.084	.088	.093	.097	.100	.102	.109	.111	.112	.114	.123
Mar	.065	.068	.074	.068	.079	.083	.088	.092	.095	.097	.105	.106	.107	.109	.118
Apr	.061	.064	.071	.064	.076	.079	.085	.089	.091	.094	.101	.103	.103	.105	.115
May	.059	.062	.068	.062	.074	.077	.082	.087	.089	.092	.099	.100	.101	.103	.112
June	.060	.063	.070	.063	.075	.078	.084	.088	.091	.093	.100	.102	.103	.105	.114
July	.060	.063	.070	.063	.075	.078	.084	.088	.091	.093	.100	.102	.103	.105	.114
Aug	.055	.058	.064	.058	.069	.073	.078	.082	.085	.087	.094	.096	.097	.099	.108
Sept	.051	.054	.060	.054	.066	.069	.074	.079	.081	.083	.091	.092	.093	.095	.104
Oct	.051	.054	.060	.054	.066	.069	.074	.079	.081	.083	.091	.092	.093	.095	.104
Nov	.050	.053	.060	.053	.065	.068	.073	.078	.080	.083	.090	.091	.092	.094	.103
Dec	.048	.051	.057	.051	.063	.066	.071	.076	.078	.080	.087	.089	.090	.092	.101

MONTH OF DISPOSAL

	2015						*2016*								
2014	July	Aug	Sep	Oct	Nov	Dec	Jan	Feb	Mar	Apr	May	June	July	Aug	Sep
Jan	.024	.029	.028	.027	.029	.032	.025	.029	.034	.035	.038	.042	.043	.047	.049
Feb	.017	.022	.021	.021	.022	.025	.018	.023	.027	.028	.031	.035	.036	.040	.042
Mar	.015	.020	.019	.018	.020	.023	.016	.020	.025	.026	.029	.033	.034	.038	.040
Apr	.011	.016	.015	.015	.016	.019	.012	.017	.021	.022	.025	.029	.030	.034	.036
May	.011	.015	.014	.014	.015	.018	.011	.016	.020	.021	.024	.028	.029	.033	.035
June	.010	.014	.013	.012	.014	.017	.010	.014	.019	.020	.023	.027	.028	.032	.034
July	.010	.015	.014	.014	.015	.018	.011	.016	.020	.021	.024	.028	.029	.033	.035
Aug	.006	.011	.010	.010	.011	.014	.007	.012	.016	.017	.020	.024	.025	.029	.031
Sep	.004	.009	.008	.007	.009	.012	.005	.009	.014	.015	.017	.021	.023	.026	.028
Oct	.003	.008	.007	.007	.008	.011	.004	.009	.013	.014	.017	.021	.022	.026	.028
Nov	.006	.011	.010	.009	.011	.014	.007	.011	.016	.017	.019	.023	.025	.028	.030
Dec	.004	.009	.008	.008	.009	.012	.005	.010	.014	.015	.018	.022	.023	.027	.029
2015	July	Aug	Sep	Oct	Nov	Dec	Jan	Feb	Mar	Apr	May	June	July	Aug	Sep
Jan	.013	.017	.016	.016	.017	.020	.013	.018	.022	.023	.026	.030	.031	.035	.037
Feb	.007	.012	.011	.011	.012	.015	.008	.013	.017	.018	.021	.025	.026	.030	.032
Mar	.006	.011	.010	.009	.011	.014	.007	.011	.016	.017	.019	.023	.025	.028	.030
Apr	.002	.007	.006	.006	.007	.010	.003	.008	.012	.013	.016	.020	.021	.025	.027
May	.000	.005	.004	.004	.005	.008	.001	.006	.010	.011	.014	.018	.019	.023	.025
June	.000	.003	.003	.002	.003	.007	.000	.004	.008	.010	.012	.016	.017	.021	.023
July	—	.005	.004	.003	.005	.008	.001	.005	.010	.011	.014	.017	.019	.022	.024
Aug	—	—	.000	.000	.000	.003	.000	.001	.005	.006	.009	.013	.014	.018	.020
Sep	—	—	—	.000	.001	.004	.000	.002	.006	.007	.010	.013	.015	.018	.020
Oct	—	—	—	—	.001	.004	.000	.002	.006	.007	.010	.014	.015	.019	.021
Nov	—	—	—	—	—	.003	.000	.001	.005	.006	.009	.013	.014	.018	.020
Dec	—	—	—	—	—	—	.000	.000	.002	.003	.006	.010	.011	.015	.017
2016	July	Aug	Sep	Oct	Nov	Dec	Jan	Feb	Mar	Apr	May	June	July	Aug	Sep
Jan	—	—	—	—	—	—	—	.005	.009	.010	.013	.017	.018	.022	.024
Feb	—	—	—	—	—	—	—	—	.004	.005	.008	.012	.013	.017	.019
Mar	—	—	—	—	—	—	—	—	—	.001	.004	.008	.009	.013	.015
Apr	—	—	—	—	—	—	—	—	—	—	.003	.007	.008	.011	.013
May	—	—	—	—	—	—	—	—	—	—	—	.004	.005	.009	.011
June	—	—	—	—	—	—	—	—	—	—	—	—	.001	.005	.007
July	—	—	—	—	—	—	—	—	—	—	—	—	—	.004	.006
Aug	—	—	—	—	—	—	—	—	—	—	—	—	—	—	.002
Sep	—	—	—	—	—	—	—	—	—	—	—	—	—	—	—
Oct	—	—	—	—	—	—	—	—	—	—	—	—	—	—	—
Nov	—	—	—	—	—	—	—	—	—	—	—	—	—	—	—
Dec	—	—	—	—	—	—	—	—	—	—	—	—	—	—	—
2017	July	Aug	Sep	Oct	Nov	Dec	Jan	Feb	Mar	Apr	May	June	July	Aug	Sep
Jan	—	—	—	—	—	—	—	—	—	—	—	—	—	—	—
Feb	—	—	—	—	—	—	—	—	—	—	—	—	—	—	—
Mar	—	—	—	—	—	—	—	—	—	—	—	—	—	—	—
Apr	—	—	—	—	—	—	—	—	—	—	—	—	—	—	—
May	—	—	—	—	—	—	—	—	—	—	—	—	—	—	—
June	—	—	—	—	—	—	—	—	—	—	—	—	—	—	—
July	—	—	—	—	—	—	—	—	—	—	—	—	—	—	—
Aug	—	—	—	—	—	—	—	—	—	—	—	—	—	—	—
Sep	—	—	—	—	—	—	—	—	—	—	—	—	—	—	—
Oct	—	—	—	—	—	—	—	—	—	—	—	—	—	—	—
Nov	—	—	—	—	—	—	—	—	—	—	—	—	—	—	—
Dec	—	—	—	—	—	—	—	—	—	—	—	—	—	—	—

MONTH OF DISPOSAL

	2016			*2017*											
2014	Oct	Nov	Dec	Jan	Feb	Mar	Apr	May	June	July	Aug	Sep	Oct	Nov	Dec
Jan	.048	.051	.057	.051	.063	.066	.071	.076	.078	.080	.087	.089	.090	.092	.101
Feb	.042	.044	.051	.044	.056	.059	.065	.069	.071	.074	.081	.082	.083	.085	.094
Mar	.039	.042	.048	.042	.053	.057	.062	.066	.069	.071	.078	.080	.080	.082	.091
Apr	.036	.038	.045	.038	.050	.053	.058	.063	.065	.067	.074	.076	.077	.079	.088
May	.035	.038	.044	.038	.049	.052	.057	.062	.064	.066	.073	.075	.076	.078	.087
June	.033	.036	.042	.036	.047	.051	.056	.060	.062	.065	.072	.073	.074	.076	.085
July	.034	.037	.043	.037	.048	.052	.057	.061	.064	.066	.073	.075	.075	.077	.086
Aug	.030	.033	.039	.033	.044	.048	.053	.057	.060	.062	.069	.070	.071	.073	.082
Sep	.028	.031	.037	.031	.042	.045	.050	.055	.057	.059	.066	.068	.069	.071	.080
Oct	.028	.030	.036	.030	.042	.045	.050	.054	.057	.059	.066	.068	.068	.070	.079
Nov	.030	.033	.039	.033	.044	.047	.053	.057	.059	.061	.068	.070	.071	.073	.082
Dec	.028	.031	.037	.031	.042	.046	.051	.055	.057	.060	.067	.068	.069	.071	.080
2015	Oct	Nov	Dec	Jan	Feb	Mar	Apr	May	June	July	Aug	Sep	Oct	Nov	Dec
Jan	.037	.040	.046	.040	.051	.054	.060	.064	.066	.069	.076	.077	.078	.080	.089
Feb	.032	.034	.041	.034	.046	.049	.054	.058	.061	.063	.070	.072	.072	.074	.083
Mar	.030	.033	.039	.033	.044	.047	.053	.057	.059	.061	.068	.070	.071	.073	.082
Apr	.026	.029	.035	.029	.040	.044	.049	.053	.055	.058	.065	.066	.067	.069	.078
May	.024	.027	.033	.027	.038	.042	.047	.051	.053	.056	.063	.064	.065	.067	.076
June	.023	.025	.032	.025	.037	.040	.045	.049	.052	.054	.061	.063	.063	.065	.074
July	.024	.027	.033	.027	.038	.041	.046	.051	.053	.055	.062	.064	.065	.067	.075
Aug	.019	.022	.028	.022	.033	.037	.042	.046	.048	.050	.057	.059	.060	.062	.070
Sep	.020	.023	.029	.023	.034	.037	.042	.047	.049	.051	.058	.060	.060	.062	.071
Oct	.020	.023	.029	.023	.034	.038	.043	.047	.049	.052	.059	.060	.061	.063	.072
Nov	.019	.022	.028	.022	.033	.037	.042	.046	.048	.050	.057	.059	.060	.062	.070
Dec	.016	.019	.025	.019	.030	.033	.038	.043	.045	.047	.054	.056	.056	.058	.067
2016	Oct	Nov	Dec	Jan	Feb	Mar	Apr	May	June	July	Aug	Sep	Oct	Nov	Dec
Jan	.023	.026	.032	.026	.037	.041	.046	.050	.052	.054	.061	.063	.064	.066	.075
Feb	.018	.021	.027	.021	.032	.036	.041	.045	.047	.050	.057	.058	.059	.061	.070
Mar	.014	.017	.023	.017	.028	.031	.036	.041	.043	.045	.052	.054	.054	.056	.065
Apr	.013	.016	.022	.016	.027	.030	.035	.039	.042	.044	.051	.052	.053	.055	.064
May	.010	.013	.019	.013	.024	.027	.032	.037	.039	.041	.048	.050	.050	.052	.061
June	.006	.009	.015	.009	.020	.024	.029	.033	.035	.037	.044	.046	.046	.048	.057
July	.005	.008	.014	.008	.019	.022	.027	.032	.034	.036	.043	.044	.045	.047	.056
Aug	.002	.004	.010	.004	.015	.019	.023	.028	.030	.032	.039	.040	.041	.043	.052
Sep	.000	.002	.008	.002	.013	.017	.022	.026	.028	.030	.037	.039	.039	.041	.050
Oct	—	.003	.009	.003	.014	.017	.022	.026	.028	.031	.037	.039	.040	.042	.050
Nov	—	—	.006	.000	.011	.014	.019	.023	.026	.028	.035	.036	.037	.039	.047
Dec	—	—	—	.000	.005	.008	.013	.017	.019	.022	.028	.030	.031	.033	.041
2017	Oct	Nov	Dec	Jan	Feb	Mar	Apr	May	June	July	Aug	Sep	Oct	Nov	Dec
Jan	—	—	—	—	.011	.014	.019	.023	.026	.028	.035	.036	.037	.039	.047
Feb	—	—	—	—	—	.003	.008	.012	.015	.017	.023	.025	.026	.028	.036
Mar	—	—	—	—	—	—	.005	.009	.011	.013	.020	.022	.022	.024	.033
Apr	—	—	—	—	—	—	—	.004	.006	.008	.015	.017	.017	.019	.028
May	—	—	—	—	—	—	—	—	.002	.004	.011	.013	.013	.015	.024
June	—	—	—	—	—	—	—	—	—	.002	.009	.010	.011	.013	.021
July	—	—	—	—	—	—	—	—	—	—	.007	.008	.009	.011	.019
Aug	—	—	—	—	—	—	—	—	—	—	—	.001	.002	.004	.012
Sep	—	—	—	—	—	—	—	—	—	—	—	—	.001	.003	.011
Oct	—	—	—	—	—	—	—	—	—	—	—	—	—	.002	.010
Nov	—	—	—	—	—	—	—	—	—	—	—	—	—	—	.008
Dec	—	—	—	—	—	—	—	—	—	—	—	—	—	—	—

Retail prices index

	Jan	*Feb*	*Mar*	*Apr*	*May*	*Jun*
1982	78.73	78.76	79.44	81.04	81.62	81.85
1983	82.61	82.97	83.12	84.28	84.64	84.84
1984	86.84	87.20	87.48	88.64	88.97	89.20
1985	91.20	91.94	92.80	94.78	95.21	95.41
1986	96.25	96.60	96.73	97.67	97.85	97.79
1987	100.00	100.40	100.60	101.80	101.90	101.90
1988	103.30	103.70	104.10	105.80	106.20	106.60
1989	111.00	111.80	112.30	114.30	115.00	115.40
1990	119.50	120.20	121.40	125.10	126.20	126.70
1991	130.20	130.90	131.40	133.10	133.50	134.10
1992	135.60	136.30	136.70	138.80	139.30	139.30
1993	137.90	138.80	139.30	140.60	141.10	141.00
1994	141.30	142.10	142.50	144.20	144.70	144.70
1995	146.00	146.90	147.50	149.00	149.60	149.80
1996	150.20	150.90	151.50	152.60	152.90	153.00
1997	154.40	155.00	155.40	156.30	156.90	157.50
1998	159.50	160.30	160.80	162.60	163.50	163.40
1999	163.40	163.70	164.10	165.20	165.60	165.60
2000	166.60	167.50	168.40	170.10	170.70	171.10
2001	171.10	172.00	172.20	173.10	174.20	174.40
2002	173.30	173.80	174.50	175.70	176.20	176.20
2003	178.40	179.30	179.90	181.20	181.50	181.30
2004	183.10	183.80	184.60	185.70	186.50	186.80
2005	188.90	189.60	190.50	191.60	192.00	192.20
2006	193.40	194.20	195.00	196.50	197.70	198.50
2007	201.60	203.10	204.40	205.40	206.20	207.30
2008	209.80	211.40	212.10	214.00	215.10	216.80
2009	210.10	211.40	211.30	211.50	212.80	213.40
2010	217.90	219.20	220.70	222.80	223.60	224.10
2011	229.00	231.30	232.50	234.40	235.20	235.20
2012	238.00	239.90	240.80	242.50	242.40	241.80
2013	245.80	247.60	248.70	249.50	250.00	249.70
2014	252.60	254.20	254.80	255.70	255.90	256.30
2015	255.40	256.70	257.10	258.00	258.50	258.90
2016	258.80	260.00	261.10	261.40	262.10	263.10
2017	265.50	268.40	269.30	270.60	271.70	272.30

Retail prices index, cont.

	Jul	Aug	Sep	Oct	Nov	Dec
1982	81.88	81.90	81.85	82.26	82.66	82.51
1983	85.30	85.68	86.06	86.36	86.67	86.89
1984	89.10	89.94	90.11	90.67	90.95	90.87
1985	95.23	95.49	95.44	95.59	95.92	96.05
1986	97.52	97.82	98.30	98.45	99.29	99.62
1987	101.80	102.10	102.40	102.90	103.40	103.30
1988	106.70	107.90	108.40	109.50	110.00	110.30
1989	115.50	115.80	116.60	117.50	118.50	118.80
1990	126.80	128.10	129.30	130.30	130.00	129.90
1991	133.80	134.10	134.60	135.10	135.60	135.70
1992	138.80	138.90	139.40	139.90	139.70	139.20
1993	140.70	141.30	141.90	141.80	141.60	141.90
1994	144.00	144.70	145.00	145.20	145.30	146.00
1995	149.10	149.90	150.60	149.80	149.80	150.70
1996	152.40	153.10	153.80	153.80	153.90	154.40
1997	157.50	158.50	159.30	159.50	159.60	160.00
1998	163.00	163.70	164.40	164.50	164.40	164.40
1999	165.10	165.50	166.20	166.50	166.70	167.30
2000	170.50	170.50	171.70	171.60	172.10	172.20
2001	173.30	174.00	174.60	174.30	173.60	173.40
2002	175.90	176.40	177.60	177.90	178.20	178.50
2003	181.30	181.60	182.50	182.60	182.70	183.50
2004	186.80	187.40	188.10	188.60	189.00	189.90
2005	192.20	192.60	193.10	193.30	193.60	194.10
2006	198.50	199.20	200.10	200.40	201.10	202.70
2007	206.10	207.30	208.00	208.90	209.70	210.90
2008	216.50	217.20	218.40	217.70	216.00	212.90
2009	213.40	214.40	215.30	216.00	216.60	218.00
2010	223.60	224.50	225.30	225.80	226.80	228.40
2011	234.70	236.10	237.90	238.00	238.50	239.40
2012	242.10	243.00	244.20	245.60	245.60	246.80
2013	249.70	251.00	251.90	251.90	252.10	253.40
2014	256.00	257.00	257.60	257.70	257.10	257.50
2015	258.60	259.80	259.60	259.50	259.80	260.60
2016	263.40	264.40	264.90	264.80	265.50	267.10
2017	272.90	274.70	275.10	275.30	275.80	278.10

Leases

SEE TOLLEY'S TAX COMPUTATIONS 216.3.

Depreciation table (TCGA 1992 Sch 8 para 1)

Yrs	%	Yrs	%	Yrs	%	Yrs	%
50 (or more)	100	37	93.497	24	79.622	11	50.038
49	99.657	36	92.761	23	78.055	10	46.695
48	99.289	35	91.981	22	76.399	9	43.154
47	98.902	34	91.156	21	74.635	8	39.399
46	98.490	33	90.280	20	72.770	7	35.414
45	98.059	32	89.354	19	70.791	6	31.195
44	97.595	31	88.371	18	68.697	5	26.722
43	97.107	30	87.330	17	66.470	4	21.983
42	96.593	29	86.226	16	64.116	3	16.959
41	96.041	28	85.053	15	61.617	2	11.629
40	95.457	27	83.816	14	58.971	1	5.983
39	94.842	26	82.496	13	56.167	0	0
38	94.189	25	81.100	12	53.191		

Formula: Fraction of expenditure disallowed—

$$\frac{AE - D}{AE}$$

Where:

AE is the percentage for duration of lease at acquisition or expenditure; and
D is the percentage for duration of lease at disposal.

Fractions of years: Add one-twelfth of the difference between the percentage for the whole year and the next higher percentage for each additional month. Odd days under 14 are not counted; 14 odd days or more count as a month.

Short leases: premiums treated as rent (TCGA 1992 Sch 8 para 5; ITTOIA 2005 ss 277–281A; CTA 2009 s 217–221A) Part of premium for grant of a short lease which is chargeable to income tax as property income:

$$P - (2\% \times (n - 1) \times P)$$

Where:

P is the amount of premium;
n is the number of complete years which lease has to run when granted.

Length of lease (complete years)	*Amount chargeable to CGT %*	*Income tax charge %*	*Length of lease (complete years)*	*Amount chargeable to CGT %*	*Income tax charge %*	*Length of lease (complete years)*	*Amount chargeable to CGT %*	*Income tax charge %*
Over 50	100	0	34	66	34	17	32	68
50	98	2	33	64	36	16	30	70
49	96	4	32	62	38	15	28	72
48	94	6	31	60	40	14	26	74
47	92	8	30	58	42	13	24	76
46	90	10	29	56	44	12	22	78
45	88	12	28	54	46	11	20	80
44	86	14	27	52	48	10	18	82
43	84	16	26	50	50	9	16	84
42	82	18	25	48	52	8	14	86
41	80	20	24	46	54	7	12	88
40	78	22	23	44	56	6	10	90
39	76	24	22	42	58	5	8	92
38	74	26	21	40	60	4	6	94
37	72	28	20	38	62	3	4	96
36	70	30	19	36	64	2	2	98
35	68	32	18	34	66	1 or less	0	100

Corporation tax

Rates for non-ring fence profits

SEE TOLLEY'S TAX COMPUTATIONS 101.2.
(CTA 2010 ss 3, 18–34; FA 2015 s 6; F(No 2)A 2015 s 7)

Financial year	***2013***	***2014***	***2015***	***2016***	***2017***	***2018***
Main rate	23%	21%	20%[2]	20%[2]	19%[2]	**19%[2]**
Small profits rate	20%	20%	N/A	N/A	N/A	**N/A**
lower limit[1]	£300,000	£300,000	N/A	N/A	N/A	**N/A**
upper limit[1]	£1.5m	£1.5m	N/A	N/A	N/A	**N/A**
marginal relief fraction	3/400	1/400	N/A	N/A	N/A	**N/A**
effective marginal rate	23.75%	21.25%	N/A	N/A	N/A	**N/A**
Tax credit: from 6 April	10%	10%	10%	N/A[5]	N/A[5]	**N/A[5]**

1 Reduced proportionally for accounting periods of less than 12 months. For financial years before 2015 the limits are divided by the number of associated companies (including the company in question).
2 For financial year 2015 onwards there is one main rate and no small profits rate.
3 For financial year 2019 the main rate will be 19%. For financial year 2020 it will be 17%.
4 The power to set the rate of corporation tax in Northern Ireland has been devolved to the Northern Ireland Assembly in relation to such financial year as HM Treasury may appoint. The Northern Ireland Executive has committed to setting a rate of 12.5% in April 2018 although the UK Government has indicated it will not legislate to implement the provisions until the NI Executive's finances are on a 'sustainable footing'.
5 Tax credits are abolished from 6 April 2016.

Marginal relief before 1 April 2015

The small profits rate applies to taxable total profits where augmented profits (see below) do not exceed the lower limit. Where a company's profits exceed the lower limit but do not exceed the upper limit, the charge to corporation tax on the company's taxable total profits is reduced by an amount calculated in accordance with a statutory formula—

$$F \times (U - A) \times \frac{N}{A}$$

where—

F is the marginal relief fraction;
U is the upper limit;
N is the amount of the taxable total profits;
A is the amount of the augmented profits—its adjusted taxable total profits plus franked investment income (other than from UK companies in the same group or owned by a consortium of which the recipient is a member). A company's adjusted taxable total profits are its profits chargeable to corporation tax as if no part of its chargeable gains and allowable losses for the period were liable to capital gains tax (ie on disposals of certain high value UK property, see p 65) instead of to corporation tax.

Bank levy see p 66. **Patent box** see p 64. **Diverted profits tax** see p 66. **Bank corporation tax surcharge** see p 66. **Tax charge on restitution interest** see p 66.

Rates for ring fence profits

(CTA 2010 ss 279A–279H)

Financial year	***2013***	***2014***	***2015***	***2016***	***2017***	***2018***
Main rate	30%	30%	30%	30%	30%	**30%**
Small profits rate	19%	19%	19%	19%	19%	**19%**
lower limit[1]	£300,000	£300,000	£300,000	£300,000	£300,000	**£300,000**
upper limit[1]	£1.5m	£1.5m	£1.5m	£1.5m	£1.5m	**£1.5m**
marginal relief fraction	11/400	11/400	11/400	11/400	11/400	**11/400**

1 Reduced proportionally for accounting periods of less than 12 months. The limits are divided by the number of related 51% group companies (before 1 April 2015, number of associated companies), including the company in question.

Marginal relief

From 1 April 2015 Applies to ring fence profits only. The small ring fence profits rate applies to taxable total profits where augmented profits (see below) do not exceed the lower limit. Where a company's ring fence profits exceed the lower limit but do not exceed the upper limit, the charge to corporation tax on the company's taxable total profits is reduced by an amount calculated in accordance with a statutory formula—

$$R \times (U - A) \times \frac{N}{A}$$

where—

R is the marginal relief fraction;

U is the upper limit;

N is the amount of the taxable total profits;

A is the amount of the augmented profits—its adjusted taxable total profits plus exempt ABGH distributions (before 6 April 2016, franked investment income) (other than from UK companies in the same group or owned by a consortium of which the recipient is a member). A company's adjusted taxable total profits are its profits chargeable to corporation tax as if no part of its chargeable gains and allowable losses for the period were liable to capital gains tax (ie on disposals of certain high value UK property, see p 65) instead of to corporation tax.

Corporation tax reliefs

Disincorporation relief *before 1 April 2018*

SEE TOLLEY'S TAX COMPUTATIONS 213.4.

(FA 2013 ss 58–61)

With effect for disincorporations between 1 April 2013 and 31 March 2018 inclusive, joint claims may be made by a company and its shareholders to allow goodwill or interests in land not held as trading stock to be transferred at a reduced value so that no corporation tax will be payable by the company on the transfer. Relief is restricted to cases where the market value of the assets allowed for disincorporation relief does not exceed £100,000. Joint claims must be made to HMRC within two years of the date of the transfer and other eligibility criteria also apply. Shareholders to whom the assets are transferred will inherit the transfer value for the purpose of capital gains tax.

Gifts of pre-eminent objects

(FA 2012 Sch 14)

Companies which gift pre-eminent objects to the nation will receive a reduction in their UK tax liability of 20% of the value of the object they are donating. The legislation has effect in relation to liabilities for tax years and accounting periods beginning on or after 1 April 2012. The gift must be accepted as pre-eminent by the Arts Council under the Cultural Gifts Scheme.

Patent box

(CTA 2010 Pt 8A)

The patent box allows companies to elect to apply a 10% corporation tax rate to a proportion of profits attributable to qualifying patents, whether paid separately as royalties or embedded in the sales price of products, and to certain other qualifying intellectual property rights such as regulatory data protection (also called 'data exclusivity'), supplementary protection certificates and plant variety rights from 1 April 2013. In the first year the proportion of profits qualifying for the 10% rate was 60% and this was increased annually to 100% from April 2017. Thus, for financial year 2014 the proportion was 70%, for 2015 it was 80%, and for 2016 it was 90%.

Real Estate Investment Trusts (REITs)

(CTA 2010 ss 518–609)

From 1 January 2007, qualifying rental income from and gains on disposals of investment properties by UK companies within the REIT scheme are exempt from corporation tax.

Research and development

(CTA 2009 ss 1039–1142; FA 2018 s 19)

Deduction scheme

SEE TOLLEY'S TAX COMPUTATIONS 117.1.

An '**SME**' incurring R&D expenditure in a 12-month accounting period can obtain relief for 230% (applying from 1 April 2015) of that expenditure (225% for expenditure incurred between 1 April 2012 and 31 March 2015). **SMEs** not yet in profit or which have not yet started to trade can claim relief upfront as a cash payment (R&D tax credit).

An '**SME**' can also claim relief where it incurs expenditure on work contracted to it by a large company or by any person otherwise than in the course of carrying on a chargeable trade; or expenditure which is subsidised; or expenditure subject to the project limit (€7.5m for expenditure incurred after 31 July 2008). The relief is 130% of the expenditure.

An '**SME**' is a company with less than 500 employees and either annual turnover of €100m or less or annual balance sheet total of €86m or less.

Large companies can claim a similar relief to that for SMEs above, including tax credits, for expenditure incurred before 1 April 2017 on certain vaccines research.

Before 1 April 2016 **large companies** incurring R&D expenditure could obtain relief for 130% of that expenditure. From that date they must use the 'Above the line' credit scheme outlined below.

'Above the line' credit scheme for large companies

SEE TOLLEY'S TAX COMPUTATIONS 117.2.

This scheme applies from 1 April 2013. Large companies (and certain SMEs with sub-contracted or subsidised R&D, or R&D subject to the project limit) can claim R&D relief as a taxable above the line (ATL) credit to the value of 12% (11% for expenditure before 1 January 2018, 10% before 1 April 2015) of their qualifying R&D expenditure (49% for ring fence trades). The credit is fully payable, net of tax, to companies with no corporation tax liability. The scheme was initially optional. Companies that did not elect to claim the ATL credit could continue claiming R&D relief under the large company deduction scheme (see above) until 31 March 2016. The ATL credit became mandatory for such companies on 1 April 2016. Universities and charities are unable to claim the credit for expenditure incurred on or after 1 August 2015.

Annual tax on enveloped dwellings

(FA 2013 ss 94–174, Schs 33–35)

From 1 April 2013 a charge is imposed on certain non-natural persons (NNPs), ie companies, partnerships with at least one company member, and collective investment schemes which hold UK residential dwellings valued above a certain limit on specified valuation dates. The limit was set at £2 million from 1 April 2013, but lowered to £1 million from 1 April 2015, and £500,000 from 1 April 2016. Returns and payment are generally due by 30 April[2] each year. If the payer is not chargeable for the full year, a later repayment claim can be made. Various reliefs from the charge apply and from 1 April 2015 companies may be able to submit relief declaration returns. **A charge to capital gains tax** at 28% also applies to the disposal of such properties, whether by UK resident or non-resident NNPs. See also p 137 regarding the 15% **stamp duty land tax** which can apply to acquisitions of such properties.

Annual tax charge

Property value[1]	**Annual tax 2013–14**	**Annual tax 2014–15**	**Annual tax 2015–16**	**Annual tax 2016–17**	**Annual tax 2017–18**	**Annual tax 2018–19**
More than £500,000 to £1m	N/A	N/A	N/A	£3,500	£3,500	**£3,600**
More than £1m to £2m	N/A	N/A	£7,000	£7,000	£7,050	**£7,250**
More than £2m to £5m	£15,000	£15,400	£23,350	£23,350	£23,550	**£24,250**
More than £5 million to £10m	£35,000	£35,900	£54,450	£54,450	£54,950	**£56,550**
More than £10m to £20m	£70,000	£71,850	£109,050	£109,050	£110,100	**£113,400**
More than £20m	£140,000	£143,750	£218,200	£218,200	£220,350	**£226,950**

1 The valuation is the market value on the last previous valuation date. The first valuation date was 1 April 2012 and then every five years thereafter. Other valuation dates can apply in certain circumstances, for example when a new property is purchased. The valuation is applied on the first day of the chargeable period if the chargeable person is within the charge on that day, otherwise the first day in the chargeable period on which they are first within the charge.

2 Returns applicable to the band applying from 1 April 2015 to residential properties worth more than £1 million and not more than £2 million were not required until 1 October 2015 with payment required by 31 October 2015.

Relief codes for relief declaration returns

	Code for type of relief
Property rental business	1
Dwellings open to the public	2
Property developers	3
Property traders	4
Financial institutions acquiring dwellings	5
Regulated home reversion plans	5A
Occupation by certain employees etc	6
Farmhouses	7
Providers of social housing	8

Bank corporation tax surcharge

(CTA 2010 ss 269D–269DO)

From 1 January 2016 a surcharge of 8% is levied on profits of banking companies and building societies.

Bank levy

(FA 2011 Sch 19 para 6)

From 1 January 2011 a bank levy is charged based on the total chargeable equity and liabilities reported in the relevant balance sheets of affected banks, banking and building society groups at the end of the chargeable period. It is payable through the existing corporation tax self-assessment system. It is not charged on the first £20 billion of chargeable liabilities.

	1.1.14–31.3.15	1.4.15–31.12.15	1.1.16–31.12.16	1.1.17–31.12.17	**1.1.18–31.12.18**	**1.1.19–31.12.19**
Short-term chargeable liabilities	0.156%	0.21%	0.18%	0.17%	**0.16%**	**0.15%**
Long-term chargeable equity and liabilities	0.078%	0.105%	0.09%	0.085%	**0.08%**	**0.075%**

Diverted profits tax

(FA 2015 ss 77–116)

From 1 April 2015 a diverted profits tax of 25% applies to counter the use of aggressive tax planning techniques by multinational enterprises to divert profits from the UK. There are two basic rules which apply. The first rule counteracts arrangements by which foreign companies exploit the permanent establishment rules, and comes into effect if a person is carrying on activity in the UK in connection with supplies of goods and services by a non-UK resident company to customers in the UK, provided that the detailed conditions are met. The second rule applies to certain arrangements which lack economic substance involving entities with an existing UK taxable presence.

Loans to participators

See Tolley's Tax Computations **104.2**.

(CTA 2010 s 455)

A charge of 32.5% of the loan made or benefit conferred applies (25% for loans made and benefits conferred before 6 April 2016).

Tax charge on restitution interest

(CTA 2010 ss 357YA–357YW)

Where tax has been overpaid by a company as a result of a mistake in law or following unlawful collection of tax by HMRC a restitution award may be made. Where the award is made as a result of a judgment or an agreement between the parties which became final on or after 21 October 2015, the interest element of the award, whether arising before, on or after 21 October 2015, is chargeable to corporation tax at a special rate of 45%.

Environmental taxes and other levies

Aggregates levy

(FA 2001 ss 16–49, Schs 4–10; SI 2004/1959; SI 2010/2598)

Levy on commercial exploitation of aggregates including rock, gravel or sand together with any other substance incorporated or naturally occurring with it. Applies to all aggregate (not recycled) extracted in the UK or territorial waters unless exempt. Before 1 April 2014 exemptions applied to quarried or mined products such as clay, shale, slate, metal and metal ores, gemstones, semi-precious gemstones and industrial minerals. From 1 April 2014, the Government had to suspend these exemptions, exclusions and reliefs as they were the subject of a State aid investigation by the European Commission. Following conclusion of the investigation, all the exemptions except that for shale were reinstated on 1 August 2015 with retrospective effect from 1 April 2014. There is an exempt process for shale which is not used as aggregate for construction purposes which applies from 1 April 2014. This enables a person who has commercially exploited and accounted for the levy chargeable on such shale to claim a tax credit for it, when it is used in this new exempt process (HMRC Brief 6/2015).

The aggregates levy has been devolved to the Scottish Parliament. From a date to be appointed a replacement tax will apply in Scotland.

From 1 April 2009	**£2.00 per tonne**

Air passenger duty

(FA 1994 s 30, Sch 5A; FA 2018 s 43)

APD was extended to smaller aircraft and business jets (reducing the de minimis weight limit from 10 tonnes to 5.7 tonnes) from 1 April 2013 and passengers on 'luxury' business jets (20 tonnes or more and fewer than 19 seats) pay APD at twice the standard rate. From 1 November 2011 to 31 December 2012 the band A rates applied to all *direct* long haul flights departing from Northern Ireland. The rates for all *direct* long haul flights (ie in bands B to D) departing from Northern Ireland from 1 January 2013 are devolved to the Northern Ireland Assembly and set at £0.

Children under the age of 2 years on the date of the flight without their own seat are exempt from charge in all classes of travel. From 1 May 2015, children under the age of 12 years on the date of the flight are exempt from charge in standard class. From 1 March 2016 this exemption applies to children under age 16.

From 1 April 2015 destinations from bands B, C and D are merged into a single band B.

Air passenger duty has been devolved to the Scottish Parliament. A replacement tax (air departure tax) was planned to apply in Scotland from April 2018 but has been deferred.

Reduced rate (lowest class of travel)

Band and distance of capital city of destination country from UK in miles			Band and distance of capital city of destination country from UK in miles					
	1.4.13–31.3.14	1.4.14–31.3.15		1.4.15–31.3.16	1.4.16–31.3.17	1.4.17–31.3.18	**1.4.18–31.3.19**	From 1.4.19
Band A (0–2,000)	£13	£13	**Band A** (0–2,000)	£13	£13	£13	**£13**	£13
Band B (2,001–4,000)	£67	£69	**Band B** (over 2,000)	£71	£73	£75	**£78**	£78
Band C (4,001–6,000)	£83	£85						
Band D (over 6,000)	£94	£97						

Standard rate (all classes other than lowest class)[1]

Band and distance of capital city of destination country from UK in miles			Band and distance of capital city of destination country from UK in miles					
	1.4.13–31.3.14	1.4.14–31.3.15		1.4.15–31.3.16	1.4.16–31.3.17	1.4.17–31.3.18	**1.4.18–31.3.19**	From 1.4.19
Band A (0–2,000)	£26	£26	**Band A** (0–2,000)	£26	£26	£26	**£26**	£26
Band B (2,001–4,000)	£134	£138	**Band B** (over 2,000)	£142	£146	£150	**£156**	£172
Band C (4,001–6,000)	£166	£170						
Band D (over 6,000)	£188	£194						

Higher rate (flights aboard aircraft of 20 tonnes and above with fewer than 19 seats)

Band and distance of capital city of destination country from UK in miles			Band and distance of capital city of destination country from UK in miles					
	1.4.13–31.3.14	1.4.14–31.3.15		1.4.15–31.3.16	1.4.16–31.3.17	1.4.17–31.3.18	**1.4.18–31.3.19**	From 1.4.19
Band A (0–2,000)	£52	£52	**Band A** (0–2,000)	£78	£78	£78	**£78**	£78
Band B (2,001–4,000)	£268	£276	**Band B** (over 2,000)	£426	£438	£450	**£468**	£515
Band C (4,001–6,000)	£332	£340						
Band D (over 6,000)	£376	£388						

1 From 1 November 2008, if a class of travel provides a seat pitch in excess of 1.016 metres (40 inches) the standard rate is the minimum rate that applies, even if it is the lowest or only class of travel.

The following specifies which countries come into which bands.

Band A territories — 0–2,000 miles from London

Albania	Greenland	Morocco
Algeria	Guernsey[3]	Netherlands
Andorra	Hungary	Norway (including Svalbard)
Austria	Iceland	Poland
Azores	Republic of Irelanc	Portugal (including Madeira)
Belarus	Isle of Man	Romania
Belgium	Italy (including Sicily and Sardinia)[2]	Russian Federation (west of the Urals)
Bosnia and Herzegovina	Jersey[3]	San Marino
Bulgaria	Republic of Kosovo	Serbia
Croatia	Latvia	Slovak Republic
Cyprus	Libya	Slovenia
Czech Republic	Liechtenstein	Spain (including the Balearic Islands and the Canary Islands)
Denmark (including the Faroe Islands)	Lithuania	Sweden
Estonia	Luxembourg	Switzerland
Finland	former Yugoslav Republic of Macedonia	Tunisia
France (including Corsica)	Malta	Turkey
Germany	Moldova	Ukraine
Gibraltar	Monaco	Western Sahara[1]
Greece	Montenegro	

1 HMRC Notice 550 Appendix 1 (updated March 2017) does not include Western Sahara.
2 HMRC Notice 550 Appendix 1 (updated March 2017) does include Vatican City even though this is not in the tables in FA 1994 Sch 5A.
3 HMRC Notice 550 Appendix 1 (updated March 2017) refers to the Channel Islands, rather than Guernsey and Jersey.

Note: From 1 April 2015 destinations from bands B, C and D are merged into a single band B.

Band B territories — 2,001–4,000 miles from London

Afghanistan	Gambia	Pakistan
Armenia	Georgia	Qatar
Azerbaijan	Ghana	Russian Federation (east of the Urals)
Bahrain	Guinea	Saint Pierre and Miquelon
Benin	Guinea-Bissau	Sao Tome and Principe
Bermuda	Iran	Saudi Arabia
Burkina Faso	Iraq	Senegal
Cameroon	Israel & Occupied Palestinian Territories	Sierra Leone
Canada	Ivory Coast	South Sudan
Cape Verde	Jordan	Sudan
Central African Republic	Kazakhstan	Syria
Chad	Kuwait	Tajikistan
Democratic Republic of Congo	Kyrgyzstan	Togo
Republic of Congo	Lebanon	Turkmenistan
Djibouti	Liberia	Uganda
Egypt	Mali	United Arab Emirates
Equatorial Guinea	Mauritania	United States of America
Eritrea	Niger	Uzbekistan
Ethiopia	Nigeria	Yemen
Gabon	Oman	

Note: From 1 April 2015 destinations from bands B, C and D are merged into a single band B.

Band C territories — 4,001–6,000 miles from London

Angola
Anguilla
Antigua and Barbuda
Aruba
Bahamas
Bangladesh
Barbados
Belize
Bhutan
Bonaire
Botswana
Brazil
British Indian Ocean Territory
British Virgin Islands
Burma
Burundi
Cayman Islands
China
Colombia
Comoros
Costa Rica
Cuba
Curaçao
Dominica
Dominican Republic
Ecuador
El Salvador
French Guiana
Grenada
Guadeloupe
Guatemala
Guyana
Haiti
Honduras
Hong Kong SAR
India
Jamaica
Japan
Kenya
North Korea
South Korea
Laos
Lesotho
Macao SAR
Madagascar
Malawi
Maldives
Martinique
Mauritius
Mayotte
Mexico
Mongolia
Montserrat
Mozambique
Namibia
Nepal
Nicaragua
Panama
Puerto Rico
Reunion
Rwanda
Saba
Saint Barthelemy
Saint Christopher and Nevis (St Kitts and Nevis)
Saint Helena, Ascension and Tristan da Cuhna
Saint Lucia
Saint Martin
Saint Vincent and the Grenadines
Seychelles
Sint Eustatius
Sint Maarten
Somalia
South Africa
Sri Lanka
Suriname
Swaziland
Tanzania
Thailand
Trinidad and Tobago
Turks and Caicos Islands
Venezuela
Vietnam
Virgin Islands
Zambia
Zimbabwe

Band D — journey ends in any other place.

Note: From 1 April 2015 destinations from bands B, C and D are merged into a single band B.

Climate change levy

(FA 2000 s 30, Sch 6)

Levy on supply for industrial or commercial purposes of energy, from 1 April 2001, in the form of electricity, gas, petroleum and hydrocarbon gas supplied in a liquid state, coal and lignite, coke and semi-coke of coal or lignite and petroleum coke.

Taxable commodity supplied	*Rate*[1]						
	1.4.13–31.3.14	1.4.14–31.3.15	1.4.15–31.3.16	1.4.16–31.3.17	1.4.17–31.3.18	**1.4.18–31.3.19**	1.4.19–31.3.20
Electricity	0.524p per kWh	0.541p per kWh	0.554p per kWh	0.559p per kWh	0.568p per kWh	**0.583p per kWh**	0.847p per kWh
Gas supplied by a gas utility or any gas supplied in a gaseous state that is of a kind supplied by a gas utility	0.182p per kWh	0.188p per kWh	0.193p per kWh	0.195p per kWh	0.198p per kWh	**0.203p per kWh**	0.339p per kWh
Gas supplied as above in Northern Ireland	0.064p per kWh until 31.10.13 then main rate applies	0.188p per kWh	0.193p per kWh	0.195p per kWh	0.198p per kWh	**0.203p per kWh**	0.339p per kWh
Any petroleum gas, or other gaseous hydrocarbon supplied in a liquid state	1.172p per kg	1.210p per kg	1.240p per kg	1.251p per kg	1.272p per kg	**1.304p per kg**	2.175p per kg
Any other taxable commodity	1.429p per kg	1.476p per kg	1.512p per kg	1.526p per kg	1.551p per kg	**1.591p per kg**	2.653p per kg

1 Rate at which payable if supply is not a reduced-rate supply. The levy is charged at a reduced rate for facilities covered by a climate change agreement, generally 35% of the full rate (to be reduced to 22% from 1 April 2019), but 20% from 1 April 2012 to 31 March 2014 for supplies of taxable commodities used in recycling of steel and aluminium (previously and subsequently exempt) and 10% from 1 April 2013 for electricity supplies (to be reduced to 7% from 1 April 2019). From 1 April 2014 supplies of taxable commodities used in metallurgical and mineralogical processes are exempt. From 1 August 2015 electricity generated from renewable sources is no longer eligible for exemption when supplied under a renewable source contract, though the exemption may still apply until 31 March 2018 to renewable source electricity generated before 1 August 2015.

Carbon price support rates for climate change levy and fuel duty

The carbon price floor was introduced from 1 April 2013. Supplies of solid fossil fuels, gas and liquefied petroleum gas used in most forms of electricity generation are liable to the CPS rates of CCL, which differs from the main CCL rates (see above) levied on consumers' use of these commodities (and electricity). Oils and bioblends are not taxable commodities for CCL purposes, and are taxed under the fuel duty regime. There are, however, CPS rates of fuel duty for oils and bioblends used in the generation of electricity. Subject to state aid approval, the carbon price floor does not apply to Northern Ireland. The CPS rate is reduced by the carbon capture percentage where there is a supply of fossil fuels to an electricity generator which uses carbon capture and storage (CCS) technology. Small scale Combined Heat and Power (CHP) stations are not subject to the CPS rate. From 1 April 2015 fossil fuels used in a CHP station to generate good quality electricity consumed on-site are also excluded.

Supplies of commodity	*Rate*			
	1.4.13–31.3.14	1.4.14–31.3.15	1.4.15–31.3.16	**1.4.16–31.3.20**
Gas supplied by a gas utility or any gas supplied in a gaseous state that is of a kind supplied by a gas utility	0.091p per kWh	0.175p per kWh	0.334p per kWh	**0.331p per kWh**
Any petroleum gas, or other gaseous hydrocarbon supplied in a liquid state	1.460p per kg	2.822p per kg	5.307p per kg	**5.28p per kg**
Coal and other taxable solid fossil fuels	44.264p per gross gigajoule	81.906p per gross gigajoule	156.86p per gross gigajoule	**154.79p per gross gigajoule**
Gas oil; rebated bioblend; kerosene[1]	1.365p per litre	2.642p per litre	4.99p per litre	**4.916p per litre**
Fuel oil; other heavy oil; rebated light oil	1.568p per litre	3.011p per litre	5.73p per litre	**5.711p per litre**

1 The CPS rates of fuel duty apply to duty paid kerosene used in electricity generation from 1 May 2014.

Fuel duty

(HODA 1979 s 6; SI 2011/2935; SI 2015/550)

A Rural Fuel Duty relief scheme for retailers of road fuel on the Inner and Outer Hebrides, the Northern Isles, the Islands of the Clyde and the Isles of Scilly originally applied from 1 January 2012 to 31 December 2017, though the Government has announced that it is extending the scheme until 31 October 2023. Retailers of road fuel within these areas are eligible to register with HMRC to claim back five pence per litre relief on unleaded petrol and diesel for retail sale within the eligible areas. The retailers have 60 days following registration for the scheme to reduce the cost of every litre of road fuel sold by the equivalent amount of the relief claimed (HMRC Brief 40/2011). The scheme is extended from 1 April 2015 to 31 March 2020 to the postal town of Hawes in North Yorkshire, and the following postcode districts: EX35, LA17, NE48, IV14, IV21, IV22, IV26, IV27, IV54, KW12, PA38, PA80, PH19, PH23, PH36, PH41 (HMRC Brief 3/2015).

	Petrol/diesel	Biodiesel or bioethanol	LPG used as road fuel	Natural gas used as road fuel	Red diesel	Fuel oil	Aqua-methanol
From 14 November 2016	**57.95p per litre**	**57.95p per litre**	**31.61p per kg**	**24.70p per kg**	**11.14p per litre**	**10.70p per litre**	**7.90p per litre**
From 6pm 23 March 2011 to 13 November 2016	57.95p per litre	57.95p per litre	31.61p per kg	24.70p per kg	11.14p per litre	10.70p per litre	57.95p per litre
From 1 January 2011 to 6pm 23 March 2011	58.95p per litre	58.95p per litre	33.04p per kg	26.15p per kg	11.33p per litre	10.88p per litre	N/A
From 1 October 2010 to 31 December 2010	58.19p per litre	58.19p per litre	31.95p per kg	25.05p per kg	11.18p per litre	10.74p per litre	N/A
From 1 April 2010 to 30 September 2010	57.19p per litre	57.19p per litre	30.53p per kg	23.60p per kg	10.99p per litre	10.55p per litre	N/A

Insurance premium tax

(FA 1994 ss 48–74, Schs 6A, 7, 7A)

IPT is a tax on premiums received under insurance contracts other than those which are specifically exempt.

	Standard rate	*Higher rate*[1]
From 1.6.17	**12.0%**	**20.0%**
1.10.16–31.5.17[3]	10.0%	20.0%
1.11.15–30.9.16[2]	9.5%	20.0%
4.1.11–31.10.15	6.0%	20.0%

1 The higher rate applies to sales of motor cars, light vans and motorcycles, electrical or mechanical domestic appliances, and travel insurance.

2 9.5% rate applies from 1 March 2016 for insurers who use a special accounting scheme rather than the cash receipt method, and where the premium relates to risks covered by the terms of a contract entered into before 1 November 2015.

3 10% rate applies from 1 February 2017 for insurers who use a special accounting scheme rather than the cash receipt method, and where the premium relates to risks covered by the terms of a contract entered into before 1 October 2016.

Landfill tax

(FA 1996 ss 39–71, 197, Sch 5; FA 2018 Sch 12; SI 1996/1527; SI 1996/1528; SI 2016/376; Notice LFT 1 para 4.5; SSI 2017/332)

Tax on disposal of material (before 1 April 2018, waste) imposed on operators of landfill sites calculated by reference to the weight and type of material deposited. Exemption applies to mining and quarrying material, dredging material, pet cemeteries, disposals of NATO material, and inert material used to fill working and old quarries. From 1 April 2018 the scope of the tax is extended to disposals of material at sites operating without the appropriate licence or permit, and the exemptions above will not apply to these sites. The power to raise landfill tax devolved to the Scottish Parliament from 1 April 2015 (see table below). That power has also been devolved to the Welsh Government from 1 April 2018 (see table below).

Period	*Active waste per tonne*	*Inert waste per tonne*[2]	*Maximum credit*[1]
From 1.4.19	£91.35	£2.90	TBA
1.4.18–31.3.19	**£88.95**	**£2.80**	**5.3%**
1.4.17–31.3.18	£86.10	£2.70	5.3%
1.4.16–31.3.17	£84.40	£2.65	4.2%
1.4.15–31.3.16	£82.60	£2.60	5.7%
1.4.14–31.3.15	£80	£2.50	5.1%
1.4.13–31.3.14	£72	£2.50	6.8%
1.4.12–31.3.13	£64	£2.50	5.6%

1 Tax credits are available to operators who make donations to environmental trusts of 90% of the donation to the maximum percentage above of the tax payable in a 12-month period (Landfill Communities Fund). Tax credits do not apply to disposals of material at sites operating without the appropriate licence or permit.

2 For details of waste materials liable at the lower rate see SI 2011/1017 as amended by SI 2012/940 and HMRC Briefs 15/2012 and 18/2012. The lower rate does not apply to disposals of material at sites operating without the appropriate licence or permit.

Scottish landfill tax

(Landfill Tax (Scotland) Act 2014; SSI 2017/23)

Tax replaces landfill tax in Scotland from 1 April 2015.

Period	*Active waste per tonne*	*Inert waste per tonne*[2]	*Maximum credit*[1]
1.4.18–31.3.19	**£88.95**	**£2.80**	**5.6%**
1.4.17–31.3.18	£86.10	£2.70	5.6%
1.4.16–31.3.17	£84.40	£2.65	5.6%
1.4.15–31.3.16	£82.60	£2.60	5.6%

1 Tax credits are available to operators who make donations to environmental trusts of 90% of the donation to the maximum percentage above of the tax payable in a 12-month period (Scottish Landfill Communities Fund).

2 For details of waste materials liable at the lower rate see SSIs 2015/45 and 2016/93.

Landfill disposals tax (Wales)

(Landfill Disposals Tax (Wales) Act 2017; SI 2017/955)

Tax replaces landfill tax in Wales from 1 April 2018.

Period	*Active waste per tonne*	*Inert waste per tonne*	*Unauthorised disposals rate*
1.4.18–31.3.19	**£88.95**	**£2.80**	**£133.45**

1 The Landfill Disposals Tax Communities Scheme will be established as a grant scheme and will not be delivered by means of a tax credit.

Vehicle excise duty

(VERA 1994 Sch 1; FA 2018 s 44)

Vehicle tax, or 'road tax' is charged according to CO_2 emissions, as follows:

Standard and first-year rates for cars registered before 1 April 2017

Band	CO_2 (g/km)	2016–17 Standard rate	2016–17 first-year rate	2017–18 Standard rate	2018–19 Standard rate
A	Up to 100	£0	£0	£0	**£0**
B	101–110	£20	£0	£20	**£20**
C	111–120	£30	£0	£30	**£30**
D	121–130	£110	£0	£115	**£120**
E	131–140	£130	£130	£135	**£140**
F	141–150	£145	£145	£150	**£155**
G	151–165	£185	£185	£190	**£195**
H	166–175	£210	£300	£220	**£230**
I	176–185	£230	£355	£240	**£250**
J	186–200	£270	£500	£280	**£290**
K	201–225	£295	£650	£305	**£315**
L	226–255	£500	£885	£520	**£540**
M	Over 255	£515	£1,120	£535	**£555**

There is an alternative fuel discount of £10 for all cars. The first-year rate of tax applies in the year of purchase of a new vehicle. In later years, the standard rate applies. A different banding system applies to cars registered on or after 1 April 2017. There are no first-year rates for cars registered before 1 April 2017. First-year rates for cars registered on or after 1 April 2017 are still based on CO_2 emissions but a standard flat rate of £140 applies to all cars except those with zero emissions. Cars with a list price above £40,000 when new, have an additional rate of £310 per year for the first 5 yrs in which the standard rate is paid. From 1 April 2018 there is a separate first-year rate for diesel cars that do not meet the Euro 6d emissions standard.

Standard and first-year rates for cars registered on or after 1 April 2017

CO_2 (g/km)	2017–18 Standard rate	2017–18 first-year rate	2018–19 Standard rate	2018–19 first-year rate	2018–19 first-year rate diesel vehicles
0	£0	£0	**£0**	**£0**	**£0**
1–50	£140	£10	**£140**	**£10**	**£25**
51–75	£140	£25	**£140**	**£25**	**£105**
76–90	£140	£100	**£140**	**£105**	**£125**
91–100	£140	£120	**£140**	**£125**	**£145**
101–110	£140	£140	**£140**	**£145**	**£165**
111–130	£140	£160	**£140**	**£165**	**£205**
131–150	£140	£200	**£140**	**£205**	**£515**
151–170	£140	£500	**£140**	**£515**	**£830**
171–190	£140	£800	**£140**	**£830**	**£1,240**
191–225	£140	£1,200	**£140**	**£1,240**	**£1,760**
226–255	£140	£1,700	**£140**	**£1,760**	**£2,070**
Over 255	£140	£2,000	**£140**	**£2,070**	**£2,070**

Light goods vehicle rates

Tax class	2016–17	2017–18	2018–19
Light goods vehicle[1]	£230	£240	**£250**
Euro 4 & 5 LGV	£140	£140	**£140**

[1] Registered on or after 1 March 2001.

Motorcycle rates

VED band	2016–17	2017–18	2018–19
Up to 150 cc	£17	£18	**£19**
151–400 cc	£39	£41	**£42**
401–600 cc	£60	£62	**£64**
Over 600 cc	£82	£85	**£88**

Income tax

Starting, basic, higher and additional rates

(ITA 2007 ss 6–21)

Band of taxable income £	Band £	Rate[1] %	Tax £	Cumulative tax £
2018–19				
0–34,500	**34,500**	**20**	**6,900**	**6,900**
34,501–150,000	**115,500**	**40**	**46,200**	**53,100**
Over 150,000	**–**	**45**	**–**	**–**
2017–18				
0–33,500	33,500	20	6,700	6,700
33,501–150,000	116,500	40	46,600	53,300
Over 150,000	–	45	–	–
2016–17				
0–32,000	32,000	20	6,400	6,400
32,001–150,000	118,000	40	47,200	53,600
Over 150,000	–	45	–	–
2015–16				
0–31,785	31,785	20	6,357	6,357
31,786–150,000	118,215	40	47,286	53,643
Over 150,000	–	45	–	–
2014–15				
0–31,865	31,865	20	6,373	6,373
31,866–150,000	118,135	40	47,254	53,627
Over 150,000	–	45	–	–
2013–14				
0–32,010	32,010	20	6,402	6,402
32,011–150,000	117,990	40	47,196	53,598
Over 150,000	–	45	–	–

1 A Scottish rate of income tax applies from 6 April 2016 — see below.

Scottish rate of income tax

SEE TOLLEY'S TAX COMPUTATIONS 1.8.
(Scotland Act 1998 s 80C; Scotland Act 2016 s 13)

Band of taxable income £	Band £	Rate %	Tax £	Cumulative tax £
2018–19				
0–2,000	**2,000**	**19**	**380**	**380**
2,001–12,150	**10,150**	**20**	**2,030**	**2,410**
12,151–31,580	**19,430**	**21**	**4,080**	**6,490**
31,581–150,000	**118,420**	**41**	**48,552**	**55,042**
Over 150,000	**–**	**46**	**–**	**–**
2017–18				
0–31,500	31,500	20	6,300	6,300
31,501–150,000	118,500	40	47,400	53,700
Over 150,000	–	45	–	–
2016–17				
0–32,000	32,000	20	6,400	6,400
32,001–150,000	118,000	40	47,200	53,600
Over 150,000	–	45	–	–

From 6 April 2016 a Scottish rate of income tax applies to Scottish taxpayers' non-dividend, non-savings income. From 2017–18 the Scottish Parliament can set its own Scottish income tax rates and bands. In 2018–19 the higher rate and additional rate are increased by 1% over UK rates, and the basic rate band is split into three, giving a total of five tax bands. In 2017–18 the tax rates remained the same as the rest of the UK but the basic rate band applying to non-dividend, non-savings income is £31,500 rather than £33,500. In 2016–17 the Scottish basic, higher and additional rates were calculated by reducing each of the UK basic, higher and additional rates by ten percentage points and then adding a Scottish rate of 10%. This means for 2016–17 the rates of income tax paid by Scottish taxpayers stayed the same as for the rest of the UK. The UK basic rate band still applies to Scottish taxpayers' dividend and savings income. The definition of a Scottish taxpayer is based on the location of an individual's main place of residence.

Taxation of savings

SEE TOLLEY'S TAX COMPUTATIONS 1.2, 1.3.

(ITA 2007 ss 6–21)

A starting rate for savings band for individuals applies. For **2015–16 onwards it is £5,000**. Previous rate bands were £2,880 for 2014–15 and £2,790 for 2013–14. Where an individual's taxable non-savings income is less than this limit, there is a **0% starting rate for 2015–16 onwards** (10% for earlier years) for savings up to the limit. Where taxable non-savings income exceeds the limit, the starting rate for savings does not apply. Savings income includes interest from banks and building societies, interest distributions from authorised unit trusts, interest on gilts and other securities including corporate bonds, purchased life annuities and discounts.

From 6 April 2016 a personal savings allowance (PSA) is available to basic and higher rate taxpayers but not to additional rate taxpayers. The allowance is **£1,000 per year for basic rate taxpayers and £500 per year for higher rate taxpayers**. Savings income above the allowance is taxable at the basic or higher rate as appropriate, with savings income generally being treated as the second top slice of income behind dividends. The PSA is not a deduction in arriving at total income or taxable income. **A 0% rate of income tax applies** to savings income covered by the PSA. It operates in conjunction with the 0% starting rate for savings and income taxable at this rate does not fall within the PSA. Also from 6 April 2016, banks, building societies and National Savings are no longer required to deduct 20% tax at source from interest payable. From 6 April 2017 there is no requirement to deduct income tax at source from interest distributions from open-ended investment companies, authorised unit trusts and investment trust companies and from interest on peer-to-peer loans. Savings income within an ISA continues to be tax-free, and does not need to be covered by the PSA.

For tax years before 2016–17, where income did not exceed the basic rate limit, there was no further tax to pay on savings income from which 20% tax had been deducted. Any tax over-deducted was repayable. Higher rate taxpayers liable to pay tax at 40% and additional rate taxpayers liable to pay tax at 45% on that part of their savings income falling above the basic rate limit or higher rate limit (as applicable) were entitled to a credit for any tax deducted at source. Non-taxpayers and those whose total savings income is eligible for the 0% starting rate could apply to have interest paid without deduction of tax.

Taxation of dividends

SEE TOLLEY'S TAX COMPUTATIONS 1.1.

(ITA 2007 ss 6–21)

For 2018–19 a **dividend allowance of £2,000** is available to all taxpayers (£5,000 for 2016–17 and 2017–18). A **0% rate of income tax applies** to dividends covered by the allowance. The rates of tax on dividend income above the allowance are 7.5% for dividend income falling within the basic rate band, 32.5% for dividend income falling within the higher rate band, and 38.1% for dividend income falling within the additional rate band. The dividend allowance is not a deduction in arriving at total income or taxable income. UK and foreign dividends (except those foreign dividends taxed under the remittance basis) form the top slice of taxable income.

For tax years before 2016–17, where income did not exceed the basic rate limit the tax rate was 10% (applied to the dividend grossed-up by a tax credit of 1/9) so that the liability was met by the tax credit. Higher rate taxpayers were liable to pay tax at 32.5% on that part of their dividend income falling above the basic rate limit. From 2013–14 additional rate taxpayers were liable to pay tax at 37.5% on that part of their dividend income falling above the higher rate limit. Tax credits are abolished from 6 April 2016.

Taxation of trusts

SEE TOLLEY'S TAX COMPUTATIONS 27.2.

	Trust rate	*Dividend trust rate*
2016–17 onwards	**45%**	**38.1%**
2013–14 to 2015–16	45%	37.5%
2011–12 to 2012–13	50%	42.5%

First slice of income: For 2006–07 onwards the first £1,000 of income arising to a trust chargeable at the trust rate or the dividend trust rate is instead chargeable at the basic, savings or dividend rate.
Vulnerable beneficiaries: From 2004–05 onwards, trustees can be taxed (on election) on trust income as if it were income of the vulnerable beneficiary taking into account the beneficiary's personal allowances, starting and basic rate bands (FA 2005 ss 23–45).

Construction industry sub-contractors

(SI 2007/46)

	Rate of tax deduction at source
Registered sub-contractors	**20%**
Unregistered sub-contractors	**30%**

Child benefit income tax charge

SEE TOLLEY'S TAX COMPUTATIONS **29.1**.

(ITEPA 2003 ss 681B–H; Social Security Administration Act 1992, s 13A)

Where an individual or their partner is in receipt of child benefit a high income child benefit charge can arise from 7 January 2013. The charge is applied to the higher earner. Taxpayers with adjusted net income between £50,000 and £60,000 are subject to an income tax charge of 1% of the amount of child benefit for every £100 of income that exceeds £50,000. For taxpayers with income above £60,000, the amount of the charge will equal the amount of child benefit received. Alternatively, a taxpayer with expected income over £60,000 can elect not to receive any child benefit. The election has effect for weeks beginning after it is made. It can be revoked at any time to restore payment of child benefit, and, where the election was made in the erroneous belief that the charge would arise, it may be revoked up to two years after the end of the tax year to which it relates in order for child benefit to be paid for the period.

Charities and Community Amateur Sports Clubs (CASCs)

Gift Aid and Gift Aid Small Donations schemes

SEE TOLLEY'S TAX COMPUTATIONS **5.1**.

Under the **Gift Aid scheme** an individual donor can claim higher rate relief and, if applicable, additional rate relief on the grossed up amount of a monetary donation against income tax and capital gains tax. The charity or CASC claims basic rate relief on the grossed up amount of the donation. Donors must make a declaration that they are UK taxpayers to allow the charity to reclaim the repayment. One declaration can cover a series of donations to the same charity and the declaration can be made in writing, including fax, email and text, or orally, although an oral declaration is not effective until a written confirmation is sent to the donor. Template declarations are provided on Gov.uk. A declaration can be backdated for up to four years prior to the declaration. The basic rate tax deemed to have been deducted by the donor at source is clawed back if the donor's tax liability is insufficient to match it. Donors may elect in their self-assessment tax returns for donations to be treated as made in the preceding tax year for higher rate (and if applicable, additional rate) relief purposes.

Relief for payments under charitable covenants is given under the Gift Aid scheme.

From April 2013 the **Gift Aid Small Donations scheme** allows charities and CASCs to claim a gift aid style payment on broadly £8,000 (£5,000 before 6 April 2016) of small cash donations (or from 6 April 2017, contactless payments) of up to £20 each in circumstances where it is often difficult to obtain a gift aid declaration, such as street collections. The donations must not have been the subject of a gift aid declaration and must not be deductible in calculating the individual's income.

(ITA 2007 ss 413–430; FA 2012 s 50; Small Charitable Donations Act 2012; SI 2015/2027)

Gifts in kind

Relief is available for gifts by traders to charities, community amateur sports clubs or educational establishments of goods produced or sold or of plant or machinery used for the purposes of the trade (CAA 2001 s 63(2)–(4); ITTOIA 2005 ss 107–109; CTA 2009 ss 105–107; CTA 2010 ss 658–671).

Gifts of land, shares and securities etc

Relief is available where a person disposes of listed shares and securities, unit trust units, AIM shares, etc or of freehold or leasehold interests in land to a charity by way of a gift or sale at an undervalue. The amount deductible from total income is the market value of the shares etc on the date of disposal plus incidental disposal costs less any consideration or value of benefits received by the donor or a connected person. This is in addition to any capital gains tax relief (ITA 2007 ss 431–446).

Payroll giving

Under the payroll giving scheme, employees authorise their employer to deduct charitable donations from their pay and receive tax relief on their donation at their top rate of tax (FA 2000 s 38; ITEPA 2003 ss 713–715; SI 1986/2211 as amended).

Inheritance tax relief see p 108. **Capital gains tax** see p 38. **Gifts of pre-eminent objects** see p 99.

Table of income tax reliefs

	2018–19	2017–18
	£	£
Basic personal allowance[6]	**11,850**	11,500
Total income limit[5]	**100,000**	100,000
Not beneficial if individual's total income exceeds	**123,700**	123,000
Transferable marriage allowance[7]	**1,190**	1,150
Age allowance		
Total income limit[1]	**N/A**	N/A
Personal allowance born after 5.4.1938 but before 6.4.1948 / age 65–74[6]	**N/A**	N/A
Not beneficial if individual's total income exceeds	**N/A**	N/A
Personal allowance born before 6.4.1938 / age 75 and over	**N/A**	N/A
Not beneficial if individual's total income exceeds	**N/A**	N/A
Married couple's allowance[2]		
Either partner aged 75 and over and born before 6 April 1935		
Minimum amount	**3,360**	3,260
Total income limit[3]	**28,900**	28,000
Maximum amount	**8,695**	8,445
Reduced to minimum if:[3, 6]		
born after 5.4.1948/under 65 and total income over	**39,570**	38,370
born after 5.4.1938 but before 6.4.1948/65–74 and total income over	**39,570**	38,370
born before 6.4.1938/75 or over and total income over	**39,570**	38,370
Blind person's allowance[4]	**2,390**	2,320
Dividend allowance[8]	**2,000**	5,000
Personal savings allowance[8]		
Basic rate taxpayer	**1,000**	1,000
Higher rate taxpayer	**500**	500
Trading allowance[9]	**1,000**	1,000
Property allowance[9]	**1,000**	1,000

1 The higher personal allowances for years before 2016–17 were available if the claimant's adjusted net income did not exceed the statutory income limit. If the limit was exceeded the maximum allowance was reduced by one-half of the excess until it was reduced to the basic personal allowance, but subject to a further reduction as outlined in note 5 if the adjusted net income exceeded £100,000.

2 The universal married couple's allowance was withdrawn for 2000–01 onwards but continues to be available to any married couple or, from 2005–06, civil partnership where at least one spouse or partner was born before 6 April 1935. The relief is given as a reduction in income tax liability restricted to the lower of 10% of the amount of the allowance or the claimant's total income tax liability.

For marriages before 5 December 2005, married couple's allowance is given to the husband (subject to right of transfer to the wife), the amount being determined by the level of the husband's income. For marriages and civil partnerships entered into on or after that date, the allowance is given to whichever of the two partners has the higher total income for the tax year in question, the amount being determined by the level of that partner's income (subject to the right to transfer half or all of the basic allowance or excess allowances to the partner). Couples married before 5 December 2005 could make a joint election to be brought within the rules for couples marrying on or after that date.

SEE TOLLEY'S TAX COMPUTATIONS 1.7.

3 The higher married couple's allowance is available if the claimant's adjusted net income does not exceed the statutory income limit (subject to relief given as a reduction in tax liability as in note 2 above). If the limit is exceeded the maximum allowance is reduced by one-half of the excess (less any reduction made in the personal age allowance as in note 1 above for years before 2016–17) but it cannot be reduced to less than the basic couple's allowance.

National insurance contributions – self-employed

SEE TOLLEY'S TAX COMPUTATIONS 507.1.

		2018–19	2017–18
Class 2	Flat rate per week	**£2.95**	£2.85
	Small profits threshold/ small earnings exception	**6,205**	6,025
Class 4	Band	**8,424–46,350**	8,164–45,000
	Rate	**37,926@9%**	36,836@9%
	Amount payable to upper limit	**3,413.34**	3,315.24
	Charge on profits above the limit	**2%**	2%

Table of income tax reliefs (cont.)

2016–17	2015–16	2014–15	2013–14	2012–13
£	£	£	£	£
11,000	10,600	10,000	9,440	8,105
100,000	100,000	100,000	100,000	100,000
122,000	121,200	120,000	118,880	116,210
1,100	1,060	N/A	N/A	N/A
N/A	27,700	27,000	26,100	25,400
N/A	N/A	10,500	10,500	10,500
N/A	N/A	28,000	28,220	30,190
N/A	10,660	10,660	10,660	10,660
N/A	27,820	28,320	28,540	30,510
3,220	3,220	3,140	3,040	2,960
27,700	27,700	27,000	26,100	25,400
8,355	8,355	8,165	7,915	7,705
37,970	37,970	37,050	35,850	34,890
37,970	37,970	38,050	37,970	39,680
37,970	38,090	38,370	38,290	40,000
2,290	2,290	2,230	2,160	2,100
5,000	N/A	N/A	N/A	N/A
1,000	N/A	N/A	N/A	N/A
500	N/A	N/A	N/A	N/A
N/A	N/A	N/A	N/A	N/A
N/A	N/A	N/A	N/A	N/A

4 The allowance is available for persons registered blind but not for persons registered partially-sighted.

5 From 2010–11, the basic personal allowance for income tax is gradually reduced to nil for individuals with adjusted net incomes in excess of £100,000. The reduction is £1 for every £2 of income over the limit. SEE TOLLEY'S TAX COMPUTATIONS 1.5.

6 For 2012–13 and earlier years differing levels of personal allowances applied based on age. From 2013–14 the differing levels applied based on specified dates of birth. For 2015–16 there was one level of basic personal allowance for individuals born after 5 April 1938, and an age allowance for those born before 6 April 1938. From 2016–17 onwards there is one personal allowance regardless of age.

7 From 2015–16 a spouse or civil partner who is not liable to income tax above the basic rate (or Scottish intermediate rate from 2018–19) is able to transfer an amount of their personal allowance to their spouse or civil partner, provided the transferee is also not liable to income tax above the basic rate (or Scottish intermediate rate from 2018–19). Married couples or civil partnerships entitled to claim the married couple's allowance will not be entitled to make a transfer. With effect from 29 November 2017, regardless of when death occurred, transfers can be made on behalf of a deceased spouse or partner or from a surviving spouse / partner to a deceased spouse / partner. SEE TOLLEY'S TAX COMPUTATIONS 1.6.

8 See p 76 for the tax rates applying where allowance is exceeded.

9 See p 98 for details.

National insurance contributions – self-employed (cont.)

2016–17	2015–16	2014–15	2013–14	2012–13
£2.80	£2.80	£2.75	£2.70	£2.65
5,965	5,965	5,885	£5,725	5,595
8,060–43,000	8,060–42,385	7,956–41,865	7,755–41,450	7,605–42,475
34,940@9%	34,325@9%	33,909@ 9%	33,695@ 9%	34,870@ 9%
3144.60	3089.25	3,051.81	3,032.55	3,138.30
2%	2%	2%	2%	2%

Cars, vans and related benefits

Cars

SEE TOLLEY'S TAX COMPUTATIONS 9.3.

The income tax charge is based on a percentage of the car's price graduated according to the level of the car's carbon dioxide measured in grams per kilometre (g/km). (ITEPA 2003 ss 114–148, 169)

CO_2 emissions (g/km)	*% of list price*		*CO_2 emissions (g/km)*	*% of list price*	
2017–18	*Petrol*	*Diesel*[1]	***2018–19***	*Petrol*	*Diesel*[1]
0–50	9%[5]	12%	**0–50**	13%[5]	17%
51–75	13%	16%	**51–75**	16%	20%
76–94	17%	20%	**76–94**	19%	23%
95–99	18%	21%	**95–99**	20%	24%
100–104	19%	22%	**100–104**	21%	25%
105–109	20%	23%	**105–109**	22%	26%
110–114	21%	24%	**110–114**	23%	27%
115–119	22%	25%	**115–119**	24%	28%
120–124	23%	26%	**120–124**	25%	29%
125–129	24%	27%	**125–129**	26%	30%
130–134	25%	28%	**130–134**	27%	31%
135–139	26%	29%	**135–139**	28%	32%
140–144	27%	30%	**140–144**	29%	33%
145–149	28%	31%	**145–149**	30%	34%
150–154	29%	32%	**150–154**	31%	35%
155–159	30%	33%	**155–159**	32%	36%
160–164	31%	34%	**160–164**	33%	37%
165–169	32%	35%	**165–169**	34%	37%
170–174	33%	36%	**170–174**	35%	37%
175–179	34%	37%	**175–179**	36%	37%
180–184	35%	37%	**180 or more**	37%	37%
185–189	36%	37%			
190 or more	37%	37%			

CO_2 emissions (g/km)		*% of list price*		*CO_2 emissions (g/km)*	*% of list price*		*CO_2 emissions (g/km)*	*% of list price*	
2013–14	***2014–15***	*Petrol*	*Diesel*[1]	***2015–16***	*Petrol*	*Diesel*[1]	***2016–17***	*Petrol*	*Diesel*[1]
1–75	1–75	5%[2]	8%	0–50	5%[3]	8%	0–50	7%[4]	10%
76–94	N/A	10%	13%	51–75	9%	12%	51–75	11%	14%
95–99	76–94	11%	14%	76–94	13%	16%	76–94	15%	18%
100–104	95–99	12%	15%	95–99	14%	17%	95–99	16%	19%
105–109	100–104	13%	16%	100–104	15%	18%	100–104	17%	20%
110–114	105–109	14%	17%	105–109	16%	19%	105–109	18%	21%
115–119	110–114	15%	18%	110–114	17%	20%	110–114	19%	22%
120–124	115–119	16%	19%	115–119	18%	21%	115–119	20%	23%
125–129	120–124	17%	20%	120–124	19%	22%	120–124	21%	24%
130–134	125–129	18%	21%	125–129	20%	23%	125–129	22%	25%
135–139	130–134	19%	22%	130–134	21%	24%	130–134	23%	26%
140–144	135–139	20%	23%	135–139	22%	25%	135–139	24%	27%
145–149	140–144	21%	24%	140–144	23%	26%	140–144	25%	28%
150–154	145–149	22%	25%	145–149	24%	27%	145–149	26%	29%
155–159	150–154	23%	26%	150–154	25%	28%	150–154	27%	30%
160–164	155–159	24%	27%	155–159	26%	29%	155–159	28%	31%
165–169	160–164	25%	28%	160–164	27%	30%	160–164	29%	32%
170–174	165–169	26%	29%	165–169	28%	31%	165–169	30%	33%
175–179	170–174	27%	30%	170–174	29%	32%	170–174	31%	34%
180–184	175–179	28%	31%	175–179	30%	33%	175–179	32%	35%
185–189	180–184	29%	32%	180–184	31%	34%	180–184	33%	36%
190–194	185–189	30%	33%	185–189	32%	35%	185–189	34%	37%
195–199	190–194	31%	34%	190–194	33%	36%	190–194	35%	37%
200–204	195–199	32%	35%	195–199	34%	37%	195–199	36%	37%
205–209	200–204	33%	35%	200–204	35%	37%	200 or more	37%	37%
210–214	205–209	34%	35%	205–209	36%	37%			
215 or more	210 or more	35%	35%	210 or more	37%	37%			

1 **Diesel cars:** A 4% (3% before 6 April 2018) supplement applies to diesel cars up to a maximum of 37%.

The supplement will not apply to cars registered on or after 1 September 2017 if they meet the Euro 6d emissions standards.

2 **For 2013–14 and 2014–15:** No benefit applies to cars which are incapable of producing carbon dioxide when driven.

3 **For 2015–16:** The 5% rate applies to cars which are incapable of producing carbon dioxide when driven.

4 **For 2016–17:** The 7% rate applies to cars which are incapable of producing carbon dioxide when driven.

5 **For 2017–18:** The 9% rate applies to cars which are incapable of producing carbon dioxide when driven.

6 **For 2018–19:** The 13% rate applies to cars which are incapable of producing carbon dioxide when driven.

7 **For 2019–20:** The relevant threshold will remain at 95g/km but the percentage applying at that threshold (the threshold percentage) will be increased to 23/27%. The minimum percentage applying if the emissions do not exceed 50g/km will be 16/20%. For emissions from 51g/km to 75g/km inclusive the rate will be 19/23%, and for emissions from 76g/km to 94g/km inclusive the rate will be 22/26%.

Cars registered after 28 February 2001

For cars registered on or after 1.3.01, the definitive CO_2 emissions figure is recorded on the vehicle registration document. For cars first registered between 1.1.98 and 28.2.01, the Vehicle Certification Agency supply relevant information on their website at carfueldata.direct.gov.uk and in their free, twice-yearly edition of the 'New Car Fuel Consumption & Emission Figures' booklet.

Cars registered on or after 1 January 1998 with no CO_2 emission figures

Cylinder capacity of car[2]	*Appropriate percentage*[1]				
	2013–14 and 2014–15	***2015–16***	***2016–17***	***2017–18***	***2018–19***
1,400cc or less	15%	15%	16%	18%	**20%**[3]
Over 1,400cc up to 2,000cc	25%	25%	27%	29%	**31%**[3]
Over 2,000cc:	35%	37%	37%	37%	**37%**
Cars incapable of producing CO_2 when driven	0%	5%	7%	9%	**13%**[3]

1 **Diesel cars:** A 4% (3% before 6 April 2018) supplement applies to diesel cars up to a maximum of 37%. The supplement will not apply to cars registered on or after 1 September 2017 if they meet the Euro 6d emissions standards.

2 **No cylinder capacity:** For a car with no cylinder capacity 37% applies.

3 **2019–20:** The percentages will be 23%, 34% and 16% respectively.

Cars registered before 1.1.98: For 2015–16 and earlier years tax is charged on 15% of the list price for engines to 1,400cc, 22% for engines of 1,401 to 2,000cc and 32% for engines above 2,000cc. For 2016–17 tax is charged on 16% of the list price for engines to 1,400cc, 27% for engines of 1,401 to 2,000cc and 37% for engines above 2,000cc. For 2017–18 the percentages are 18%, 29%, and 37% respectively. For **2018–19** the percentages are 20%, 31% and 37% respectively. For 2019–20 the percentages will be 23%, 34%, and 37% respectively. Cars without a cylinder capacity are taxed on 37% (32% before 2016–17) of the list price.

Automatic cars for disabled drivers: CO_2 figure reduced to equivalent for manual car (ITEPA 2003 s 138).

Car unavailable for part of year: Value of the benefit is reduced proportionately (ITEPA 2003 s 143).

National Insurance: Also used to calculate the national insurance contributions payable by employers on the benefit of cars they provide for the private use of their employees, see p 118.

The cash equivalent is reduced proportionately where the car is not available for the whole tax year. The amount (as so reduced) is reduced by any payments made by the employee for private use.

List price of car:

(1) Includes qualifying accessories, excluding accessories provided after car made available if its list price was less than £100. Accessories designed for use only by disabled people also excluded. From 6 April 2011 accessories do not include certain security enhancements provided to meet the threat to an employee's personal physical security arising from the nature of the employment. Where a car is manufactured so as to be capable of running on road fuel gas, its price is proportionately reduced by so much of that price as is reasonably attributable to it being manufactured in that way. Where a new car is converted to run on road fuel gas, the equipment is not regarded as an accessory. With effect from 6 April 2009 disabled drivers of automatic cars who hold a disabled person's badge can use the list price of an equivalent manual car.

(2) Reduced by capital contributions made by employee up to £5,000.

(3) Classic cars (aged 15 years or more and with a market value of £15,000 or more at end of tax year): substitute market value at end of tax year if higher than adjusted list price. Reduction for capital contributions applies.

(ITEPA 2003 ss 120–132)

Vans and fuel for vans

SEE TOLLEY'S TAX COMPUTATIONS **9.3**.

(ITEPA 2003 ss 114–119, 154–164, 168, 169A, 170; SI 2016/1174, SI 2017/1176)

Van benefit[1]	*Vans which emit CO_2 when driven*	*Vans which do not emit CO_2 when driven*[2]
2018–19	**£3,350**	**£1,340**
2017–18	£3,230	£646
2016–17	£3,170	£634
2015–16	£3,150	£630
2014–15	£3,090	Nil
2013–14	£3,000	Nil

1 Vehicle weight up to 3,500kg

2 For 2013–14 and 2014–15 no benefit applies to vans which are incapable of producing CO_2 when driven. For 2015–16, 2016–17 and 2017–18, 20% of the van benefit charge for vans which emit CO_2 applies. 40% of the charge applies in 2018–19, 60% of the charge will apply in 2019–20, 80% in 2020–21, and 90% in 2021–22, with the rates equalised in 2022–23.

3 No charge applies to employees who have to take their van home and private use is restricted other than for ordinary commuting (insignificant use is disregarded).

Van fuel benefit	
2018–19	**£633**
2017–18	£610
2016–17	£598
2015–16	£594
2014–15	£581
2013–14	£564

The fuel charge applies where the van benefit charge applies (though not where the reduced charge for zero-emission vans applies) and fuel is provided for private use.

Related benefits

Parking facilities: No taxable benefit for work place provision of car or van parking spaces, or parking for bicycles or motorcycles (ITEPA 2003 s 237).

Cycles and cyclist's safety equipment: No taxable benefit in respect of the provision to employees of bicycles or cycling safety equipment for travel to and from work (ITEPA 2003 s 244) nor for subsequent transfer to the employee at market value (ITEPA 2003 s 206).

On-call emergency vehicles: No tax or NIC charge where emergency service workers have private use of their emergency vehicle when on call (ITEPA 2003 s 248A).

Bus services: No taxable benefit in respect of the provision of works buses with a seating capacity of 9 or more provided to employees (or their children) to travel to and from work (ITEPA 2003 s 242).

Car and motorcycle hire: restricted allowances

SEE TOLLEY'S TAX COMPUTATIONS **116.1**.

(ITTOIA 2005 ss 48–50B; CTA 2009 ss 56–58B; SI 2016/984)

Hire period from April 2009 (subject to transitional provisions), the disallowance is a flat rate of 15%. This applies only to cars with CO_2 emissions exceeding 110g/km from 1 April 2018 (130g/km before 1 April 2018, 160g/km before 1 April 2013 (corporation tax) or 6 April 2013 (income tax)).

Hire period before April 2009, if a car with a retail price when new of more than £12,000 is acquired under a rental lease the maximum allowable deduction in computing trading profits is restricted to:

$$\frac{£12{,}000 + P}{2P} \times R$$

P = retail price of car when new. R = annual rental.

Capital allowances see p 29.

Car fuel: company cars

SEE TOLLEY'S TAX COMPUTATIONS **9.3**.

(ITEPA 2003 ss 149–153; SI 2016/1174, SI 2017/1176)

The same percentage figures on p 80 used to calculate the car benefit charge for the company car, which are directly linked to the car's CO_2 emissions, are used to calculate the benefit charge for fuel provided for private motoring. The relevant percentage figure is multiplied by £21,100 for 2013–14, by £21,700 for 2014–15, by £22,100 for 2015–16, by £22,200 for 2016–17, by £22,600 for 2017–18, and by **£23,400 for 2018–19**.

Benefit is reduced to nil if employee is required to, and does, make good all fuel provided for private use. No taxable benefit where employer only provides fuel for business travel. Charge is proportionately reduced where employee stops receiving free fuel part way through tax year, but where free fuel is subsequently provided in same tax year, full year's charge is payable. Benefit is proportionately reduced where a car is not available or is incapable of being used for part of a year (being at least 30 days).

CO_2 emissions (g/km)	Petrol	Diesel	CO_2 emissions (g/km)	Petrol	Diesel	CO_2 emissions (g/km)	Petrol	Diesel
2016–17	**£**	**£**	***2017–18***	**£**	**£**	***2018–19***	**£**	**£**
0–50	1,554	2,220	0–50	2,034	2,712	**0–50**	3,042	3,978
51–75	2,442	3,108	51–75	2,938	3,616	**51–75**	3,744	4,680
76–94	3,330	3,996	76–94	3,842	4,520	**76–94**	4,446	5,382
95–99	3,552	4,218	95–99	4,068	4,746	**95–99**	4,680	5,616
100–104	3,774	4,440	100–104	4,294	4,972	**100–104**	4,914	5,850
105–109	3,996	4,662	105–109	4,520	5,198	**105–109**	5,148	6,084
110–114	4,218	4,884	110–114	4,746	5,424	**110–114**	5,382	6,318
115–119	4,440	5,106	115–119	4,972	5,650	**115–119**	5,616	6,552
120–124	4,662	5,328	120–124	5,198	5,876	**120–124**	5,850	6,786
125–129	4,884	5,550	125–129	5,424	6,102	**125–129**	6,084	7,020
130–134	5,106	5,772	130–134	5,650	6,328	**130–134**	6,318	7,254
135–139	5,328	5,994	135–139	5,876	6,554	**135–139**	6,552	7,488
140–144	5,550	6,216	140–144	6,102	6,780	**140–144**	6,786	7,722
145–149	5,772	6,438	145–149	6,328	7,006	**145–149**	7,020	7,956
150–154	5,994	6,660	150–154	6,554	7,232	**150–154**	7,254	8,190
155–159	6,216	6,882	155–159	6,780	7,458	**155–159**	7,488	8,424
160–164	6,438	7,104	160–164	7,006	7,684	**160–164**	7,722	8,658
165–169	6,660	7,326	165–169	7,232	7,910	**165–169**	7,956	8,658
170–174	6,882	7,548	170–174	7,458	8,136	**170–174**	8,190	8,658
175–179	7,104	7,770	175–179	7,684	8,362	**175–179**	8,424	8,658
180–184	7,326	7,992	180–184	7,910	8,362	**180 or more**	8,658	8,658
185–189	7,548	8,214	185–189	8,136	8,362			
190–194	7,770	8,214	190 or more	8,362	8,362			
195–199	7,992	8,214						
200 or more	8,214	8,214						

CO_2 emissions (g/km)	Petrol	Diesel	CO_2 emissions (g/km)	Petrol	Diesel	CO_2 emissions (g/km)	Petrol	Diesel
2013–14	**£**	**£**	***2014–15***	**£**	**£**	***2015–16***	**£**	**£**
1–75	1,055	1,688	–	–	–	0–50	1,105	1,768
76–94	2,110	2,743	1–75	1,085	1,736	51–75	1,989	2,652
95–99	2,321	2,954	76–94	2,387	3,038	76–94	2,873	3,536
100–104	2,532	3,165	95–99	2,604	3,255	95–99	3,094	3,757
105–109	2,743	3,376	100–104	2,821	3,472	100–104	3,315	3,978
110–114	2,954	3,587	105–109	3,038	3,689	105–109	3,536	4,199
115–119	3,165	3,798	110–114	3,255	3,906	110–114	3,757	4,420
120–124	3,376	4,009	115–119	3,472	4,123	115–119	3,978	4,641
125–129	3,587	4,220	120–124	3,689	4,340	120–124	4,199	4,862
130–134	3,798	4,431	125–129	3,906	4,557	125–129	4,420	5,083
135–139	4,009	4,642	130–134	4,123	4,774	130–134	4,641	5,304
140–144	4,220	4,853	135–139	4,340	4,991	135–139	4,862	5,525
145–149	4,431	5,064	140–144	4,557	5,208	140–144	5,083	5,746
150–154	4,642	5,275	145–149	4,774	5,425	145–149	5,304	5,967
155–159	4,853	5,486	150–154	4,991	5,642	150–154	5,525	6,188
160–164	5,064	5,697	155–159	5,208	5,859	155–159	5,746	6,409
165–169	5,275	5,908	160–164	5,425	6,076	160–164	5,967	6,630
170–174	5,486	6,119	165–169	5,642	6,293	165–169	6,188	6,851
175–179	5,697	6,330	170–174	5,859	6,510	170–174	6,409	7,072
180–184	5,908	6,541	175–179	6,076	6,727	175–179	6,630	7,293
185–189	6,119	6,752	180–184	6,293	6,944	180–184	6,851	7,514
190–194	6,330	6,963	185–189	6,510	7,161	185–189	7,072	7,735
195–199	6,541	7,174	190–194	6,727	7,378	190–194	7,293	7,956
200–204	6,752	7,385	195–199	6,944	7,595	195–199	7,514	8,177
205–209	6,963	7,385	200–204	7,161	7,595	200–204	7,735	8,177
210–214	7,174	7,385	205–209	7,378	7,595	205–209	7,956	8,177
215 or more	7,385	7,385	210 or more	7,595	7,595	210 or more	8,177	8,177

Mileage allowances

Advisory fuel rates for company cars

Engine size	*Cost per mile*		
	Petrol	*Diesel*	*LPG*
From 1 March 2018			
1,400cc or less	**11p**	**–**	**7p**
1,600cc or less	**–**	**9p**	**–**
1,401–2,000cc	**14p**	**–**	**8p**
1,601–2,000cc	**–**	**11p**	**–**
Over 2,000cc	**22p**	**13p**	**13p**
1 December 2017–28 February 2018			
1,400cc or less	11p	–	7p
1,600cc or less	–	9p	–
1,401–2,000cc	14p	–	9p
1,601–2,000cc	–	11p	–
Over 2,000cc	21p	13p	14p
1 September 2017–30 November 2017			
1,400cc or less	11p	–	7p
1,600cc or less	–	9p	–
1,401–2,000cc	13p	–	8p
1,601–2,000cc	–	11p	–
Over 2,000cc	21p	12p	13p
1 June 2017–31 August 2017			
1,400cc or less	11p	–	7p
1,600cc or less	–	9p	–
1,401–2,000cc	14p	–	9p
1,601–2,000cc	–	11p	–
Over 2,000cc	21p	13p	14p
1 March 2017–31 May 2017			
1,400cc or less	11p	–	7p
1,600cc or less	–	9p	–
1,401–2,000cc	14p	–	9p
1,601–2,000cc	–	11p	–
Over 2,000cc	22p	13p	14p
1 December 2016–28 February 2017			
1,400cc or less	11p	–	7p
1,600cc or less	–	9p	–
1,401–2,000cc	14p	–	9p
1,601–2,000cc	–	11p	–
Over 2,000cc	21p	13p	13p
1 September 2016–30 November 2016			
1,400cc or less	11p	–	7p
1,600cc or less	–	9p	–
1,401–2,000cc	13p	–	9p
1,601–2,000cc	–	11p	–
Over 2,000cc	20p	13p	13p
1 June 2016–31 August 2016			
1,400cc or less	10p	–	7p
1,600cc or less	–	9p	–
1,401–2,000cc	13p	–	9p
1,601–2,000cc	–	10p	–
Over 2,000cc	20p	12p	13p
1 March 2016–31 May 2016			
1,400cc or less	10p	–	7p
1,600cc or less	–	8p	–
1,401–2,000cc	12p	–	8p
1,601–2,000cc	–	10p	–
Over 2,000cc	19p	11p	13p

Engine size	*Cost per mile*		
	Petrol	*Diesel*	*LPG*
1 December 2015–29 February 2016			
1,400cc or less	11p	–	7p
1,600cc or less	–	9p	–
1,401–2,000cc	13p	–	9p
1,601–2,000cc	–	11p	–
Over 2,000cc	20p	13p	13p
1 September 2015–30 November 2015			
1,400cc or less	11p	–	7p
1,600cc or less	–	9p	–
1,401–2,000cc	14p	–	9p
1,601–2,000cc	–	11p	–
Over 2,000cc	21p	13p	14p
1 June 2015–31 August 2015			
1,400cc or less	12p	–	8p
1,600cc or less	–	10p	–
1,401–2,000cc	14p	–	9p
1,601–2,000cc	–	12p	–
Over 2,000cc	21p	14p	14p
1 March 2015–31 May 2015			
1,400cc or less	11p	–	8p
1,600cc or less	–	9p	–
1,401–2,000cc	13p	–	10p
1,601–2,000cc	–	11p	–
Over 2,000cc	20p	14p	14p
1 December 2014–28 February 2015			
1,400cc or less	13p	–	9p
1,600cc or less	–	11p	–
1,401–2,000cc	16p	–	11p
1,601–2,000cc	–	13p	–
Over 2,000cc	23p	16p	16p
1 September 2014–30 November 2014			
1,400cc or less	14p	–	9p
1,600cc or less	–	11p	–
1,401–2,000cc	16p	–	11p
1,601–2,000cc	–	13p	–
Over 2,000cc	24p	17p	16p
1 June 2014–31 August 2014			
1,400cc or less	14p	–	9p
1,600cc or less	–	12p	–
1,401–2,000cc	16p	–	11p
1,601–2,000cc	–	14p	–
Over 2,000cc	24p	17p	16p
1 March 2014–31 May 2014			
1,400cc or less	14p	–	9p
1,600cc or less	–	12p	–
1,401–2,000cc	16p	–	11p
1,601–2,000cc	–	14p	–
Over 2,000cc	24p	17p	17p
1 December 2013–28 February 2014			
1,400cc or less	14p	–	9p
1,600cc or less	–	12p	–
1,401–2,000cc	16p	–	11p
1,601–2,000cc	–	14p	–
Over 2,000cc	24p	17p	16p

1 Payments at or below these rates are tax and NIC free. The table figures will be accepted for VAT purposes.
2 Other rates may be used if the employer can demonstrate that they are justified.
3 Rates are currently reviewed by HMRC quarterly.

Authorised mileage rates

SEE TOLLEY'S TAX COMPUTATIONS 9.2.

	Rate per business mile	
Cars or vans	*First 10,000 miles*	*Over 10,000 miles*
2011–12 onwards[1]	**45p**	**25p**

1 Where the employer pays less than the authorised rate the employee can claim tax relief for the difference (ITEPA 2003 ss 229–232, 235, 236).

	Rate per business mile
Car passengers Allowance for each fellow passenger carried	
2002–03 onwards	**5p**
Cycles	
2002–03 onwards[1]	**20p**
Motorcycles	
2002–03 onwards[1]	**24p**

1 Where the employer pays less than the authorised rate the employee can claim tax relief for the difference (ITEPA 2003 ss 229–232, 235, 236).

Travel expenses of members of local authorities

(ITEPA 2003 s 235A)

From April 2016 there is an exemption for qualifying payments made by a local authority in respect of travel expenses incurred by a member on a journey between home and permanent workplace provided the member's home is in the area of the authority or within 20 miles of the boundary of the area. The exemption for mileage payments will be limited to the authorised mileage rates above.

Employment benefits and expenses payments

Pages 87 to 91 cover some common benefits and expenses payments not detailed separately elsewhere. From 6 April 2016 employees (other than lower-paid ministers of religion) earning at a rate of less than £8,500 per year will pay income tax on their benefits in kind in the same way as other employees earning at a rate of £8,500 or more. Previously all 'lower-paid' employees (ie those whose annual remuneration plus benefits was less than £8,500) were exempted from certain benefits.

Accommodation, supplies, etc used in employment duties

SEE TOLLEY'S TAX COMPUTATIONS 9.4.

(ITEPA 2003 s 316)

The provision of accommodation, supplies or services used by employees in performance of employment duties is not taxable provided:

(a) if the benefit is provided on premises occupied by the employer, any private use by the employee (or the employee's family or household) is not significant; or

(b) in any other case, the sole purpose of providing the benefit is to enable the employee to perform those duties, any private use is not significant and the benefit is not an excluded benefit (eg the provision of a motor vehicle, boat or aircraft).

Amounts which would otherwise be deductible

SEE TOLLEY'S TAX COMPUTATIONS 9.3.

(ITEPA 2003 ss 289A–289E)

From 6 April 2016 an exemption applies to expenses and benefits paid or reimbursed by the employer where the employee would be due a deduction. The exemption does not apply if the payment or reimbursement is offered in conjunction with a relevant salary sacrifice arrangement.

Assets given to employees

SEE TOLLEY'S TAX COMPUTATIONS 9.3.

(ITEPA 2003 ss 203, 204)

If new, tax chargeable on cost to employer (market value in the case of a 'lower-paid' minister of religion, and before 2016–17 in the case of all 'lower-paid' employees). If used, tax chargeable on greater of:

(a) market value at the time of transfer; and

(b) where the asset is first applied for the provision of a benefit after 5 April 1980 and a person has been chargeable to tax on its use, market value when first so applied less amounts charged to tax for use up to and including the year of transfer.

Buses to shops

(SI 2002/205)

The provision of buses for journeys of ten miles or less from the workplace to shops etc on a working day is not taxable.

Cheap loans

SEE TOLLEY'S TAX COMPUTATIONS 9.3.

(ITEPA 2003 ss 174–190; SI 2015/411; SI 2017/305)

A taxable benefit arises on employer-related loans to all employees other than 'lower-paid' ministers of religion (previously to directors or employees earning £8,500 or more a year), on the difference between the interest paid and interest payable at the 'official rate' below. There is no tax charge where:

(a) all the employer-related loans (or all loans not qualifying for tax relief) do not exceed £10,000 (£5,000 before 6 April 2014);

(b) all the interest payable is or would be eligible for tax relief; and

(c) the loans are ordinary commercial loans.

The provisions can apply to alternative finance arrangements entered into after 21 March 2006.

The 'official rate' is:

From 6 April 2017	**2.50%**
6 April 2015 to 5 April 2017	3.00%
6 April 2014 to 5 April 2015	3.25%
6 April 2010 to 5 April 2014	4.00%

The average rate for the tax year is:

2017–18	**2.50%**
2016–17	3.00%
2015–16	3.00%
2014–15	3.25%
2013–14	4.00%

The official rate is set in advance for the whole of the following tax year, subject to review if the typical mortgage rates were to fall sharply during a tax year.

Childcare provision

(ITEPA 2003 ss 318–318D; CPA 2014; SI 2006/882; SI 2015/537; SI 2018/462)

No liability arises:

(a) where the premises (which are not wholly or mainly used as a private dwelling) are made available by the employer; or

(b) where the scheme is provided under arrangements with other persons, by one or more of those persons; or

(c) where (a) or (b) does not apply, on the first £55 per week of registered or approved childcare, or where the employee joins the scheme after 5 April 2011, the first £55 (basic rate taxpayers), £28 per week (higher rate taxpayers), £25 per week (additional rate taxpayers, £22 per week before 6 April 2013) of registered or approved childcare.

From April 2017 a 'tax-free childcare' scheme was introduced under which the Government will make a top-up payment of 25% of payments into a childcare account up to a maximum of £8,000 per year (£16,000 for a disabled child). Government support is therefore capped at a maximum of £2,000 each year per qualifying child (£4,000 for a disabled child). A child is a qualifying child until the last day of the week containing 1 September after the child's 11th birthday (16th in the case of a disabled child). There is no liability to income tax or NIC under the scheme. The scheme has now been rolled out to all eligible parents and replaces those under (b) and (c) above for new entrants from 4 October 2018, though existing recipients will continue to receive tax and NIC relief for as long as they remain eligible, provided that their employer continues to operate the scheme.

Christmas parties and annual functions

(ITEPA 2003 s 264; SI 2003/1361)

Not taxable if cost does not exceed £150 per head per tax year and open to staff generally. Otherwise, fully taxable. Expenditure may be split between more than one function. (Not taxable on 'lower-paid' ministers of religion, and before 2016–17 on all 'lower-paid' employees.)

Credit tokens

(ITEPA 2003 ss 90–96A, 363)

Where money goods or services are provided to employees through credit tokens, the cost to the employer, less any employee contribution, is taxable on the employee, except if they were used to buy certain non-taxable benefits.

Cyclists' breakfasts

(SI 2002/205; SI 2012/1808)

Before 6 April 2013 breakfast provided for employees arriving at the workplace by bicycle in recognition of having cycled to work is not taxable. No limit on number of such breakfasts per year. This exemption is removed from 2013–14 onwards.

Disabled employees

(ITEPA 2003 ss 246, 247; SI 2002/1596)

The provision of, or payment for, transport for disabled employees for ordinary commuting is tax free. This also applies to the provision of equipment, services or facilities to disabled employees to help them carry out their duties of employment.

Electricity for an electric car or van

It is proposed to exempt retrospectively from 6 April 2018 electricity provided in workplace charging points for electric or plug-in hybrid cars and vans owned by employees.

Emergency service vehicles

(ITEPA 2003 s 248A)

There is no tax charge on any benefit arising from use of an emergency vehicle by an employee of an emergency service where private use is prohibited.

Employees' liability insurance

(ITEPA 2003 s 346)

This is non-taxable.

Eye tests and corrective appliances

(ITEPA 2003 s 320A)

No liability arises where the provision of tests or special corrective appliances are required under health and safety legislation and are available as required to employees generally.

Homeworkers

(ITEPA 2003 s 316A)

Employer contributions to additional household costs not taxable where employee works at home. Supporting evidence required if contributions exceed £4 per week (£18 per month for monthly paid employees).

Incidental overnight expenses

SEE TOLLEY'S TAX COMPUTATIONS 9.6.

(ITEPA 2003 ss 240, 241)

Not taxable where employee stays away from home on business and payment from employer does not exceed:

(a) £5 per night in the UK; or
(b) £10 per night overseas.

Living accommodation

SEE TOLLEY'S TAX COMPUTATIONS 9.4.

(ITEPA 2003 ss 97–113)

A taxable benefit (the '*basic charge*') arises on the annual rental value (or actual rent if greater) less any sums made good by the employee. There is an *additional charge* (if the basic charge is not calculated on the full open market rental value) where the cost of accommodation (including costs of any capital improvements less amounts made good by the employee) exceeds £75,000. The additional charge is the excess cost over £75,000 multiplied by the official rate for cheap loans (see above) in force at the start of the tax year less any rent paid by the employee in excess of the basic charge.

For leases of ten years or less entered into on or after 22 April 2009, a lease premium paid is to be treated as if it were rent and spread over the period of the lease accordingly.

The charges are apportioned in the case of multiple occupation or if the property is provided for only part of the year or part is used exclusively for business purposes.

Exemption: No taxable benefit arises where living accommodation is provided:

(a) for the proper performance of duties;
(b) by reason that it is customary to do so; or
(c) by reason of special threat to the employee's security.

The above exemptions apply to a full-time working director whose interest in the company does not exceed 5%, otherwise only exemption (c) applies to directors.

Living expenses

SEE TOLLEY'S TAX COMPUTATIONS 9.4.

(ITEPA 2003 ss 313–315)

A taxable charge arises on the cost to the employer of the employee's living expenses. For the provision of assets such as furniture, see 'Use of employer's assets' below.

Where the exemption for living accommodation above applies, the tax charge relating to living expenses (including the provision of furniture and items normal for domestic occupation) is restricted to 10% of the employee's net earnings from the related employment less any sums made good by the employee.

Expenditure on alteration and structural repairs which are normally the landlord's responsibility do not give rise to a taxable benefit.

Long service awards

(ITEPA 2003 s 323; SI 2003/1361)

Not taxable provided the employee has at least 20 years' service and cost to the employer does not exceed £50 for each year of service. No similar award may be made within ten years of such an award.

Meals

(ITEPA 2003 s 317)

Subsidised or free meals provided for staff generally at the workplace are not taxable. This relief does not apply if the provision of meals is made under salary sacrifice or flexible remuneration arrangements.

Medical check-ups, insurance and treatment

SEE TOLLEY'S TAX COMPUTATIONS 9.6.

(ITEPA 2003 ss 320B, 325; SI 2014/3226; HMRC Employment Income Manual EIM21765)

Check-ups:

From 2009–10 onwards one screening and one check-up each year not taxable.

Insurance: Premiums paid on behalf of employees (other than 'lower-paid' ministers of religion, and before 2016–17 all 'lower-paid' employees) are taxable unless for treatment outside the UK whilst the employee is performing duties abroad.

Recommended medical treatment: From 1.1.15 any benefit in kind or payment of earnings, up to an annual cap of £500 per employee, is not taxable where an employer meets the cost of certain recommended medical treatment in connection with an employee's return to work after a period of absence due to ill-health or injury.

Pensions advice

(SI 2002/205; ITEPA 2003 ss 308B, 308C)

Payments provided to employees in respect of advice on pensions (including on general financial and tax issues relating to pensions) are not taxable if the cost is no more than £500 (£150 before 6 April 2017 and restricted to advice on pensions).

From 6 April 2015 payments by employers in respect of independent advice provided to employees in relation to conversions and transfers of pension scheme benefits are exempt.

Personal expenses

SEE TOLLEY'S TAX COMPUTATIONS 9.2.

(ITEPA 2003 ss 70–72, 336–341)

Unless covered by specific exemptions, payments to an employee by reason of his employment in respect of expenses or allowances are taxable. Deduction is allowed for expenses the employee is obliged to incur which are:

(a) qualifying travelling expenses (broadly those necessarily incurred other than for ordinary commuting or private travel); or

(b) other amounts incurred wholly, exclusively and necessarily in the performance of employment duties.

Relocation expenses

SEE TOLLEY'S TAX COMPUTATIONS 9.5.

(ITEPA 2003 ss 271–289)

Qualifying removal expenses and benefits up to £8,000 per move in connection with job-related residential moves are not taxable. Included are expenses of disposal, acquisition, abortive acquisition, transport of belongings, travelling and subsistence, bridging loans and duplicate expenses (replacement domestic items).

Salary sacrifice and flexible benefit arrangements

(ITEPA 2003 ss 69A, 69B)

From 2017–18 the range of benefits that attract income tax and NIC advantages when provided as part of optional remuneration arrangements is limited but savings can still be made on employer pension contributions and advice, employer-provided childcare, cycle to work schemes, and ultra-low emission company cars. Arrangements in place before 6 April 2017 could continue unaffected until 5 April 2018 (with a further extension until 5 April 2021 for existing longer term agreements covering cars, living accommodation and school fees).

Scholarships

(ITEPA 2003 ss 211–215)

An employee is taxable on the cost of any scholarship from a trust fund which does not satisfy a 25% distribution test or which is paid because of the employee's employment.

Subscriptions and fees

(ITEPA 2003 ss 343–345)

Not taxable where paid to professional bodies and the employee has a contractual or professional requirement to be a member of the body.

Third party gifts

(ITEPA 2003 ss 270, 324; SI 2003/1361)

Gifts during the tax year of goods and non-cash vouchers up to £250 not taxable where provided by a party unconnected with the employer and not for services provided in connection with employment.

Trivial benefits

(ITEPA 2003 ss 323A–323C)

From 6 April 2016 there is an exemption for qualifying trivial benefits in kind costing less than £50, extending to qualifying benefits provided to former employees. An annual cap of £300 applies to office holders of close companies, and employees who are family members of those office holders.

Use of employer's assets

SEE TOLLEY'S TAX COMPUTATIONS 9.3.

(ITEPA 2003 ss 203–206, 242, 244, 319, 320; FA 2005 s 17; FA 2006 ss 60, 61 HMRC Brief 02/2012)

Tax is chargeable on all employees other than 'lower-paid' ministers of religion (previously all 'lower-paid' employees) on the annual rental value of land and, for other assets, at 20% of the market value when they are first lent or the rental charge to the employer if higher. No taxable benefit arises on:

(a) the loan of a mobile phone for private use. From 6 April 2006 this is restricted to one mobile phone per employee and no longer extends to the employee's family or household but phones first loaned before 6 April 2006 are not affected by the change. HMRC's view from January 2012 is that exemption applies to smartphones with retrospective effect;

(b) the use of works buses (see p 82);

(c) cycles and cycle safety equipment (see p 82);
(d) to 5 April 2006, the loan of computer equipment for private use, provided use is not restricted to directors or senior staff and value of benefit does not exceed £2,500 (computers made available for private use before 6 April 2006 are not affected by the change).

No benefit arises on the subsequent purchase by an employee at market value of computer or cycling equipment previously on loan.

From 2017–18 the benefit is reduced by periods during which the asset is unavailable for private use by the employee or his family/household, or where the asset is shared by two or more employees.

Vouchers

SEE TOLLEY'S TAX COMPUTATIONS **9.6**.

(ITEPA 2003 ss 73–89, 95, 96, 268–270, 362; FA 2012 Sch 39)

Vouchers are taxable as follows.

(a)	Cash vouchers	On amount for which voucher can be exchanged.
(b)	Non-cash vouchers	On cost to employer less any contribution from employee (except where used to obtain certain non-taxable benefits).
(c)	Luncheon vouchers	Before 6 April 2013 on excess over 15p per working day[1].
(d)	Transport vouchers	On cost to employer less any contribution from employee.

1 The 15p exemption on luncheon vouchers is repealed from 2013–14 onwards.

Employment exemption

Employee-ownership trusts

(ITEPA 2003 ss 312A–312I)

From 1 October 2014 an exemption from income tax applies to qualifying bonus payments of up to £3,600 per tax year made to employees, and qualifying former employees, by a company which is owned directly or indirectly by an employee-ownership trust which meets certain qualifying conditions.

For CGT relief relating to such companies see p 38.

Employment income

PAYE and national insurance thresholds

	2013–14	*2014–15*	*2015–16*	*2016–17*	*2017–18*	***2018–19***
	£	£	£	£	£	£
Weekly NI	148/149	153	155/156	155/156	157	**162**
Weekly PAYE	182	192	204	212	221	**228**
Monthly NI	641/646	663	672/676	672/676	680	**702**
Monthly PAYE	787	833	883	917	958	**988**

For full list of national insurance rates see p 111.

PAYE settlement agreements

SEE TOLLEY'S TAX COMPUTATIONS **506.1**.

(SI 2003/2682 Part 6)

These are voluntary agreements between the employer and HMRC under which the employer agrees to meet the tax payable on certain expenses and benefits in kind that are given to his employees. Once an agreement has been signed for a tax year, there is no need to:

- enter the items covered on form P11D (and before 2016–17, form P9D);
- operate PAYE on them, or
- calculate a liability for included items which are liable for Class 1 or Class 1A NICs.

The employer pays Class 1B NICs on the items included in PAYE settlement agreements and on the total amount of tax payable. To be effective for a tax year, an agreement must be signed before 6 July following the end of the year and tax must be paid by 19 October following (or 22 October where paid electronically). They are most suited for payments and benefits provided on an irregular basis, or where benefits are for a group of employees and apportionment is difficult.

From 2018–19, the requirement for employers to agree annually with HMRC which employee expenses and benefits may be included is removed. Employers will now be able to create an enduring agreement with HMRC which will remain in place for subsequent tax years unless varied or cancelled by the employer or HMRC.

Personal service companies

SEE TOLLEY'S TAX COMPUTATIONS **20.1**.

(ITEPA 2003 ss 48–61)

These provisions are commonly known under the name 'IR35' and apply where personal services are provided to a client through an intermediary – normally the worker's personal service company. The effect of the legislation is to treat the worker as an employee of the client for working out the 'deemed employment payment'. The computation involves taking into account all payments and benefits, including those paid direct to the worker for a tax year other than by the intermediary for his services. Certain, restricted, allowable expenses, are deducted from 'earnings'. Finally, any payments or benefits received by the worker from the intermediary are deducted. Tax (under PAYE) and NIC is calculated and the amounts due are payable by the worker and his company. From 2013–14 the provisions are extended to office holders.

For public sector engagements from April 2017 the liability to pay the correct employment taxes moves from the worker's own company to the public sector body or agency/third party paying the company, and the amount will be deducted from the amount paid to the company. The normal 5% flat rate deduction from payments for the worker's services cannot be made in computing the deemed employment payment.

Managed service companies

(ITEPA 2003 ss 61A–61J)

Where an individual provides his services through a managed service company (as defined) all payments made to him by the company are deemed to be employment income and PAYE and NIC have to be applied.

National minimum wage

(SI 2018/455)

Hourly rate

Age of worker	*apprentice rate*[2]	*Under 18*[1]	*18–20*	*21 or more*[3]	*21–24*[3]
From 1 April 2018	**£3.70**	**£4.20**	**£5.90**	**N/A**	**£7.38**
1.4.17–31.3.18	£3.50	£4.05	£5.60	N/A	£7.05
1.10.16–31.3.17	£3.40	£4.00	£5.55	N/A	£6.95
1.4.16–30.9.16	£3.30	£3.87	£5.30	N/A	£6.70
1.10.15–5.4.16	£3.30	£3.87	£5.30	£6.70	N/A
1.10.14–30.9.15	£2.73	£3.79	£5.13	£6.50	N/A
1.10.13–30.9.14	£2.68	£3.72	£5.03	£6.31	N/A

1 Applies to all workers under 18 who are no longer of compulsory school age.
2 From 1 October 2010 the apprentice rate applies to apprentices aged under 19 and other apprentices in their first year of apprenticeship.
3 From 1 April 2016 workers age 25 and over are entitled to the national living wage.

National living wage

(SI 2018/455)

Applies for employees aged 25 and over.

Hourly rate

Age of worker	25 and over
From 1 April 2018	**£7.83**
1.4.17–31.3.18	£7.50
1.4.16–31.3.17	£7.20

Basis of assessment

(ITEPA 2003 ss 14–41E)

	Services performed			
	Wholly in UK	*Partly in UK*	*Partly abroad*	*Wholly abroad*
Persons domiciled in UK				
Non-resident[2]	All	That part	None	None
Resident[2]	All	All[1]	All[1]	All[1]
Persons domiciled outside the UK				
UK employer				
Non-resident	All	That part	None	None
Meets requirement for 3-year period of non-residence[3]	All	That part	Remittances	Remittances
Resident	All	All[1]	All[1]	All[1]
Foreign employer				
Non-resident	All	That part	None	None
Meets requirement for 3-year period of non-residence	All	That part	Remittances	Remittances
Resident[4]	All	That part	Remittances	Remittances

[1] Exemption for seafarers if at least half of qualifying period of over 364 days worked abroad (including 183 consecutive days). Deduction extended in April 2011 with retrospective effect to seafarers who are resident for tax purposes in a European Economic Area or European Union State, other than the United Kingdom. Extended with effect from the date of Royal Asset to Finance Bill 2018 to employees of the Royal Fleet Auxiliary (ITEPA 2003 ss 378–385, HMRC Brief 10/2012).

[2] A statutory residence test was introduced from 6 April 2013 and ordinary residence was abolished from that date, subject to transitional provisions in certain cases for individuals who were resident but not ordinarily resident in the UK at the end of the tax year 2012–13. Before 6 April 2013 resident but not ordinarily resident taxpayers were taxed broadly on all UK earnings and remittances for duties performed abroad.

[3] An employee meets the requirement for a 3-year period of non-residence for a tax year X if he has been non-resident for three consecutive tax years and year X is any of the three years immediately following that spell of non-residence.

[4] From 2014–15 an anti-avoidance measure will tax UK resident non-domiciles on an arising basis in respect of certain overseas employment income where separate employment contracts have been artificially arranged to separate the UK and overseas employment to obtain a tax advantage.

Termination payments

SEE TOLLEY'S TAX COMPUTATIONS 6.1.

(ITEPA 2003 ss 401–416; FA 2018 s 10)

The following lump sum payments are exempt from tax:

(a) Payments in connection with the cessation of employment on the death, injury or disability of the employee.

(b) Payments under tax-exempt pension schemes by way of compensation for loss of employment (or of earnings due to ill-health) or which can properly be regarded as a benefit earned by past service.

(c) Certain payments of terminal grants to members of the armed forces.

(d) Certain benefits under superannuation schemes for civil servants in Commonwealth overseas territories.

(e) Payments in respect of foreign service broadly before 14 September 2017 (but see note below) where the period of foreign service comprises:
   (i) 75% of the whole period of service; or
   (ii) the whole of the last 10 years of service; or
   (iii) where the period of service exceeded 20 years, one-half of that period, including any 10 of the last 20 years.

   Otherwise, a proportion of the payment is exempt, as follows:

$$\frac{\text{length of foreign service}}{\text{length of total service}} \times \text{amount otherwise chargeable}$$

(f) The first £30,000 of genuine ex gratia payments (where there is no 'arrangement' by the employer to make the payment).

(g) Statutory redundancy payments (included in computing £30,000 limit in (*f*) above).

Foreign service relief is abolished for termination payments and benefits to employees who are UK resident in the tax year in which the employment is terminated. This applies where the date of the termination is on or after 6 April 2018 and the termination payment, or other benefit, is received after 13 September 2017. Foreign service relief continues in termination cases where the employee is non-UK resident in the year of termination, and for UK residents where the payment or benefit is in connection with a change of duties or earnings rather than with termination of the employment. Reductions for foreign service are also retained for seafarers and extended to employees of the Royal Fleet Auxiliary.

Fixed rate expenses

For most classes of industry fixed rate allowances for the upkeep of tools and special clothing have been agreed between HMRC and the trade unions concerned. Alternatively, the individual employee may claim as a deduction his or her actual expenses (ITEPA 2003 s 367). (HMRC Employment Income Manual EIM32712.)

Industry	*Occupation*	*Deduction*
Agriculture	All workers[1]	100
Airlines	See note 5 below	
Aluminium	(*a*) Continual casting operators, process operators, de-dimplers, driers, drill punchers, dross unloaders, firemen[2], furnace operators and their helpers, leaders, mouldmen, pourers, remelt department labourers, roll flatteners	140
	(*b*) Cable hands, case makers, labourers, mates, truck drivers and measurers, storekeepers	80
	(*c*) Apprentices	60
	(*d*) All other workers[1]	120
Banks and building societies	Uniformed doormen and messengers	60
Brass and copper	Braziers, coppersmiths, finishers, fitters, moulders, turners and all other workers	120
Building	(*a*) Joiners and carpenters	140
	(*b*) Cement works, roofing felt and asphalt labourers	80
	(*c*) Labourers and navvies	60
	(*d*) All other workers	120
Building materials	(*a*) Stone masons	120
	(*b*) Tilemakers and labourers	60
	(*c*) All other workers	80
Clothing	(*a*) Lacemakers, hosiery bleachers, dyers, scourers and knitters, knitwear bleachers and dyers	60
	(*b*) All other workers	60
Constructional engineering[3]	(*a*) Blacksmiths and their strikers, burners, caulkers, chippers, drillers, erectors, fitters, holders up, markers off, platers, riggers, riveters, rivet heaters, scaffolders, sheeters, template workers, turners, welders	140
	(*b*) Banksmen, labourers, shop-helpers, slewers, straighteners	80
	(*c*) Apprentices and storekeepers	60
	(*d*) All other workers	100
Electrical and electricity supply	(*a*) Those workers incurring laundry costs only	60
	(*b*) All other workers	120
Engineering (trades ancillary to)	(*a*) Pattern makers	140
	(*b*) Labourers, supervisory and unskilled workers	80
	(*c*) Apprentices and storekeepers	60
	(*d*) Motor mechanics in garage repair shops	120
	(*e*) All other workers	120
Fire service	Uniformed firefighters and fire officers	80
Food	All workers	60
Forces personnel	See note 7 below	
Forestry	All workers	100
Glass	All workers	80
Healthcare staff in the NHS, private hospitals and nursing homes	(*a*) Ambulance staff on active service	185 (140 before 6 April 2014)
	(*b*) Nurses and midwives, chiropodists, dental nurses, occupational, speech, physiotherapists and other therapists, healthcare assistants, phlebotomists and radiographers	125 (100 before 6 April 2014)
	(*c*) Plaster room orderlies, hospital porters, ward clerks, sterile supply workers, hospital domestics, hospital catering staff	125 (100 before 6 April 2014)
	(*d*) Laboratory staff, pharmacists, pharmacy assistants	80 (60 before 6 April 2014)
	(*e*) Uniformed ancillary staff: maintenance workers, grounds staff, drivers, parking attendants and security guards, receptionists and other uniformed staff	80 (60 before 6 April 2014)
Heating	(*a*) Pipe fitters and plumbers	120
	(*b*) Coverers, laggers, domestic glaziers, heating engineers and their mates	120
	(*c*) All gas workers, all other workers	100
Iron mining	(*a*) Fillers, miners and underground workers	120
	(*b*) All other workers	100
Iron and steel	(*a*) Day labourers, general labourers, stockmen, time keepers, warehouse staff and weighmen	80
	(*b*) Apprentices	60
	(*c*) All other workers	140
Leather	(*a*) Curriers (wet workers), fellmongering workers, tanning operatives (wet)	80
	(*b*) All other workers	60

Industry	*Occupation*			*Deduction*
Particular engineering[4]	(*a*)	Pattern makers		140
	(*b*)	Chainmakers, cleaners, galvanisers, tinners and wire drawers in the wire drawing industry, tool-makers in the lock making industry		120
	(*c*)	Apprentices and storekeepers		60
	(*d*)	All other workers		80
Police force	Uniformed police officers (ranks up to and including Chief Inspector) Community Support officers and other police service employees — see note 6 below			140
Precious metals	All workers			100
Printing	(*a*)	Letterpress section — electrical engineers (rotary presses), electrotypers, ink and roller makers, machine minders (rotary), maintenance engineers (rotary presses) and stereotypers		140
	(*b*)	Bench hands (periodical and bookbinding section), compositors (letterpress section), readers (letterpress section), telecommunications and electronic section wire room operators, warehousemen (paper box making section)		60
	(*c*)	All other workers		100
Prisons	Uniformed prison officers			80
Public service	(i)	Dock and inland waterways		
		(*a*)	Dockers, dredger drivers, hopper steerers	80
		(*b*)	All other workers	60
	(ii)	Public transport		
		(*a*)	Garage hands (including cleaners)	80
		(*b*)	Conductors and drivers	60
Quarrying	All workers			100
Railways	(See the appropriate category for craftsmen, eg engineers, vehicles etc.) All other workers			100
Seamen	Carpenters			
	(*a*)	Passenger liners		165
	(*b*)	Cargo vessels, tankers, coasters and ferries		140
Shipyards	(*a*)	Blacksmiths and their strikers, boilermakers, burners, carpenters, caulkers, drillers, furnacemen (platers), holders up, fitters, platers, plumbers, riveters, sheet iron workers, shipwrights, tubers, welders		140
	(*b*)	Labourers		80
	(*c*)	Apprentices and storekeepers		60
	(*d*)	All other workers		100
Textiles and textile printing	(*a*)	Carders, carding engineers, overlookers and technicians in spinning mills		120
	(*b*)	All other workers		80
Vehicles	(*a*)	Builders, railway vehicle repairers, and railway wagon lifters		140
	(*b*)	Railway vehicle painters and letterers, builders' and repairers' assistants		80
	(*c*)	All other workers		60
Wood & furniture	(*a*)	Carpenters, cabinet makers, joiners, wood carvers and woodcutting machinists		140
	(*b*)	Artificial limb makers (other than in wood), organ builders and packing case makers		120
	(*c*)	Coopers not providing own tools, labourers, polishers and upholsterers		60
	(*d*)	All other workers		100

1 'All workers' and 'all other workers' refer only to manual workers who have to bear the cost of upkeep of tools and special clothing. They do not extend to other employees such as office staff.
2 'Firemen' means persons engaged to light and maintain furnaces.
3 'Constructional engineering' means engineering undertaken on a construction site, including buildings, shipyards, bridges, roads and other similar operations.
4 'Particular engineering' means engineering undertaken on a commercial basis in a factory or workshop for the purposes of producing components such as wire, springs, nails and locks.
5 A basic flat rate expenses allowance of £1,022 (£850 before 2013–14) applies to all uniformed commercial pilots, co-pilots and other flight deck crew working in the UK (but not stewards/stewardesses). A further £110 (£100 before 2013–14) allowance is allowed for the cost of travel to certain regular specified activities. From 2013–14 stewards/stewardesses may claim basic flat rate expenses of £720.
6 The allowance for police officers applies to community support officers. Other police service employees who must clean their own uniform can claim a deduction of £60.
7 A flat-rate expenses allowance applies in relation to the laundering of uniforms for naval ratings and other ranks. The annual amount is £80 for the Royal Navy and £100 for the Army, RAF and Royal Marines.
8 Correct as at 6 April 2018.

Apprenticeship levy

(FA 2016 ss 98–121)

From April 2017 an apprenticeship levy applies to UK employers in both the private and public sectors. It is set at a rate of 0.5% of an employer's pay bill and paid through PAYE. Each employer receives an allowance of £15,000 to offset against their levy payment. This means that the levy will only be paid on any pay bill in excess of £3 million. The pay bill is the total of employee earnings subject to Class 1 secondary National Insurance Contributions, as if disregarding the secondary and upper secondary thresholds.

Investment reliefs

Community investment tax relief

(ITA 2007 ss 333–382; CTA 2010 ss 218–269)

Investments made by an individual or company in an accredited community development finance institution (CDFI) are eligible for tax relief up to 25%. The investment may be a loan or a subscription for shares or securities. Tax relief may be claimed for the tax year or accounting period in which the investment is made and each of the four subsequent years. Relief for each year is broadly 5% of the invested amount, but from April 2013 any unused balance of the 5% annual relief can be carried forward, although not beyond the 5-year investment period, and only as long as some part of the investment remains within the CDFI. In addition, to comply with European State aid rules, from 1 April 2013 there is a limit on the amounts of relief a company can obtain in any 3-year period — the amount of CITR relief and any de minimis aid from other sources must not exceed €200,000.

Enterprise investment scheme

(ITA 2007 ss 156–257; FA 2018 Sch 4)

The EIS applies to investments in qualifying unquoted companies trading in the UK. Eligible shares must be held for at least three years from the issue date or commencement of trade if later. The following reliefs apply subject to this and other conditions.

Relief on investment

See Tolley's Tax Computations 10.1 onwards.

Maximum investment: if amount over £1,000,000 invested in Knowledge Intensive Companies	**From date to be determined but not before 6 April 2018**	**£2,000,000**
Maximum investment: otherwise	**From 2012–13**	**£1,000,000**
Maximum carry-back to preceding year	**From 2009–10**	**No restriction (subject to annual maximum)**
Rate of relief	**From 2011–12**	**30%**[1]

1 Given as a deduction against income tax liability.

Other reliefs (TCGA 1992 ss 150A–150C, Sch 5B)

See Tolley's Tax Computations 210.1, 210.2, 210.3.

(a) A gain on a disposal of shares on which EIS relief has been given and not withdrawn is exempt from capital gains tax (see p 38).

(b) Deferral relief is available for gains on assets where the disposal proceeds are reinvested in eligible shares in a qualifying company within one year before and three years after the disposal.

(c) A loss on a disposal of shares on which EIS relief has been given may be relieved against income tax or capital gains tax.

Seed enterprise investment scheme

(ITA 2007 ss 257A–257HG)

From 6 April 2012 SEIS applies to investments in companies with fewer than 25 employees and assets up to £200,000 carrying on or preparing to carry on new business. Eligible shares must be held for at least three years from the issue date. The following reliefs apply subject to this and other conditions.

Relief on investment

See Tolley's Tax Computations 25.1, 25.2.

Maximum investment:	**From 2012–13**	**£100,000**
Maximum carry-back to preceding year	**From 2013–14**	**No restriction (subject to annual maximum)**
Rate of relief	**From 2012–13**	**50%**[1]

1 Given as a deduction against income tax liability.

Other reliefs (TCGA 1992 ss 150E, 150G, Sch 5BB)

SEE TOLLEY'S TAX COMPUTATIONS **227.1, 227.2, 227.3**.

(a) A gain on a disposal of shares on which SEIS relief has been given and not withdrawn is exempt from capital gains tax.

(b) Reinvestment relief is available for certain gains on assets where the disposal proceeds are reinvested in SEIS and SEIS relief is claimed (see p 39).

Social investment tax relief

(ITA 2007 ss 257J–257TE)

Between 6 April 2014 and 5 April 2019 income tax relief is available to both resident and non-UK resident individuals who subscribe for qualifying shares or make qualifying debt investments in a social enterprise which meets the requirements, and who have a UK tax liability against which to set the relief. The investment must be held for a period of three years. The following reliefs apply subject to conditions.

Relief on investment

Maximum investment:	**From 2014–15**	**£1,000,000**
Maximum carry-back to preceding year	**From 2015–16**	**No restriction (subject to annual maximum)**
Rate of relief	**From 2014–15**	**30%[1]**

1 Given as a deduction against income tax liability.

Other reliefs

SEE TOLLEY'S TAX COMPUTATIONS **231.1, 231.2, 231.3**.

(a) A gain on a disposal of shares on which SITR income tax relief has been given and not withdrawn is exempt from capital gains tax where shares held for at least 3 years.

(b) Deferral relief is available for gains arising on assets in the period 6 April 2014 to 5 April 2019 where the disposal proceeds are reinvested in shares or debt investments which also qualify for the SITR income tax relief (see p 39).

Venture capital trusts

SEE TOLLEY'S TAX COMPUTATIONS **32.1, 32.2, 32.3**.

(ITA 2007 ss 258–332)

An individual who subscribes for ordinary shares in a VCT obtains income tax reliefs at the rates in the table below subject to conditions. The shares must be held for at least five years.

Relief on investment

Maximum annual investment:	**From 2004–05**	**£200,000**
Rate of relief:	**From 2006–07**	**30%**

Other reliefs

(a) Dividends on shares within investment limit exempt from income tax (unless the investor's main purpose is tax avoidance) (ITTOIA 2005 s 709).

(b) Capital gains reliefs (see p 39).

Urban Regeneration Companies

Relief is available from 1 April 2003 for expenditure incurred by businesses in making contributions to designated Urban Regeneration Companies (ITTOIA 2005 ss 82, 86; CTA 2009 ss 82, 86).

Individual savings accounts ('ISAs')

(TA 1988 s 333; ITTOIA 2005 ss 694–701; SI 1998/1870; SI 2018/359)

Savers can subscribe to an ISA up to the following limits per tax year.

	2013–14	6.4.14–30.6.14	1.7.14–5.4.15	2015–16	2016–17	2017–18	**2018–19**
Overall annual subscription limit	£11,520	£11,880	£15,000[1]	£15,240	£15,240	£20,000	**£20,000**
Cash limit	£5,760	£5,940	£15,000[1]	£15,240	£15,240	£20,000	**£20,000**

1 From 1 July 2014 ISAs were reformed into a simpler product, the 'New ISA'. All existing ISAs became New ISAs and ISA savers are able to subscribe the full subscription amount to a cash account.

2 The subscription limit applies to each spouse or civil partner. From 2015–16 an additional ISA allowance is available for spouses or civil partners following the death of an ISA saver on or after 3 December 2014, equal to the value of that deceased saver's ISAs.

3 From 6 April 2016 there is the facility to offer a flexible account, whereby withdrawals during the year may be replaced without the replacement counting towards the subscription limit.

4 Shares acquired under a tax-favoured share incentive plan or SAYE option scheme may be transferred to an ISA within 90 days without tax consequences.

5 From 6 April 2018 and subject to certain time limits, investments retained in an ISA during the administration of a deceased saver's estate will retain their tax-advantaged status.

Reliefs

(a) Investments under the scheme are free from income tax and capital gains tax. When an investment is transferred to an investor he is deemed to have made a disposal and reacquisition at market value and any notional gain is exempt from capital gains tax.

(b) Withdrawals may be made at any time without loss of tax relief.

Lifetime ISA

From 6 April 2017 individuals aged between 18 and 40 are able to save up to £4,000 per year into one Lifetime ISA and receive a 25% bonus from the Government at the end of the year. Contributions can continue to be made with the bonus paid up to the age of 50. Funds, including the Government bonus, can be used to buy a first home up to the value of £450,000 at any time from 12 months after opening the account, and can be withdrawn tax-free from age 60 for use in retirement. Withdrawals prior to that will forfeit the Government bonus (plus added interest) and also attract a charge. If an individual has a Help to Buy: ISA he could transfer those savings into the Lifetime ISA in 2017–18, or continue saving into both, or open a Help to Buy: ISA after opening a Lifetime ISA, but he will only be able to use the bonus from one of the ISAs to buy a house.

Help to Buy: ISAs

Help to Buy: ISAs are available from 1 December 2015 to 30 November 2019 for first-time house buyers. The Government will provide a top-up of 25% of savings up to a maximum monthly savings amount of £200, and the total bonus available will be capped at £3,000 on £12,000 of savings. It is possible to deposit an additional £1,000 when the account is first opened and there is no limit to how long the account may remain open. The interest on the account and the bonus will be tax-free. The bonus will be paid at the time of completion of the purchase of the property provided the property is worth a maximum of £450,000 in London and £250,000 elsewhere in the UK. Accounts are limited to one per person rather than one per property. See above regarding Lifetime ISAs held at the same time as Help to Buy: ISAs.

Junior individual savings accounts (Junior ISAs)

(ITTOIA 2005 s 695A; SI 1998/1870; SI 2018/359)

The Junior ISA scheme is available to all UK resident children under 18 who do not have a Child Trust Fund account or, from 6 April 2015, to those who wish to transfer a Child Trust Fund account to a Junior ISA. Children are able to have one cash and one stocks and shares Junior ISA at any time.

	2013–14	6.4.14–30.6.14	1.7.14–5.4.15	2015–16	2016–17	2017–18	**2018–19**
Overall annual subscription limit	£3,720	£3,840	£4,000	£4,080	£4,080	£4,128	**£4,260**

Miscellaneous income tax reliefs

Trading allowance and property allowance

(ITTOIA 2005 ss 783A–783AR, 783B–783BQ)

From 6 April 2017 a trading allowance and a property allowance of £1,000 each per year are available to certain individuals. They are not available on income of partners or close company participators, or where rent-a-room relief could be claimed. Where total receipts are no more than £1,000, the allowance is given automatically, no tax is payable and the income need not be declared. An election can be made for relief not to apply at all, or for partial relief to apply where receipts exceed £1,000 so that the allowance rather than expenses is deducted from gross receipts.

Employee shareholder shares

(ITEPA 2003 ss 226A–226D; SI 2013/1755)

From 1 September 2013 the first £2,000 of the value of shares acquired through the adoption of the 'employee shareholder' employment status is not subject to income tax or national insurance, provided the Employee Shareholder Agreement was entered into before 1 December 2016 (or 2 December 2016 where professional advice was given in relation to the share offer on 23 November 2016 before 1.30pm). For the capital gains tax rules see p 38.

Foster carers and shared lives carers (Qualifying care)

SEE TOLLEY'S TAX COMPUTATIONS 30.9.

(ITTOIA 2005 ss 803–828; SI 2018/317)

Generally, local authority payments to foster carers are not taxable to the extent they do no more than meet the actual costs of caring. In other cases, and for shared lives carers from 6 April 2010:

- where gross receipts do not exceed the 'individual limit' and shared lives care is not being provided to more than three people, the carer is treated as having a nil profit and nil loss for the tax year concerned;

- where gross receipts exceed the 'individual limit' and shared lives care is not being provided to more than three people, the carer can choose to either be taxed on the excess or compute profit or loss using the normal business rules.

In addition from 2017–18 the relief is extended to include shared lives schemes that are self-funded by the person receiving care.

The 'individual limit' is made up of a fixed amount of £10,000 per residence for a full tax year plus an amount per adult or child for each week or part week that the individual provides qualifying care. The weekly amounts are £200 for a child under 11 years and £250 for a child of 11 or over and an adult.

Gift of pre-eminent objects

(FA 2012 Sch 14)

With effect in relation to liabilities for tax years and accounting periods beginning on or after 1 April 2012, individuals who gift pre-eminent objects to the nation will receive a reduction in their UK tax liability of 30% of the value of the object they are donating. The tax reduction can be against income or capital gains tax and can be spread forward across a period of up to five years starting with the tax year in which the object is offered. The gift must be accepted as pre-eminent by the Arts Council under the Cultural Gifts Scheme.

Landlord's energy-saving allowance

(ITTOIA 2005 ss 312–314; CTA 2009 ss 251–253; SI 2007/831; SI 2007/3278; SI 2008/1520)

From 6 April 2004 to 5 April 2015 individual landlords who let residential property and pay income tax could claim a deduction from the property business profits for expenditure in the dwelling-houses let to install:

- loft insulation or cavity wall insulation; or
- (from 7 April 2005) solid wall insulation; or
- (from 6 April 2006) draught-proofing and insulation for hot water systems; or
- (from 6 April 2007) floor insulation.

Expenditure is restricted to £1,500 per building until 5 April 2007 and to £1,500 per dwelling-house from 6 April 2007.

The relief was extended to corporate landlords of residential property for expenditure on or after 8 July 2008.

Life assurance premium relief

(TA 1988 s 266, Sch 14 para 7; FA 2012 Sch 39)

For premiums due and payable ***before 6 April 2015***, or payable before that date and actually paid before 6 July 2015, relief for premiums paid on qualifying life assurance policies for contracts made before 14 March 1984 is available by deduction of 12.5% from admissible premiums.

Maintenance payments

SEE TOLLEY'S TAX COMPUTATIONS 16.2.

(ITTOIA 2005 ss 727, 729; ITA 2007 ss 453–456)

Where either party to the marriage or civil partnership was born before 6 April 1935 tax relief may be claimed by the payer in respect of the lower of:

- the amount of the payments in the year concerned and
- the minimum amount of the married couple's allowance for the year concerned (see p 78).

The relief is restricted to 10% of the relevant amount. The payment must be made to the former/separated spouse or civil partner. It is made gross and is not taxable in the hands of the recipient.

Rent-a-room relief

SEE TOLLEY'S TAX COMPUTATIONS 22.3.

(ITTOIA 2005 ss 784–802)

Gross annual receipts from letting furnished accommodation in the only or main home are exempt from tax up to a maximum of £7,500 (£4,250 before 6 April 2016) (provided no other taxable income is derived from a trade, letting or arrangement from which the rent-a-room receipts are derived).

If the gross receipts exceed £7,500 (£4,250 before 6 April 2016), the taxpayer can pay tax on the net receipts after deduction of expenses. Alternatively, the taxpayer can elect to pay tax on the amount by which the gross receipts exceed £7,500, without relief for the actual expenses.

An individual's maximum is halved to £3,750 (£2,125 before 6 April 2016) if during the 'relevant period' for the year (normally the tax year) some other person received income from letting accommodation in that property.

An election can be made to disapply the relief for a particular tax year (for example, if the individual would otherwise make an allowable loss).

Simplified fixed rate deductions

SEE TOLLEY'S TAX COMPUTATIONS 31.1.

(ITTOIA 2005 ss 94B–94I; FA 2018 s 36)

From 2013–14 individuals carrying on a trade, profession or vocation as self-employed sole traders or in partnership with other individuals can choose certain simplified expenses when calculating their profits for income tax purposes. From 2017–18 deductions for vehicle expenditure are available to those carrying on a property business. Conditions apply.

Vehicle expenditure

Kind of vehicle	Rate per business mile
Car or goods vehicle	45p for the first 10,000 miles
	25p after that
Motor cycle	24p

Use of home for business purposes

Hours worked per month	Amount per month
25 or more	£10
51 or more	£18
101 or more	£26

Premises used both as a home and for business

Note: Amount below is the non-business use amount to be deducted from the total expenses claimed. The flat rate includes all household goods and services, food and non-alcoholic drinks and utilities. It does not include mortgage interest, rent of the premises, council tax or rates. A reasonable apportionment of these expenses should be made based on the extent of the private occupation of the premises — HMRC Brief 14/2013.

Number of occupants	Disallowance amount per month
1	£350
2	£500
3 or more	£650

Capped income tax reliefs

(ITA 2007 s 24A)

From 2013–14 a limit on previously uncapped income tax reliefs is imposed. The limit is set at the greater of £50,000 or 25% of the individual's adjusted total income for the tax year. The specified reliefs which, taken together, will be limited to the extent that they can be relieved by individuals against general income are:

Trade loss relief against general income (ITA 2007 s 64)
Early trade losses relief (ITA 2007 s 72)
Post-cessation trade relief (ITA 2007 s 96)
Property loss relief against general income (ITA 2007 s 120)
Post-cessation property relief (ITA 2007 s 125)
Employment loss relief against general income (ITA 2007 s 128)
Former employees deduction for liabilities (ITEPA 2003 s 555)
Share loss relief on non-Enterprise Investment Scheme / Seed Enterprise Investment Scheme shares (ITA 2007 Pt 4 Ch 6)
Losses on deeply discounted securities (ITTOIA 2005 ss 446, 454)
Qualifying loan interest (ITA 2007 Pt 8 Ch 1)

Pension provision

(FA 2004 ss 149–284, Schs 28–36; SI 2018/206)

Tax relief on contributions

SEE TOLLEY'S TAX COMPUTATIONS 19.1.

Individual contributions: An individual may make unlimited contributions and tax relief is available on contributions up to the higher of:

- the full amount of relevant earnings; or
- £3,600 provided the scheme operates tax relief at source,

and subject to the annual allowance.

Employer contributions: Employer contributions to registered schemes are deductible for tax purposes, with statutory provision for spreading abnormally large contributions over a period of up to four years. The contributions are not treated as taxable income of the employee, although from 6 April 2013 this relief does not extend to payments for the benefit of family members.

Annual allowance

SEE TOLLEY'S TAX COMPUTATIONS 19.3.

Each individual has an annual allowance as set out in the table below. If the annual increase in an individual's rights under all registered schemes exceeds the annual allowance, the excess is chargeable at the individual's marginal rate. The individual is liable for the tax, unless he makes an election for the scheme to pay the charge if it exceeds £2,000. In such cases a consequential adjustment is made to the individual's entitlement to benefits.

Annual allowance	2012–13	2013–14	2014–15 to 2015–16	**2016–17 onwards**
Maximum	£50,000[1]	£50,000[1]	£40,000[1, 2]	**£40,000**[1, 2]
Minimum[3]	N/A	N/A	N/A	**£10,000**[3]

1 From 2011–12 unused allowance can be carried forward three years. For these purposes the annual allowance for 2008–09 to 2010–11 is assumed to be £50,000.

2 Where members make use of flexible access to their money purchase funds from 6 April 2015 the annual allowance is effectively divided between money purchase inputs and defined benefit inputs, resulting in a 'money purchase annual allowance' of £4,000 (£10,000 before 6 April 2017) and an 'alternative annual allowance' that applies to any defined benefit inputs of £36,000 (£30,000 before 6 April 2017). The money purchase annual allowance cannot be increased by amounts brought forward.

3 A tapered reduction in the annual allowance applies from 6 April 2016 for those with an 'adjusted income' (i.e. including pension contributions) over £150,000. The reduction is £1 for every £2 of income over £150,000 and the minimum allowance will be £10,000.

Taxable benefits

SEE TOLLEY'S TAX COMPUTATIONS 19.2, 19.3.

'Tax-free' lump sum: The maximum 'tax-free' lump sum that can be paid to a member under a registered scheme is broadly the lower of:

- 25% of the value of the pension rights; and
- 25% of the member's lifetime allowance.

Lifetime allowance: Each individual has a lifetime allowance for contributions as set out in the table below. The excess over the lifetime allowance of the benefits crystallising (usually when a pension begins to be paid) is taxable at the following rates:

- 55% if taken as a lump sum;
- 25% in other cases.

Any tax due may be deducted from the individual's benefits.

Lifetime allowance	2012–13	2013–14	2014–15 to 2015–16	2016–17 to 2017–18	**2018–19**
	£1,500,000	£1,500,000	£1,250,000	£1,000,000	**£1,030,000**

Transitional. There are transitional provisions for the protection of lump sum and other pension rights accrued before 6 April 2006. Fixed protection also applies to protect pension rights from 6 April 2012, from 6 April 2014 and from 6 April 2016 when the lifetime allowance is decreased. 'Individual protection 2014' and 'individual protection 2016' are also available.

Age restrictions

Minimum pension age: The minimum pension age is 55. A pension cannot be paid before the minimum age except on grounds of ill health. Protection applies to those with existing contractual rights to draw a pension earlier and for members of pre-6 April 2006 approved schemes with early retirement ages. A reduced lifetime allowance will apply in the case of early retirement before minimum pension age except in the case of certain professions such as the police and the armed forces (SI 2005/3451).

Share schemes

Share incentive plans ('SIPs')

SEE TOLLEY'S TAX COMPUTATIONS 28.4.

(TCGA 1992 ss 236A, 238A, Schs 7C, 7D Pt 1; ITEPA 2003 ss 488–515, Sch 2)

Free share plan

2014–15 onwards	*annual maximum*	**£3,600**
2000–01 to 2013–14	*annual maximum*	£3,000

Partnership share plan

2014–15 onwards	*annual maximum*	**£1,800 or 10% of annual salary if lower**
2003–04 to 2013–14	*annual maximum*	£1,500 or 10% of annual salary if lower

Matching shares

2000–01 onwards	*Maximum number of shares given by employer to employee for each partnership share bought*	2

Shares are free of tax and NICs if held in the plan for five years. Dividends are tax-free if reinvested in shares (restricted to a maximum of £1,500 per employee per tax year before 6 April 2013). Shares withdrawn from the plan at any time are exempt from capital gains tax and treated as acquired by the employee at their market value at that time.

If shares are withdrawn within between three and five years (with exceptions such as on death, injury, disability, retirement, redundancy, or, from 17 July 2013, certain cash takeovers), liability to income tax and NICs arises on the lower of their value on entering and on leaving the plan. If shares are withdrawn within three years (with similar exceptions), liability is on their value on leaving the plan.

Employer self-certification replaces HMRC approval from 6 April 2014.

Enterprise management incentives

SEE TOLLEY'S TAX COMPUTATIONS 28.5.

(TCGA 1992 s 238A, Sch 7D Pt 4; ITEPA 2003 ss 527–541, Sch 5)

Note that the tax reliefs associated with EMIs outlined below are a state aid for which approval expired on 6 April 2018. HMRC are seeking to extend approval but EMI share options granted from 7 April 2018 until fresh state aid approval is received may be treated as non-tax advantaged employment-related securities options and the following reliefs may not apply to them.

Certain independent trading companies with gross assets not exceeding £30 million may grant share options then worth up to £250,000 (£120,000 for options granted before 16 June 2012, £100,000 for options granted before 6 April 2008) to an eligible employee. The total value of shares in respect of which unexercised qualifying options exist must not exceed £3 million. Limited to companies with fewer than 250 full-time equivalent employees for options granted on or after 21 July 2008.

Where the conditions of the scheme are complied with:

(a) There is no charge to tax or NICs when the option is granted provided the option to acquire the shares is not at less than their market values at that date, and there is no charge on exercise providing the option is exercised within ten years.

(b) Capital gains tax will be payable when the shares are sold, though for disposals on or after 6 April 2013, shares acquired through exercising EMI options on or after 6 April 2012 are eligible for capital gains tax entrepreneurs' relief if certain conditions are met.

Save as you earn (SAYE) share option schemes

(TCGA 1992 s 238A, Sch 7D Pt 2; ITEPA 2003 ss 516–519, Sch 3)

The scheme is linked to a savings arrangement, on which bonuses are exempt from tax, to provide funds for the acquisition of shares when the option is exercised at the end of a three or five-year contract. A five-year contract may offer the option of repayment on the seventh anniversary, although the 7-year savings period is withdrawn with effect from 23 July 2013. Employees who were already saving under existing SAYE contracts before 23 July 2013 were not affected by this change.

From 1 September 2018 all employees will be able to take a pause of up to 12 months from saving into their SAYE scheme.

Monthly contributions to SAYE scheme

	up to 5 April 2014	**From 6 April 2014**
Minimum	£5–10[1]	**£5–£10**[1]
Maximum	£250	**£500**

1 The company may choose a minimum savings contribution between £5 and £10.

See HMRC website (www.gov.uk/government/publications/change-in-bonus-rates-for-save-as-you-earn-saye-share-option-schemes) for the latest bonus rates.

Where the conditions of the scheme are complied with, no income tax charge arises on the employee in respect of:

(a) the grant of an option to acquire shares at a discount of up to 20% of the share price at time of the grant;
(b) the exercise of the option (options must not be exercised before the bonus date subject to exceptions such as on injury, disability, redundancy, retirement, death or, from 17 July 2013, certain cash takeovers); or
(c) any increase in the value of the shares.

Capital gains tax is chargeable on disposal of the shares: the CGT base cost is the consideration given by the employee for both the shares and the option.

Employer self-certification replaces HMRC approval from 6 April 2014.

Company share option plans ('CSOPs')

(TCGA 1992 s 238A, Sch 7D Pt 3; ITEPA 2003 ss 521–526, Sch 4)

Limit on value of shares under option held by employee at any one time

From 29 April 1996	**£30,000**

Scheme shares must be fully paid up, not redeemable and, for options granted before 17 July 2013, not subject to special restrictions. Only full-time directors or qualifying employees may participate in the scheme.

Where the conditions of the scheme are complied with, no tax charge arises on the employee in respect of:

(a) the grant of an option to acquire shares[1];
(b) the exercise of the option[2]; or
(c) any increase in the value of the shares.

Capital gains tax is chargeable on disposal of the shares: the CGT base cost is the consideration given by the employee for both the shares and the option.

Employer self-certification replaces HMRC approval from 6 April 2014.

1 At the time the option is granted the price at which shares can be acquired must not be less than the market value of shares of the same class at that time.

2 The option must be exercised between three and ten years after the grant (or may be exercised less than three years after the grant where the individual ceases to be an employee due to injury, disability, redundancy or retirement, or, from 17 July 2013, where there are certain cash takeovers of constituent companies). For options granted before 9 April 2003, the options had to be exercised between three and ten years after the grant (without exception) and not less than three years after a previous exempt exercise of another option under the same or another approved company share option scheme.

Tax credits

(TCA 2002)

Tax credits are administered and paid by HMRC, and are non-taxable. Claims must be made after the commencement of the tax year and can be backdated for a maximum of one month. Universal credit will replace tax credits. New claimants in some areas started to claim universal credit from October 2013. Existing claimants will be gradually phased onto universal credit, and this is expected to be completed by 2021 (see p 134).

Child tax credit and working tax credit

	2017–18 Annual amount	***2018–19*** Annual amount
Child tax credit	**£**	**£**
Family element[1]	545	**545**
Child element (for each child or young person)[2]	2,780	**2,780**
Addition for disabled child or young person	3,175	**3,275**
Enhancement for severe disabled child or young person	1,290	**1,325**
Working tax credit	**£**	**£**
Basic element	1,960	**1,960**
Lone parent and couple element	2,010	**2,010**
30-hour element	810	**810**
Disability element	3,000	**3,090**
Severe disability element	1,290	**1,330**
Childcare element – up to 70% of eligible costs	Weekly	**Weekly**
– maximum eligible cost for one child	175	**175**
– maximum eligible cost for two or more children	300	**300**

1 Only one family element per family. It is not payable to those starting a family after 5 April 2017.

[2] No child element is payable for third and subsequent children born after 5 April 2017. Does not apply to disabled child element or severely disabled child element and multiple births are protected.

Income thresholds and withdrawal rates	***2017–18***	***2018–19***
Income threshold for those entitled to CTC and WTC	£6,420	**£6,420**
Withdrawal rate	41%	**41%**
Income threshold for those entitled to CTC only	£16,105	**£16,105**
Income rise disregard	£2,500	**£2,500**
Income fall disregard	£2,500	**£2,500**

Calculation of award. Tax credits are awarded on an annual basis. They are initially based on the income of the claimant or joint claimants for the preceding tax year and adjusted based on actual income in the tax year in which the credit is claimed. Income broadly includes all taxable income excluding the first £300 of income from pensions, savings, property or foreign assets. If current year's income is greater than the previous year's income by less than £2,500 (£5,000 for 2013–14 to 2015–16, £10,000 for 2012–13), the award is not adjusted. If current year's income is greater than the previous year's income by £2,500 or more (£5,000 for 2013–14 to 2015–16, £10,000 for 2012–13), the award is adjusted to reflect current year's income less £2,500. An income fall disregard of £2,500 applies from 6 April 2012. Thus from 2012–13, where previous year's income exceeds the current year's income by not more than £2,500, the previous year's income will be used, but where the previous year's income exceeds the current year's income by more than £2,500, the current year's income plus £2,500 will be used. In any other case current year's income is used. Where circumstances change during a tax year and different rates apply, the award is recalculated on a proportional, daily basis. Such changes must be notified to HMRC within one month if tax credit entitlement will be reduced as a result.

Eligibility. CTC is payable to UK resident single parents and couples responsible for a child or young person. WTC is payable to UK residents who are at least 16 years old and, in the case of single persons, who work at least 16 hours a week. In the case of a couple, from 6 April 2012, they must jointly work at least 24 hours a week and one must work at least 16 hours a week, or where only one of the couple works that person must work for at least 24 hours a week. Additionally, the claimant (or one of them if a couple) must either:

- be at least 25 years old and work at least 30 hours a week; or
- have a dependent child or children; or
- have a mental or physical disability which puts them at a disadvantage in getting a job and have previously been in receipt of some form of disability benefit; or
- from 6 April 2011, be over 60 and work at least 16 hours a week, regardless of whether they have dependent children.

Renewal claim. Claims for tax credit must be renewed by 31 July.

Inheritance tax

Rates of inheritance tax

(IHTA 1984 s 7, Schs 1, 1A; HMRC Inheritance Tax Manual IHTM14593)

From 15 March 1988 onwards

SEE TOLLEY'S TAX COMPUTATIONS 305.1, 305.2.

	Rate
Cumulative gross transfer rate:	
for gross transfers on death over the cumulative chargeable transfer limit	**40%**
reduced rate on death	**36%**[1]
for gross lifetime transfers over the cumulative chargeable transfer limit	**20%**
Grossing-up net transfer rate for each £1 over the chargeable transfer limit:	
for net transfers on death not bearing own tax	**2/3**
for net lifetime transfers	**1/4**

1 For deaths occurring on or after 6 April 2012 a reduced rate of 36% applies where at least 10% of the net estate is left to charity or registered community amateur sports clubs.

Nil rate bands[3]

SEE TOLLEY'S TAX COMPUTATIONS 310.3, 310.5.
(IHTA 1984 ss 8–8D)

Period	*Limit*	*Period*	*Limit*
	£		£
2009–10 to 2020–21[2]	325,000[1]	1998–99	223,000
2008–09	312,000[1]	1997–98	215,000
2007–08	300,000[1]	1996–97	200,000
2006–07	285,000	1995–96	154,000
2005–06	275,000	10.3.92–5.4.95	150,000
2004–05	263,000	6.4.91–9.3.92	140,000
2003–04	255,000	1990–91	128,000
2002–03	250,000	1989–90	118,000
2001–02	242,000	15.3.88–5.4.89	110,000
2000–01	234,000	17.3.87–14.3.88	90,000
1999–2000	231,000	18.3.86–16.3.87	71,000

1 Any nil-rate band which is unused on a person's death can be transferred to their surviving spouse or civil partner for the purposes of the charge to tax on the death of the survivor on or after 9 October 2007.
2 The nil rate band is frozen at £325,000 until 5 April 2021.
3 An additional **residence nil-rate band** applies when a home is passed on death to direct descendants of the deceased on or after 6 April 2017. Initially the band was £100,000; for **2018–19 it is £125,000** and will increase in stages up to £175,000 in 2020–21. Any unused band is transferable to a spouse or civil partner. There is a tapered withdrawal of the band for estates valued at more than £2 million. It also applies where an individual downsizes from a higher value residence to a lower value one or ceases to own a home on or after 8 July 2015 and assets of equivalent value are passed on death to direct descendants.

Capital transfer tax nil rate bands

Period	***Limit***	***Period***	***Limit***
	£		**£**
6.4.85–17.3.86	67,000	26.3.80–8.3.82	50,000
13.3.84–5.4.85	64,000	27.10.77–25.3.80	25,000
15.3.83–12.3.84	60,000	13.3.75–26.10.77	15,000
9.3.82–14.3.83	55,000		

Estate duty nil rate bands (England, Scotland and Wales)

Period	***Limit***	***Period***	***Limit***
	£		**£**
22.3.72–12.3.75	15,000	9.4.62–3.4.63	4,000
31.3.71–21.3.72	12,500	30.7.54–8.4.62	3,000
16.4.69–30.3.71	10,000	10.4.46–29.7.54	2,000
4.4.63–15.4.69	5,000	16.8.14–9.4.46	100

Delivery of accounts: due dates

(IHTA 1984 s 216)

Type of transfer	*Due date*
Chargeable lifetime transfers	Later of: (*a*) 12 months after the end of the month in which the transfer took place; and (*b*) three months after the date on which the person delivering the account became liable
Relevant property settlements periodic and exit charges	6 months after end of the month in which the chargeable event occurred. (For chargeable events before 6 April 2014, as for chargeable lifetime transfers, see above)[1]
PETs which become chargeable	12 months after the end of the month in which the transferor died
Gifts with reservation chargeable on death	12 months after the end of the month in which the death occurred
Transfers on death	Later of: (*a*) 12 months after the end of the month in which the death occurred; and (*b*) three months after the date on which the personal representatives first act or the person liable first has reason to believe that he is liable to deliver an account
National heritage property	6 months after the end of the month in which the chargeable event occurred

1 Where higher IHT is payable as a result of IHTA 1984 Sch A1 or the F(No 2)A 2017 domicile changes, the delivery date is the last day of December 2017 if later than normal due date.

Delivery of accounts: excepted transfers and estates

(SI 2004/2543; SI 2008/606)

Date of transfer or death	*6 April 2000–5 April 2002*	*6 April 2002–5 April 2003*	*6 April 2003–31 Aug 2006*	*From 1 Sept 2006*
Excepted transfers:	*Value below*	*Value below*	*Value below*	*Value below*
Total chargeable transfers since 6 April	£10,000	£10,000	£10,000	£10,000
Total chargeable transfers during last ten years	£40,000	£40,000	£40,000	£40,000
Excepted estates:				
Total gross value[1]	£210,000	£220,000	(see (*a*) below)	(see (*a*) below)
Total gross value of property outside UK	£50,000	£75,000	£75,000	£100,000
Aggregate value of 'specified transfers'[2]	£75,000	£100,000	£100,000	£150,000
Settled property passing on death	–	£100,000	£100,000	£150,000

For chargeable transfers after 5 April 2007, no account need be delivered where:

(i) the transfer is of cash or quoted shares or securities and the value of the transfer and other chargeable transfers made in the preceding seven years does not exceed the IHT threshold; or

(ii) the value of the transfer and other chargeable transfers made in the preceding seven years does not exceed 80% of the IHT threshold and the value of the transfer does not exceed the net amount of the threshold available to the transferor at the time of the transfer.

For footnotes see the list below.

Excepted estates

For deaths occurring after 5 April 2004, no account need be delivered where the deceased died domiciled in the UK provided either conditions (a) or (b) below are met, and both conditions (c) and (d) below are met.

(a) the aggregate of the gross value of the estate, and of any 'specified transfers'[2] or 'specified exempt transfers'[3] does not exceed the appropriate IHT threshold[4];

(b) the aggregate of the gross value of the estate, and of any 'specified transfers'[2] or 'specified exempt transfers'[3] does not exceed £1,000,000; for deaths after 28 February 2011 at least part of the estate passes to the person's spouse, civil partner or to a charity; and after deducting from that aggregate figure any exempt spouse, civil partner and charity transfers and total estate liabilities[6], it does not exceed the appropriate IHT threshold[4];

(c) the gross value of settled property or foreign assets do not exceed the limits in the above table; and

(d) there were no chargeable lifetime transfers in the seven years before death other than specified transfers not exceeding the limits in the above table[5].

Where the deceased was never domiciled in the UK, no account need be delivered provided that the value of the estate in the UK is wholly attributable to cash and quoted shares and securities not exceeding £150,000.

1 See table above — This limit applies to the aggregate gross value of the estate and of 'specified transfers' and 'specified exempt transfers'. For deaths after 28 February 2011 transfers treated as normal expenditure out of income made within 7 years before death and totalling more than £3,000 in any tax year will be treated as chargeable transfers for these purposes.

2 'Specified transfers' are chargeable transfers of cash, quoted shares and securities and, after 6 April 2002, interests in or over land and, after 5 April 2004, personal chattels or corporeal moveable property. For deaths after 28 February 2011 transfers treated as normal expenditure out of income made within 7 years before death and totalling more than £3,000 in any tax year will be treated as chargeable transfers for these purposes.

3 'Specified exempt transfers' are transfers in the seven years before death between spouses or civil partners, gifts to charity, political parties or housing associations, transfers to maintenance funds for historical buildings, etc or to employee trusts.

4 For deaths after 5 April 2010 the IHT threshold for these purposes is increased by 100% where—

(a) the deceased is a surviving spouse or civil partner;

(b) a claim has been made for the transfer of the unused nil-rate band of their deceased spouse or civil partner;

(c) all of the first deceased spouse's or civil partner's nil-rate band was unused; and

(d) the first deceased met certain other criteria similar to those listed above for excepted estates.

5 For deaths after 28 February 2011 transfers treated as normal expenditure out of income made within 7 years before death and totalling more than £3,000 in any tax year will be treated as chargeable transfers for these purposes.

6 For deaths on or after 1 April 2014 total estate liabilities do not include those which are not discharged on or after death out of the estate in money or money's worth, or those which are prevented by any other provision in IHTA 1984 from being taken into account, or those attributable to financing the acquisition of, or maintenance or enhancement of the value of, excluded property.

Excepted settlements

No account need be delivered of property comprised in an excepted settlement (i.e. one with no qualifying interest in possession) where a chargeable event occurs after 5 April 2007 and cash not exceeding £1,000 is the only property comprised in the settlement. Other conditions to be fulfilled are that, the settlor has not provided further property, the trustees are UK resident throughout the settlement's existence and there are no related settlements.

Inheritance tax reliefs

The following is a summary of the main reliefs and exemptions under the Inheritance Tax Act 1984 (Parts II and V). The legislation should be referred to for conditions and exceptions.

Agricultural property
SEE TOLLEY'S TAX COMPUTATIONS **302.1, 302.2**.

Transfer with vacant possession (or right to obtain it within 12 months); transfer on or after 1 September 1995, of land let (or treated as let) on or after that date.	100% of agricultural value
Any other case.	50% of agricultural value

Note: The 100% relief is extended in limited circumstances by Concession F17.

Annual gifts — £3,000
SEE TOLLEY'S TAX COMPUTATIONS **310.1**.

Business property
SEE TOLLEY'S TAX COMPUTATIONS **304.1**.

Unincorporated business.	100%
Unquoted shares (including shares in AIM or USM companies) (held for 2 years or more).[1]	100%
Unquoted securities which alone, or together with other such securities and unquoted shares, give the transferor control of the company (held for 2 years or more).[1]	100%
Settled property used in life tenant's business.	100%
Controlling holding in fully quoted companies.	50%
Land, buildings, machinery or plant used in business of company or partnership.	50%

1 Tax charges arising and transfers occurring after 5 April 1996. 10 March 1992–5 April 1996 minority holding of shares or securities of up to 25% in unquoted or USM company qualified for 50% relief; larger holdings qualified for 100% relief.

Charities, gifts to — Exempt
From 1 April 2002, Community Amateur Sports Clubs are treated as charities.

Marriage/civil partnership gifts
SEE TOLLEY'S TAX COMPUTATIONS **320.1**.

Made by:		
	parent	£5,000
	remoter ancestor	£2,500
	party to marriage/civil partnership	£2,500
	other person	£1,000

National purposes
SEE TOLLEY'S TAX COMPUTATIONS **316.1 ONWARDS**.

Property given or bequeathed to bodies listed in IHTA 1984 Sch 3. — Exempt

Political parties, gifts to — Exempt

Potentially exempt transfers
SEE TOLLEY'S TAX COMPUTATIONS **305.1**.

Exempt if made 7 or more years before the date of death. Except for gifts with reservation etc, they include:

(a) transfers by individuals to other individuals or certain trusts for the disabled;
(b) transfers after 21 March 2006 by individuals to a bereaved minor's trust on the coming to an end of an immediate post-death interest;
(c) transfers before 22 March 2006 by individuals to accumulation and maintenance trusts;
(d) transfers by individuals into interest in possession trusts in which, for transfers after 21 March 2006, the beneficiary has a disabled person's interest; and
(e) certain transfers on the termination or disposal of an individual's beneficial interest in possession in settled property (in restricted circumstances following FA 2006).

Quick succession relief
SEE TOLLEY'S TAX COMPUTATIONS **319.1**.

Estate increased by chargeable transfer followed by death within 5 years.	
Death within 1st year.	100%
Each additional year: decreased by	20%
Small gifts to same person	£250
Spouses/civil partners with separate domicile (one not being in the UK)	
SEE TOLLEY'S TAX COMPUTATIONS **310.4**.	
Total exemption.	£325,000[1]

[1] For transfers of value before 6 April 2013 the total exemption was £55,000. From 6 April 2013 the limit is increased to the level of the prevailing IHT nil-rate band (see p 105). For transfers of value made on or after 6 April 2013 individuals can elect to be treated as domiciled in the UK if, at any time on or after 6 April 2013 and during the period of 7 years ending with the date on which the election is made, they have a UK-domiciled spouse or civil partner. The election may be made in some cases where the UK-domiciled individual had died. Personal representatives may make an election on behalf of a deceased person in certain circumstances. Other conditions apply.

Tapering relief

The value of the estate on death is taxed as the top slice of cumulative transfers in the 7 years before death. Transfers on or within 7 years of death are taxed on their value at the date of the gift on the death rate scale, but using the scale in force at the date of death, subject to the following taper:

Years between gift and death	*Percentage of full charge at death rates*
0–3	100
3–4	80
4–5	60
5–6	40
6–7	20

Penalties see p 16.

National insurance contributions

(SI 2001/1004)

From 6 April 2018

SEE TOLLEY'S TAX COMPUTATIONS 504.1, 506.1, 505.1 ONWARDS.

Class 1 contributions[1]			
Earnings limits and threshold	Weekly £	Monthly £	Yearly £
Lower earnings limit	116	503	6,032
Primary threshold	162	702	8,424
Secondary threshold	162	702	8,424
Upper secondary threshold[3, 4]	892	3,863	46,350
Upper earnings limit	892	3,863	46,350
Rates			
Employees' contributions			
Weekly earnings:	£162.01–£892	12%	
	Over £892	2%	
Employers' contributions[3, 4]			
Weekly earnings:	Over £162[3, 4]	13.8%	
Women at reduced rate			
Employees' contributions			
Weekly earnings:	£162.01–£892	5.85%	
	Over £892	2%	
Employers' contributions			
Weekly earnings:	Over £162	13.8%	
Employment allowance[2]		**£3,000**	
Class 1A and Class 1B contributions		13.8%	

1 Employees' rates are nil for children under 16 and those over state pensionable age but employers' contributions are still payable. Employees' NICs are not payable on earnings up to the primary threshold, employers' NICs are not payable on earnings up to the secondary threshold.

2 An employment allowance of £3,000 per year (£2,000 from 6 April 2014 to 5 April 2016) applies for businesses, charities and CASCs to be offset against their employer Class 1 secondary NICs. The allowance is claimed as part of the normal payroll process through RTI. Only one company in a group may claim. There are some excluded employers such as certain employers of domestic staff, public authorities and those which carry out functions wholly or mainly of a public nature. From 6 April 2015 the allowance was extended to employers of care and support workers where the duties of employment relate to the employer's personal, family or household affairs. From 6 April 2016 the allowance is no longer available to companies whose only employee is the director.

3 From 6 April 2015 employers with employees under the age of 21 are no longer required to pay Class 1 secondary NICs on earnings up to the upper secondary threshold for those employees.

4 From 6 April 2016 employers with apprentices under the age of 25 are longer required to pay Class 1 secondary NICs on earnings up to the upper secondary threshold for those employees.

6 April 2017–5 April 2018

Class 1 contributions[1]			
Earnings limits and threshold	Weekly £	Monthly £	Yearly £
Lower earnings limit	113	490	5,876
Primary threshold	157	680	8,164
Secondary threshold	157	680	8,164
Upper secondary threshold[3, 4]	866	3,750	45,000
Upper earnings limit	866	3,750	45,000
Rates			
Employees' contributions			
Weekly earnings:	£157.01–£866	12%	
	Over £866	2%	
Employers' contributions[3, 4]			
Weekly earnings:	Over £157[3, 4]	13.8%	
Women at reduced rate			
Employees' contributions			
Weekly earnings:	£157.01–£866	5.85%	
	Over £866	2%	
Employers' contributions			
Weekly earnings:	Over £157	13.8%	
Employment allowance[2]		**£3,000**	
Class 1A and Class 1B contributions		13.8%	

1 Employees' rates are nil for children under 16 and those over state pensionable age but employers' contributions are still payable. Employees' NICs are not payable on earnings up to the primary threshold, employers' NICs are not payable on earnings up to the secondary threshold.

2 An employment allowance of £3,000 per year (£2,000 from 6 April 2014 to 5 April 2016) applies for businesses, charities and CASCs to be offset against their employer Class 1 secondary NICs. The allowance is claimed as part of the normal payroll process through RTI. Only one company in a group may claim. There are some excluded employers such as certain employers of domestic staff, public authorities and those which carry out functions wholly or mainly of a public nature. From 6 April 2015 the allowance was extended to employers of care and support workers where the duties of employment relate to the employer's personal, family or household affairs. From 6 April 2016 the allowance is no longer available to companies whose only employee is the director.

3 From 6 April 2015 employers with employees under the age of 21 are no longer required to pay Class 1 secondary NICs on earnings up to the upper secondary threshold for those employees.

4 From 6 April 2016 employers with apprentices under the age of 25 are longer required to pay Class 1 secondary NICs on earnings up to the upper secondary threshold for those employees.

6 April 2016–5 April 2017

Class 1 contributions[1]			
Earnings limits and threshold	Weekly £	Monthly £	Yearly £
Lower earnings limit	112	486	5,824
Primary threshold	155	672	8,060
Secondary threshold	156	676	8,112
Upper secondary threshold[3, 4]	827	3,583	43,000
Upper earnings limit	827	3,583	43,000
Rates[5]			
Employees' contributions			
Weekly earnings:	£155.01–£827	12%	
	Over £827	2%	
Employers' contributions[3, 4]			
Weekly earnings:	Over £156[3, 4]	13.8%	
Women at reduced rate			
Employees' contributions			
Weekly earnings:	£155.01–£827	5.85%	
	Over £827	2%	
Employers' contributions			
Weekly earnings:	Over £156	13.8%	
Employment allowance[2]		**£3,000**	
Class 1A and Class 1B contributions		13.8%	

1 Employees' rates are nil for children under 16 and those over state pensionable age but employers' contributions are still payable. Employees' NICs are not payable on earnings up to the primary threshold, employers' NICs are not payable on earnings up to the secondary threshold.

2 An employment allowance of £3,000 per year (£2,000 from 6 April 2014 to 5 April 2016) applies for businesses, charities and CASCs to be offset against their employer Class 1 secondary NICs. The allowance is claimed as part of the normal payroll process through RTI. Only one company in a group may claim. There are some excluded employers such as certain employers of domestic staff, public authorities and those which carry out functions wholly or mainly of a public nature. From 6 April 2015 the allowance was extended to employers of care and support workers where the duties of employment relate to the employer's personal, family or household affairs. From 6 April 2016 the allowance is no longer available to companies whose only employee is the director.

3 From 6 April 2015 employers with employees under the age of 21 are no longer required to pay Class 1 secondary NICs on earnings up to the upper secondary threshold for those employees.

4 From 6 April 2016 employers with apprentices under the age of 25 are longer required to pay Class 1 secondary NICs on earnings up to the upper secondary threshold for those employees.

5 Contracting out is no longer possible from 6 April 2016 as the single-tier state pension was introduced.

6 April 2015–5 April 2016

Class 1 contributions[1]				
Earnings limits and threshold		Weekly £	Monthly £	Yearly £
Lower earnings limit		112	486	5,824
Primary threshold		155	672	8,060
Secondary threshold		156	676	8,112
Upper secondary threshold[5]		815	3,532	42,385
Upper earnings limit		815	3,532	42,385
Upper accruals point		770	3,337	40,040
		Not contracted out	**Contracted out** *Salary-related schemes*[3]	
Employees' contributions				
Weekly earnings:	£155.01–770	12%	10.6%	
	£770.01–£815	12%	12%	
	Over £815	2%	2%	
	– rebate £112–£155		1.4%[2, 3]	
Employers' contributions[4, 5]				
Weekly earnings:	£156.01–£770[5]	13.8%	10.4%	
	Over £770[5]	13.8%	13.8%	
	– rebate £112–£156		3.4%[2, 3]	
Women at reduced rate				
Employees' contributions				
Weekly earnings:	£155.01–£815	5.85%		
	Over £815	2%		
Employers' contributions	Normal employers' contributions apply as above			
Employment allowance[4]			**£2,000**	
Class 1A and Class 1B contributions			13.8%	

1 Employees' rates are nil for children under 16 and those over state pensionable age but employers' contributions are still payable. Employees' NICs are not payable on earnings up to the primary threshold, employers' NICs are not payable on earnings up to the secondary threshold.

2 The rebate is given on earnings between the lower earnings limit and the primary threshold for employees, and between the lower earnings limit and the secondary threshold for employers. The rebate for employees is given to employers to the extent that insufficient contributions have been paid by the employee for offset.

3 From 2012 the rebates for defined benefit schemes (salary-related schemes) are 3.4% for employers and 1.4% for employees. Contracting out on a defined contribution basis (money purchase schemes) is abolished from 6 April 2012. Contracting out via a personal pension plan is also not possible from 6 April 2012.

4 From 6 April 2014 an employment allowance of £2,000 per year applies for businesses, charities and CASCs to be offset against their employer Class 1 secondary NICs. The allowance is claimed as part of the normal payroll process through RTI. Only one company in a group may claim. There are some excluded employers such as certain employers of domestic staff, public authorities and those which carry out functions wholly or mainly of a public nature. From 6 April 2015 the allowance is extended to employers of care and support workers where the duties of employment relate to the employer's personal, family or household affairs.

5 From 6 April 2015 employers with employees under the age of 21 are no longer required to pay Class 1 secondary NICs on earnings up to the upper secondary threshold for those employees.

6 April 2014–5 April 2015

Class 1 contributions[1]				
Earnings limits and threshold		Weekly £	Monthly £	Yearly £
Lower earnings limit		111	481	5,772
Secondary threshold		153	663	7,956
Primary threshold		153	663	7,956
Upper earnings limit		805	3,489	41,865
Upper accruals point		770	3,337	40,040
		Not contracted out	**Contracted out** *Salary-related schemes*[3]	
Employees' contributions				
Weekly earnings:	£153.01–770	12%	10.6%	
	£770.01–£805	12%	12%	
	Over £805	2%	2%	
	– rebate £111–£153		1.4%[2, 3]	
Employers' contributions[4]				
Weekly earnings:	£153.01–£770	13.8%	10.4%	
	Over £770	13.8%	13.8%	
	– rebate £111–£153		3.4%[2, 3]	
Women at reduced rate				
Employees' contributions				
Weekly earnings:	£153.01–£805	5.85%		
	Over £805	2%		
Employers' contributions	Normal employers' contributions apply as above			
Employment allowance[4]		**£2,000**		
Class 1A and Class 1B contributions		13.8%		

1 Employees' rates are nil for children under 16 and those over state pensionable age but employers' contributions are still payable. Employees' NICs are not payable on earnings up to the primary threshold, employers' NICs are not payable on earnings up to the secondary threshold. The primary and secondary thresholds are the same in 2014–15.

2 The rebate is given on earnings between the lower earnings limit and the primary threshold for employees, and between the lower earnings limit and the secondary threshold for employers. The rebate for employees is given to employers to the extent that insufficient contributions have been paid by the employee for offset.

3 From 2012 the rebates for defined benefit schemes (salary-related schemes) are 3.4% for employers and 1.4% for employees. Contracting out on a defined contribution basis (money purchase schemes) is abolished from 6 April 2012. Contracting out via a personal pension plan is also not possible from 6 April 2012. Contracting out via defined benefit schemes will no longer be possible from 6 April 2016 when the single-tier state pension is introduced.

4 From 6 April 2014 an employment allowance of £2,000 per year applies for businesses, charities and CASCs to be offset against their employer Class 1 secondary NICs. The allowance is claimed as part of the normal payroll process through RTI. Only one company in a group may claim. There are some excluded employers such as domestic employers, public authorities and those which carry out functions wholly or mainly of a public nature.

6 April 2013–5 April 2014

Class 1 contributions[1]				
Earnings limits and threshold		Weekly £	Monthly £	Yearly £
Lower earnings limit		109	473	5,668
Secondary threshold[3]		148	641	7,696
Primary threshold[3]		149	646	7,755
Upper earnings limit		797	3,454	41,450
Upper accruals point		770	3,337	40,040
		Not contracted out	**Contracted out** *Salary-related schemes*[5]	
Employees' contributions				
Weekly earnings:	£149.01–770	12%	10.6%	
	£770.01–£797	12%	12%	
	Over £797	2%	2%	
	– rebate £109–£149		1.4%[2, 5]	
Employers' contributions[4]				
Weekly earnings:	£148.01–£770	13.8%	10.4%	
	Over £770	13.8%	13.8%	
	– rebate £109–£148		3.4%[2, 5]	
Women at reduced rate				
Employees' contributions				
Weekly earnings:	£149.01–£797	5.85%		
	Over £797	2%		
Employers' contributions	Normal employers' contributions apply as above			
Class 1A and Class 1B contributions		13.8%		

1 Employees' rates are nil for children under 16 and those over state pensionable age but employers' contributions are still payable. Employees' NICs are not payable on earnings up to the primary threshold, employers' NICs are not payable on earnings up to the secondary threshold.

2 The rebate is given on earnings between the lower earnings limit and the primary threshold for employees, and between the lower earnings limit and the secondary threshold for employers. The rebate for employees is given to employers to the extent that insufficient contributions have been paid by the employee for offset.

3 From 6 April 2011 the primary threshold applies for employees' contributions and the secondary threshold applies for employers' contributions.

4 An employer NIC 'holiday' applies to new businesses started in certain regions between 22 June 2010 and 5 September 2013. Between 6 September 2010 and 5 September 2013 the businesses may qualify for a deduction of up to £5,000 of their employer Class 1 contributions for each of the first ten employees hired in the first year of business.

5 From 2012 the rebates for defined benefit schemes (salary-related schemes) are 3.4% for employers and 1.4% for employees. Contracting out on a defined contribution basis (money purchase schemes) is abolished from 6 April 2012. Contracting out via a personal pension plan is also not possible from 6 April 2012.

Class 2, 3 and 4 contributions

SEE TOLLEY'S TAX COMPUTATIONS 507.1, 513.1, 503.1 ONWARDS.

	2018–19	2017–18	2016–17
Class 2 (self-employed)[1]			
Flat rate—per week	**£2.95**	£2.85	£2.80
Share fishermen—per week	**£3.60**	£3.50	£3.45
Volunteer development workers—per week	**£5.80**	£5.65	£5.60
Small profits threshold—per year	**£6,205**	£6,025	£5,965
Class 3 (voluntary contributions)			
Flat rate—per week	**£14.65**	£14.25	£14.10
Class 4 (self-employed)[1]			
Lower annual profits limit	**£8,424**	£8,164	£8,060
Upper annual profits limit	**£46,350**	£45,000	£43,000
Rate between lower and upper limits	**9%**	9%	9%
Rate on profits above upper limit	**2%**	2%	2%
Maximum contributions			
Class 1 or Class 1/Class 2[2]	**£4,642.80**	£4,509.24	£4,273.92
– plus rate on earnings above upper limit	**2%**	2%	2%
Class 4 limiting amount[3]	**£3,569.69**	£3,466.29	£3,293.00
– plus rate on profits above upper limit	**2%**	2%	2%

1 Not payable if pensionable age is reached by the beginning of the tax year. Class 2 will be abolished from April 2019.

2 Where an earner has more than one employment (including self-employment), liability for Class 1 or Class 1 and Class 2 contributions cannot exceed a maximum amount equal to 53 employees' Class 1 contributions at the maximum standard rate, plus 2% on earnings over the individual's upper earnings limit (which varies depending on individual circumstances).

3 Where Class 4 contributions are payable in addition to Class 1 and/or Class 2 contributions, liability for Class 4 contributions cannot exceed such an amount as, when added to the Class 1/Class 2 contributions payable (after applying the maximum if appropriate), equals the limiting amount. The limiting amount is the maximum Class 4 contributions payable (including 2% on earnings over the upper profit limit) plus 53 Class 2 contributions.

	2015–16	2014–15	2013–14
Class 2 (self-employed)[1]			
Flat rate—per week	£2.80	£2.75	£2.70
Share fishermen—per week	£3.45	£3.40	£3.35
Volunteer development workers—per week	£5.60	£5.55	£5.45
Small earnings exception—per year	£5,965	£5,885	£5,725
Class 3 (voluntary contributions)			
Flat rate—per week	£14.10	£13.90	£13.55
Class 4 (self-employed)[1]			
Lower annual profits limit	£8,060	£7,956	£7,755
Upper annual profits limit	£42,385	£41,865	£41,450
Rate between lower and upper limits	9%	9%	9%
Rate on profits above upper limit	2%	2%	2%
Maximum contributions			
Class 1 or Class 1/Class 2[2]	£4,197.60	£4,146.72	£4,121.28
– plus rate on earnings above upper limit	2%	2%	2%
Class 4 limiting amount[3]	£3,237.65	£3,197.56	£3,175.65
– plus rate on profits above upper limit	2%	2%	2%

1 Not payable if pensionable age is reached by the beginning of the tax year.

2 Where an earner has more than one employment (including self-employment), liability for Class 1 or Class 1 and Class 2 contributions cannot exceed a maximum amount equal to 53 employees' Class 1 contributions at the maximum standard rate, plus 2% on earnings over the individual's upper earnings limit (which varies depending on individual circumstances).

3 Where Class 4 contributions are payable in addition to Class 1 and/or Class 2 contributions, liability for Class 4 contributions cannot exceed such an amount as, when added to the Class 1/Class 2 contributions payable (after applying the maximum if appropriate), equals the limiting amount. The limiting amount is the maximum Class 4 contributions payable (including 2% on earnings over the upper profit limit) plus 53 Class 2 contributions. Before 2015–16, if a contributor expected to exceed this amount he could apply for deferment of Class 4 contributions for the year in question. Deferment had no effect on the 2% payable on earnings over the upper profit limit, which was still payable. Collection of Class 2 contributions via self-assessment means deferment is no longer necessary.

Employers' contributions: benefits in kind

Class 1A NICs are payable by employers on most taxable benefits in kind, excluding benefits:

(1) included in a PAYE settlement agreement (see p 91);
(2) provided to 'lower-paid' ministers of religion, and before 6 April 2016 all 'lower-paid' employees (including benefits in kind and expenses payments);
(3) otherwise not required to be included on a P11D;
(4) on which Class 1 NICs were due;
(5) which were covered by a dispensation before 6 April 2016 (see below).

From 6 April 2016 the dispensations regime is abolished and replaced with a new exemption for paid or reimbursed amounts that would otherwise be deductible. Also from 6 April 2016 employees (other than lower-paid ministers of religion) earning at a rate of less than £8,500 per year pay income tax on their benefits in kind in the same way as other employees earning at a rate of £8,500 or more.

Class 1 and Class 1A Benefits provided under optional remuneration arrangements are not covered by existing exemptions except in limited circumstances. Where this is the case Class 1 or Class 1A NICs are due as appropriate.

Class 1B contributions are payable by employers by reference to the value of any items included in a PAYE settlement agreement (PSA) which would otherwise be earnings for Class 1 or Class 1A, including the amount of tax paid. Income tax and Class 1B contributions on a PSA are payable by 19 October after the end of the tax year to which the PSA relates (or 22 October if paid electronically).

Common benefits subject to Class 1 and Class 1A NICs (CWG5 2018)

Benefit		*NICs Class*	*PAYE or P11D*
Assets transferred to employees but not readily convertible assets		1A	P11D
Assets placed at employee's disposal for mixed business and private use		1A	P11D
Car fuel supplied for private motoring in company car		1A	P11D
Car/van fuel supplied for private motoring in privately owned car/van	– supplied using company credit card, garage account, agency card or employer's own fuel pump	1A	P11D
	– any other circumstances	1	P11D
Cars available for private use		1A	P11D
Car parking facilities other than at or near place of work or as part of business travel		1A	P11D
Car parking fees paid for or reimbursed to employee other than at or near place of work or as part of business travel		1	P11D
Childcare where employer contracts with provider and either the value exceeds the permitted maximum or the qualifying conditions are not met		1A	P11D
Childcare where employee reimbursed or additional salary provided to meet cost		1	PAYE
Christmas boxes	– cash	1	PAYE
	– goods	1A	P11D
Clothing and uniforms			
– cash payment to employee for clothing that can be worn at any time		1	PAYE or P11D[1]
– clothing provided by employer that can be worn at any time		1A	P11D
Council tax, unless employee provided with living accommodation which is not a benefit		1	P11D
Credit and charge cards – personal expenses on employer's card		1	P11D
Entertaining staff — expenses/ allowances	– employer contract with provider	1A	P11D
	– employee contract with provider	1	PAYE or P11D[1]
Expenses not covered by an exemption— any profit element in payment		1	P11D[4]
Food, groceries, farm produce	– employer contract with provider	1A	P11D
	– employee contract with provider	1	PAYE or P11D[1]
Goods transferred to employee	– employer contract with provider	1A	P11D
	– employee contract with provider	1	PAYE or P11D[1]
Holidays	– employer contract with provider	1A	P11D
	– employee contract with provider, or holiday vouchers	1	PAYE or P11D[1]
Income tax paid but not deducted from employee, or paid on notional payments not borne by employee within 90 days of receipt of each notional payment		1	P11D
Insurance premiums for pensions etc on employee's death or retirement, employee contract with provider		1	PAYE or P11D[1]
Living accommodation (beneficial)		1A	P11D

Benefit		*NICs Class*	*PAYE or P11D*
Loans	– non-qualifying	1A	P11D
	– written off	1	P11D
Meals vouchers (other than 15p a day of value before 6 April 2013)		1	P11D
Meals provided other than at canteen or at business premises open to all staff on a reasonable scale where all employees may obtain free or subsidised meals not provided in connection with salary sacrifice or flexible remuneration arrangements		1A	P11D
Medical, dental insurance or treatment provided in the UK by employer	– employer contract with provider	1A	P11D
	– employee contract with provider	1	PAYE or P11D[1]
Mobile phone[5] — cost of private calls, employee contract with provider		1	PAYE or P11D[1]
Personal bills		1	PAYE or P11D[1]
Readily convertible assets[2]		1	PAYE
Relocation payments	– qualifying over £8,000	1A	P11D
	– non-qualifying benefits or qualifying expenses paid after relevant day	1A	P11D
	– non-qualifying expenses	1	P11D
Round sum allowances (not identified as business expense)		1	P11D
Scholarships awarded to students because of parent's employment or payment of school fees	– employer contract with provider	1A	P11D
	– employee contract with provider	1	PAYE or P11D[1]
Social functions unless ITEPA 2003 s 264 satisfied		1A	P11D
Sporting or recreational facilities unless ITEPA 2003 s 261 satisfied		1A	P11D
Subscriptions, professional and fees not allowable as tax deduction	– employer contract with provider	1A	P11D
	– employee contract with provider	1	PAYE or P11D[1]
Telephones	– employer contract with provider, unless private use is insignificant or employee reimburses cost of all private calls	1A	P11D
	– employee contract with provider, unless used exclusively for business. If mixed use, not applicable to business calls if supported by evidence	1	PAYE or P11D[1]
Training payments	– employer contract with provider, unless work-related or encouraged or required by employer	1A	P11D
	– employee contract with provider, unless work-related or encouraged or required by employer	1	PAYE or P11D[1]
Vans available for commuting and other private use		1A[3]	P11D
Van fuel provided for use in van available for commuting and other private use		1A[3]	P11D
Vouchers (other than exceptions for childcare, meals, etc)		1	P11D

1 Payments by employer to provider should be entered on P11D. Reimbursements to the employee are subject to PAYE.

2 See detailed information in HMRC booklet CWG2(2018) para 5.13.1.

3 No Class 1A due if van is available mainly for employee's business travel and commuting and other private use is insignificant.

4 Specific and distinct business expenses within the payments should be recorded in appropriate section of P11D.

5 No limit to number of mobile phones which employer can contract to provide NIC free solely for business with insignificant private use. Only one mobile per employee NIC free for private use where employer contracts. No mobile phone may be provided NICs free to a member of an employee's family or household.

Overseas

Average rates of exchange

Average for year ending	***31.03.16***	***31.12.16***	***31.03.17***	***31.12.17***	***31.03.18***
Abu Dhabi (Dirham)	5.545785	5.056488	4.870015	4.7113	4.847200
Afghanistan (Afghani)	Not quoted	Not quoted	Not quoted	Not quoted	Not quoted
Albania (Lek)	190.5769	170.723375	165.255417	153.870608	151.855608
Algeria (Dinar)	156.345498	150.356917	145.760208	141.838817	147.292983
Angola (Readj Kwanza)	194.43726	223.259667	219.334167	212.751217	228.398717
Antigua (EC$)	4.076723	3.716987	3.579938	3.462775	3.562625
Argentina (Peso)	15.815366	20.039292	19.813125	21.101775	22.835108
Armenia (Dram)	725.102419	661.087208	635.039167	618.424358	635.050192
Aruba (Florin)	2.70257	2.464473	2.37361	2.296008	2.362217
Australia (A$)	2.048381	1.852649	1.766681	1.6733	1.701108
Austria (Euro)	1.368138	1.240784	1.2077	1.14615	1.137292
Azerbaijan (New Manat)	1.776242	2.182317	2.166667	2.208425	2.236083
Bahamas ($ pegged to US$)	1.508298	1.376045	1.327506	1.282692	1.319675
Bahrain (Dinar)	0.569447	0.519127	0.499965	0.48375	0.497683
Bangladesh (Taka)	117.868189	108.051708	104.331667	103.933367	108.245867
Barbados (BD$)	3.019789	2.753181	2.651663	2.565383	2.639350
Belarus (Rouble)	25,925.56886	2.57286	2.54075	2.575008	2.635217
Belgium (Euro)	1.368138	1.240784	1.2077	1.14615	1.137292
Belize (Dollar)	3.018125	2.753017	2.654854	2.5669	2.638883
Benin (CFA Franc)	897.121292	814.319917	791.886667	751.841017	746.023517
Bermuda ($ pegged to US$)	1.508298	1.376045	1.327506	1.282692	1.319675
Bhutan (Ngultrum)	98.517936	92.449	89.215625	83.8606	85.167267
Bolivia (Boliviano)	10.412043	9.505183	9.170683	8.871158	9.118975
Bosnia-Herzegovina (Marka)	2.674975	2.428067	2.361131	2.24175	2.224400
Botswana (Pula)	15.818653	15.039908	14.237492	13.265775	13.344942
Brazil (Real)	5.396725	4.854893	4.433554	4.091392	4.223092
Brunei ($)	2.091509	3.408618	3.34355	1.778117	1.794625
Bulgaria (Lev)	2.675091	2.428196	2.361273	2.241908	2.224542
Burkina Faso (CFA Franc)	897.121292	814.319917	791.886667	751.841017	746.023517
Burundi (Franc)	2,366.003657	2,222.357583	2,181.28875	2,206.898908	2,294.578075
Cambodia (Riel)	6,125.978626	5,330.036625	5,123.295	5,190.532042	5,336.462042
Cameroon Republic (CFA Franc)	897.121292	814.319917	791.886667	751.841017	746.023517
Canada (Can$)	1.975398	1.817877	1.730748	1.663342	1.692158
Cape Verde Islands (Escudo)	151.102058	136.919417	133.193333	126.771108	125.851942
Cayman Islands (CI$)	1.238113	1.128863	1.087065	1.051642	1.082142
Central African (CFA Franc)	897.121292	814.319917	791.886667	751.841017	746.023517
Chad (CFA Franc)	897.121292	814.319917	791.886667	751.841017	746.023517
Chile (Peso)	1,011.773945	937.166708	886.574792	833.321158	839.937825
China (Renminbi Yuan)	9.582777	9.098112	8.870269	8.694692	8.793500
Colombia (Peso)	4,393.427606	4,207.046542	3,943.479375	3,780.095633	3,868.970633
Comoros (Franc)	672.839977	610.738583	593.913958	563.880142	559.516808
Congo Brazzaville (CFA Franc)	897.121292	814.319917	791.886667	751.841017	746.023517
Congo Dem Rep (Zaire) (Congolese Franc)	1,388.737494	1,217.051375	1,272.947917	1,837.751325	2,010.992158
Costa Rica (Colon)	805.544166	745.827167	724.224375	726.811292	752.461292
Cote d'Ivoire (CFA Franc)	897.121292	814.319917	791.886667	751.841017	746.023517
Croatia (Kuna)	10.388589	9.354187	9.058758	8.554467	8.478242
Cuba (Peso)	1.509685	1.376575	1.325902	1.282692	1.319675
Cyprus (Euro)	1.368138	1.240784	1.2077	1.14615	1.137292
Czech Republic (Koruna)	37.128996	33.553167	32.624567	30.30255	29.617358
Denmark (Krone)	10.204585	9.239276	8.985713	8.526183	8.463283
Djibouti (Franc)	268.334328	244.655458	235.63375	227.953592	234.526925
Dominica (EC$)	4.076723	3.716987	3.579938	3.462775	3.562625
Dominican Republic (Peso)	68.159266	63.174	61.189167	60.624808	63.080642

Average for year ending	***31.03.16***	***31.12.16***	***31.03.17***	***31.12.17***	***31.03.18***
Dubai (Dirham)	5.545785	5.056488	4.870015	4.7113	4.847200
Ecuador (US$)	1.508298	1.376045	1.327506	1.282692	1.319675
Egypt (£)	11.760721	12.756667	15.525625	23.020958	23.559292
El Salvador (Colon)	13.119923	12.041875	11.59625	11.218608	11.544442
Equatorial Guinea (CFA Franc)	897.121292	814.319917	791.886667	751.841017	746.023517
Eritrea (Nakfa)	22.643617	20.6435	19.882083	19.236392	19.790558
Estonia (Euro)	1.368138	1.240784	1.2077	1.14615	1.137292
Ethiopia (Birr)	31.528464	29.935083	29.262083	30.404417	32.895250
European Community (Euro)	1.368138	1.240784	1.2077	1.14615	1.137292
Fiji Islands (F$)	3.197892	2.88288	2.758275	2.641267	2.695158
Finland (Euro)	1.368138	1.240784	1.2077	1.14615	1.137292
France (Euro)	1.368138	1.240784	1.2077	1.14615	1.137292
French Polynesia (CFP franc)	162.612789	148.136792	144.055417	136.771283	135.713783
Gabon (CFA franc)	897.121292	814.319917	791.886667	751.841017	746.023517
Gambia (Dalasi)	60.858828	57.703958	57.026875	58.403417	61.422583
Georgia (Lari)	3.548008	3.206053	3.165079	3.230683	3.262392
Germany (Euro)	1.368138	1.240784	1.2077	1.14615	1.137292
Ghana (Cedi)	5.877119	5.395412	5.328192	5.711967	5.933550
Greece (Euro)	1.368138	1.240784	1.2077	1.14615	1.137292
Grenada/Wind. Isles (EC$)	4.076723	3.716987	3.579938	3.462775	3.562625
Guatemala (Quetzal)	11.568525	10.486725	10.041267	9.4389	9.671450
Guinea Bissau (CFA Franc)	897.121292	814.319917	791.886667	751.841017	746.023517
Guinea Republic (Franc)	11,360.92819	9,424.586583	9,557.783333	11,730.00364	11,950.680308
Guyana (G$)	303.457213	285.108708	274.8625	266.302267	273.924767
Haiti (Gourde)	80.510608	86.077125	85.69875	83.77875	85.080417
Honduras (Lempira)	33.305926	31.304417	30.48125	30.10485	30.987350
Hong Kong (HK$)	11.694423	10.676933	10.296783	9.989125	10.295567
Hungary (Forint)	424.226477	386.828917	375.333958	353.952192	351.979692
Iceland (Krona)	197.546906	168.441917	156.928542	138.308883	138.964717
India (Rupee)	98.517936	92.449	89.215625	83.8606	85.167267
Indonesia (Rupiah)	20,451.65261	18,335.22346	17,584.31896	17,144.69078	17,681.332450
Iran (Rial)	Not quoted	Not quoted	Not quoted	Not quoted	Not quoted
Iraq (Dinar)	1,768.418649	1,616.382625	1,567.59125	1,516.901792	1,561.088458
Ireland (Euro)	1.368138	1.240784	1.2077	1.14615	1.137292
Israel (Shekel)	5.851666	5.285135	5.057563	4.650458	4.676292
Italy (Euro)	1.368138	1.240784	1.2077	1.14615	1.137292
Jamaica (J$)	178.29906	171.248417	167.475417	164.746542	168.302375
Japan (Yen)	181.381545	150.168417	144.307083	143.837608	146.289275
Jordan (Dinar)	1.070389	0.976191	0.940108	0.909492	0.935658
Kazakhstan (Tenge)	391.130298	469.985917	443.701458	418.35025	429.597750
Kenya (Shilling)	151.6759	139.787417	135.004375	132.611608	136.063275
Korea North (Won)	Not quoted	Not quoted	Not quoted	Not quoted	Not quoted
Korea South (Won)	1,741.725521	1,598.662625	1,529.039792	1,456.988333	1,468.298333
Kuwait (Dinar)	0.456362	0.415885	0.401694	0.389458	0.399008
Kyrgyz Republic (Som)	101.800558	96.609792	91.083333	88.318475	90.690142
Laos (New Kip)	12,280.30938	11,193.88567	10,799.85042	10,584.8802	10,924.060200
Latvia (Euro from 1.1.14, previously Lat)	1.368138	1.240784	1.2077	1.14615	1.137292
Lebanon (£)	2,276.813075	2,076.391292	1,999.26	1,936.109733	1,993.559733
Lesotho (Loti)	20.590709	20.421333	18.895	17.011558	17.009892
Liberia ($ pegged to US$)	1.508298	1.385863	1.327506	1.282692	1.319675
Libya (Dinar)	2.055243	1.873744	1.82859	1.791	1.815833
Lithuania (Euro from 1.1.15, Litas)	1.368138	1.240784	1.2077	1.14615	1.137292
Luxembourg (Euro)	1.368138	1.240784	1.2077	1.14615	1.137292
Macao (Pataca)	12.057558	11.001733	10.592617	10.286858	10.603683
Macedonia (Denar)	84.124579	76.4425	74.335625	70.574492	70.028658
Madagascar (Malagasy Ariary)	4,825.506009	4,370.964	4,223.932083	4,014.998958	4,119.578125
Malawi (Kwacha)	838.537291	975.086042	944.816875	930.329008	957.419008
Malaysia (Ringgit)	6.092072	5.660823	5.525885	5.540642	5.533767
Maldive Islands (Rufiyaa)	22.968374	21.074542	20.336667	19.79605	20.366883

Average for year ending	***31.03.16***	***31.12.16***	***31.03.17***	***31.12.17***	***31.03.18***
Mali Republic (CFA Franc)	897.121292	814.319917	791.886667	751.841017	746.023517
Malta (Euro)	1.368138	1.240784	1.2077	1.14615	1.137292
Mauritania (Ouguiya)	484.156051	481.10375	471.101667	459.318083	470.815583
Mauritius (Rupee)	53.80344	48.857917	47.026042	44.459367	44.805200
Mexico (Peso)	24.979304	25.431792	25.433958	24.309267	24.355933
Moldova (Leu)	29.115332	27.330792	26.318958	23.918608	23.550275
Mongolia (Tugrik)	2,993.241942	2,891.671958	2,935.9775	3,134.000608	3,200.468108
Montserrat (EC$)	4.076723	3.716987	3.579938	3.462775	3.562625
Morocco (Dirham)	14.798226	13.476167	13.060625	12.498817	12.579650
Mozambique (Metical)	64.096872	83.258833	87.956667	82.467542	81.167542
Myanmar (Burma) (Kyat)	1,824.413732	1,693.940542	1,659.734167	1,750.151058	1,793.330225
Nepal (Rupee)	157.621228	147.969542	142.607917	134.177958	136.268792
Netherlands (Euro)	1.368138	1.240784	1.2077	1.14615	1.137292
New Caledonia (CFP Franc)	162.612789	148.136792	144.055417	136.771283	135.713783
New Zealand (NZ$)	2.222953	1.984533	1.881252	1.799358	1.841325
Nicaragua (Gold Cordoba)	41.574764	39.258144	38.249977	38.418908	40.021408
Niger Republic (CFA Franc)	897.121292	814.319917	791.886667	751.841017	746.023517
Nigeria (Naira)	300.565604	347.059917	372.817917	422.033433	449.370933
Norway (Krone)	12.468953	11.563583	11.078125	10.603592	10.743592
Oman (Rial Omani)	0.581332	0.53006	0.510533	0.493758	0.507983
Pakistan (Rupee)	156.175647	144.189208	138.893542	134.740892	140.586725
Panama (Balboa)	1.509849	1.376654	1.325902	1.282692	1.319675
Papua New Guinea (Kina)	4.309964	4.301563	4.192831	4.084467	4.220958
Paraguay (Guarani)	8,196.462577	7,789.234917	7,464.89875	7,229.70655	7,398.514883
Peru (New Sol)	4.932809	4.635137	4.4238	4.1948	4.287767
Philippines (Peso)	69.612753	65.009792	63.514375	64.701333	66.973833
Poland (Zloty)	5.76733	5.402822	5.256254	4.896733	4.803675
Portugal (Euro)	1.368138	1.240784	1.2077	1.14615	1.137292
Qatar (Riyal)	5.497479	5.01264	4.82779	4.674633	4.809233
Romania (Leu)	6.092487	5.575248	5.422944	5.2299	5.230075
Russia (Rouble-Market)	96.035998	92.835625	84.216875	74.800833	76.261667
Rwanda (R Franc)	1,099.592742	1,075.026417	1,056.958125	1,072.778517	1,114.911850
Saotome & Principe (Dobra)	32,924.74188	27,787.62243	26,963.36918	28,151.87599	27,909.510992
Saudi Arabia (Riyal)	5.656204	5.160259	4.978908	4.810008	4.948550
Senegal (CFA Franc)	897.121292	814.319917	791.886667	751.841017	746.023517
Serbia (Dinar)	165.383875	152.777667	148.926458	139.563283	137.004950
Seychelles (Rupee)	19.969996	18.33075	17.704583	17.40575	18.005750
Sierra Leone (Leone)	6,440.172736	6,389.390333	7,017.53375	9,467.215617	10,019.493117
Singapore (S$)	2.090721	1.896978	1.834148	1.777417	1.793925
Slovakia (Euro)	1.368138	1.240784	1.2077	1.14615	1.137292
Slovenia (Euro)	1.368138	1.240784	1.2077	1.14615	1.137292
Solomon Islands (SI$)	12.003711	10.874433	10.367517	9.966892	10.244017
Somali Republic (Schilling)	962.529826	819.771	776.039167	747.50125	774.117917
South Africa (Rand)	20.614979	20.428208	18.90375	17.011558	17.009892
Spain (Euro)	1.368138	1.240784	1.2077	1.14615	1.137292
Sri Lanka (Rupee)	209.096951	200.72675	195.195625	195.30165	202.270817
St Christopher & Nevis (EC$)	4.076723	3.716987	3.579938	3.462775	3.562625
St Lucia (EC$)	4.076723	3.716987	3.579938	3.462775	3.562625
St Vincent (EC$)	4.076723	3.716987	3.579938	3.462775	3.562625
Sudan Republic (£)	9.130853	8.427427	8.224729	8.493742	10.180292
Surinam (Dollar)	5.329725	8.26306	9.132498	9.594867	9.870767
Swaziland (Lilangeni)	20.59096	20.421575	18.895	17.011558	17.009892
Sweden (Krona)	12.771428	11.667417	11.421667	11.012592	11.036758
Switzerland (Franc)	1.467847	1.35263	1.3093	1.263125	1.280883
Syria (Pound)	Not quoted	Not quoted	Not quoted	Not quoted	Not quoted
Taiwan (New T$)	48.42813	44.499375	42.342708	39.182842	39.664508
Tajikistan (Somoni)	Not quoted	Not quoted	Not quoted	Not quoted	Not quoted
Tanzania (Schilling)	3,196.90593	3,009.647958	2,909.941875	2,865.612017	2,959.310350
Thailand (Baht)	52.675466	48.517458	46.692083	43.756075	43.854408
Togo Republic (CFA Franc)	897.121292	814.319917	791.886667	751.841017	746.023517
Tonga Islands (Pa'Anga)	2.048381	1.852649	1.766681	1.6733	1.701108
Trinidad and Tobago (TT$)	9.641411	9.113027	8.867246	8.662525	8.918300

Average for year ending	***31.03.16***	***31.12.16***	***31.03.17***	***31.12.17***	***31.03.18***
Tunisia (Dinar)	2.990621	2.921115	2.901442	3.065167	3.194825
Turkey (Lira)	4.244572	4.076891	4.175619	4.643	4.821650
Turkmenistan (New Manat)	5.229315	4.821745	4.644727	4.493717	4.624408
Uganda (New Schilling)	5,057.432026	4,676.453958	4,556.602917	4,621.574158	4,771.053325
Ukraine (Hryvnia)	34.492042	34.921333	34.161667	33.94875	35.263750
United Arab Emirates (Dirham)	5.545785	5.056488	4.870015	4.7113	4.847200
Uruguay (Peso Uruguayo)	43.36413	41.794083	39.41375	36.797542	37.831708
USA (US$)	1.508298	1.376045	1.327506	1.282692	1.319675
Uzbekistan (Sum)	4,000.185779	4,039.4335	4,029.228958	6,171.072883	7,987.388717
Vanuatu (Vatu)	164.816234	152.664458	146.318125	140.846692	143.826692
Venezuela (Bolivar Fuerte)	9.514275	12.311973	13.1331	12.978875	2,921.778875
Vietnam (Dong)	33,402.43577	30,756.86363	29,726.64333	29,144.08545	29,988.879617
Wallis & Futuna Islands (CFP Franc)	162.612789	148.136792	144.055417	136.771283	135.713783
Western Samoa (Tala)	3.880187	3.509119	3.351075	3.216367	3.300658
Yemen (Republic of) (Rial)	324.63136	329.298792	329.275	320.979883	330.259050
Zambia (Kwacha)	14.447917	14.221917	13.219792	12.184633	12.531300
Zimbabwe (Dollar)	546.427136	498.20875	479.838958	464.202292	477.586458

Rates of exchange on year-end dates

	31.03.16	***31.12.16***	***31.03.17***	***31.12.17***	***31.03.18***
Australia (A$)	1.8684	1.7065	1.6279	1.7295	1.8288
Canada (Can$)	1.8591	1.6571	1.6605	1.6949	1.8086
Denmark (Krone)	9.397	8.7108	8.6547	8.3876	8.5022
European Community (Euro)	1.2613	1.1715	1.1637	1.1266	1.1406
Hong Kong (HK$)	11.14	9.5802	9.7076	10.57	11.00
Japan (Yen)	161.54	144.12	139.03	152.38	149.18
Norway (Krone)	11.88	10.63	10.66	11.06	11.01
South Africa (Rand)	21.13	16.89	16.03	16.74	16.62
Sweden (Krona)	11.65	11.22	11.12	11.07	11.74
Switzerland (Franc)	1.3764	1.2559	1.2444	1.3183	1.3433
USA (US$)	1.4373	1.2357	1.2493	1.3528	1.4028

Note: The material on pp 121–124 is reproduced from information provided by HMRC and is Crown copyright. The rates for 31.3.18 are correct at 11 April 2018.

Double taxation agreements (including protocols and regulations)

Agreements in force covering taxes on income and capital gains

Country	*SI/SR & O*
Albania	**2013/3145**
Algeria	**2015/1888**
Antigua & Barbuda	**1947/2865**
	1968/1096
Argentina	**1997/1777**
Armenia[1]	**2011/2722**
Australia	**2003/3199**
Austria	**1970/1947**
	1979/117
	1994/768
	2010/2688
Azerbaijan[1]	**1995/762**
Bahrain	**2012/3075**
Bangladesh	**1980/708**
Barbados	**2012/3076**
Belarus[1]	**1986/224**
Belgium	**1987/2053**
	2010/2979
Belize	**1947/2866**
	1968/573
	1973/2097
Bolivia	**1995/2707**
Bosnia Herzegovina[2]	**1981/1815**
Botswana	**2006/1925**
British Virgin Islands	**2009/3013**
Brunei	**1950/1977**
	1968/306
	1973/2098
	2013/3146
Bulgaria	**2015/1890**
Canada	**1980/709**
	1980/1528
	1985/1996
	2003/2619
	2014/3274
	2015/2011
Cayman Islands	**2010/2973**
Chile	**2003/3200**
China[4]	**2011/2724**
	2013/3142
Croatia[2]	**2015/1889**
Cyprus	**1975/425**
	1980/1529
Czech Republic[3]	**1991/2876**
Denmark	**1980/1960**
	1991/2877
	1996/3165
Egypt	**1980/1091**
Estonia[1]	**1994/3207**
Ethiopia	**2011/2725**
Falkland Islands	**1997/2985**
Faroes	**2007/3469**
Fiji	**1976/1342**
Finland	**1970/153**
	1973/1327
	1980/710
	1985/1997
	1991/2878
	1996/3166

Country	*SI/SR & O*
France	**2009/226**
Gambia	**1980/1963**
Georgia[1]	**2004/3325**
	2010/2972
Germany	1967/25
	1971/874
	2010/2975[5]
	2014/1874
Ghana	**1993/1800**
Greece	**1954/142**
Grenada	**1949/361**
	1968/1867
Guernsey	**1952/1215**
	1994/3209
	2009/3011
	2015/2008
	2016/750
Guyana	**1992/3207**
Hong Kong	**2010/2974**
Hungary	**2011/2726**
Iceland	**2014/1879**
India	**1993/1801**
	2013/3147
Indonesia	**1994/769**
Irish Republic	**1976/2151**
	1976/2152
	1995/764
	1998/3151
Isle of Man	**1955/1205**
	1991/2880
	1994/3208
	2009/228
	2016/749
Israel	**1963/616**
	1971/391
Italy	**1990/2590**
Ivory Coast	**1987/169**
Jamaica	**1973/1329**
Japan	**2006/1924**
	2014/1881
Jersey	**1952/1216**
	1994/3210
	2009/3012
	2015/2009
	2016/752
Jordan	**2001/3924**
Kazakhstan[1]	**1994/3211**
	1998/2567
Kenya	**1977/1299**
Kiribati (and Tuvalu)	**1950/750**
	1968/309
	1974/1271
Korea (South)	**1996/3168**
Kosovo[2]	**2015/2007**
Kuwait	**1999/2036**
Kyrgyzstan[1]	
Latvia[1]	**1996/3167**
Lesotho	**1997/2986**
Liechtenstein	**2012/3077**

Country	***SI/SR & O***
Libya	**2010/243**
Lithuania[1]	**2001/3925**
	2002/2847
Luxembourg	**1968/1100**
	1980/567
	1984/364
	2010/237
Macedonia[2]	**2007/2127**
Malawi	**1956/619**
	1964/1401
	1968/1101
	1979/302
Malaysia	**1997/2987**
	2010/2971
Malta	**1995/763**
Mauritius	**1981/1121**
	1987/467
	2003/2620
	2011/2442
Mexico	**1994/3212**
	2010/2686
Moldova[1]	**2008/1795**
Mongolia	**1996/2598**
Montenegro[2]	**1981/1815**
Montserrat	**1947/2869**
	1968/576
	2011/1083
Morocco	**1991/2881**
Myanmar (Burma)	**1952/751**
Namibia	**1962/2352**
	1962/2788
	1967/1489
	1967/1490
Netherlands	**2009/227**
	2013/3143
New Zealand	**1984/365**
	2004/1274
	2008/1793
Nigeria	**1987/2057**
Norway	**2013/3144**
Oman	**1998/2568**
	2010/2687
Pakistan	**1987/2058**
Panama	**2013/3149**
Papua New Guinea	**1991/2882**
Philippines	**1978/184**
Poland	**2006/3323**
Portugal	**1969/599**
Qatar	**2010/241**
	2011/1684

Country	***SI/SR & O***
Romania	**1977/57**
Russian Federation[1]	**1994/3213**
St Kitts and Nevis	**1947/2872**
Saudi Arabia	**2008/1770**
Senegal	**2015/1892**
Serbia[2]	**1981/1815**
Sierra Leone	**1947/2873**
	1968/1104
Singapore	**1997/2988**
	2010/2685
	2012/3078
Slovak Republic[3]	**1991/2876**
Slovenia[2]	**2008/1796**
Solomon Islands	**1950/748**
	1968/574
	1974/1270
South Africa	**2002/3138**
	2011/2441
Spain	**2013/3152**
Sri Lanka	**1980/713**
Sudan	**1977/1719**
Swaziland	**1969/380**
Sweden	**2015/1891**
Switzerland	**1978/1408**
	1982/714
	1994/3215
	2007/3465
	2010/2689
	2012/3079
Taiwan	**2002/3137**
Tajikistan[1]	**2014/3275**
Thailand	**1981/1546**
Trinidad and Tobago	**1983/1903**
Tunisia	**1984/133**
Turkey	**1988/932**
Turkmenistan[1]	**2016/1217**
Tuvalu (and Kiribati)	**1950/750**
	1968/309
	1974/1271
Uganda	**1993/1802**
Ukraine	**1993/1803**
Ukraine[1]	**1993/1803**
United Arab Emirates	**2016/754**
Uruguay	**2016/753**
USA	**2002/2848**
Uzbekistan[1]	**1994/770**
Venezuela	**1996/2599**
Vietnam	**1994/3216**
Zambia	**2014/1876**
Zimbabwe	**1982/1842**

1 Following dissolution of the USSR, new agreements are now in force with Armenia, Azerbaijan, Estonia, Georgia, Kazakhstan, Latvia, Lithuania, Moldova, the Russian Federation, Tajikistan, Turkmenistan, Ukraine and Uzbekistan. *SI 1986/224* (former USSR agreement) is treated as continuing to apply to Belarus until coming into force of the agreement signed on 26 September 2017. The UK did not apply the terms of the convention in the case of residents of Tajikistan for profits arising on or after 1 April 2014 (corporation tax) and for income and gains arising on or after 6 April 2014 (income and capital gains tax). The former USSR agreement was similarly treated as continuing to apply by the UK until 31 March 2002 for Armenia, Georgia, Kyrgyzstan, Moldova and Lithuania (none of which considered itself bound by that convention) but as ceasing so to apply after that date (but new treaties now in force with Armenia, Lithuania, Moldova and Georgia). (SP 4/01). A new agreement was signed with Kyrgyzstan on 13 June 2017 but is not yet in force.

2 *SI 1981/1815* (former Yugoslavia agreement) treated as remaining in force between the UK and, respectively, Bosnia-Herzegovina, Croatia and Serbia and Montenegro until superseded by new agreements. (SP 3/04.) The agreement was also treated as applying to Kosovo. New Croatia agreement came into force on 19 November 2015. New Kosovo agreement came into force on 16 December 2015.

3 *SI 1991/2876* (former Czechoslovakia agreement) treated as remaining in force between the UK and, respectively, Czech Republic and Slovak Republic. (SP 5/93.)

4 Hong Kong Special Administrative Region has its own agreement.

5 Treaty replaces 1967/25 with effect from 1 January 2011 or 6 April 2011 depending on type of income. However, where a resident of Germany was, before 30 December 2010, in receipt of a UK pension (including State Pension) or annuity relievable under Article X of prior treaty 1967/25, the individual may elect for the terms of the prior treaty to continue to apply to the pension or annuity.

Tax information exchange agreements in force

Country	*SI*	*Country*	*SI*
Anguilla	**2010/2677**	Isle of Man	**2009/228**
Antigua and Barbuda	**2011/1075**	Jersey	**2009/3012**
Aruba	**2011/2435**	Liberia	**2011/2434**
Bahamas	**2010/2684**	Liechtenstein	**2010/2678**
Belize	**2011/1685**	Macao	**2015/801**
Bermuda	**2008/1789**	Monaco	**2015/804**
British Virgin Islands	**2009/3013**	San Marino	**2011/1688**
Curaçao, Sint Maarten and BES Islands (formerly the Netherlands Antilles)	**2011/2433**	St Christopher and Nevis	**2011/1077**
Dominica	**2011/1686**	St Lucia	**2011/1076**
Gibraltar	**2010/2680**	St Vincent and Grenadines	**2011/1078**
Grenada	**2011/1687**	Turks and Caicos Islands	**2010/2679**
Guernsey	**2009/3011**	Uruguay	**2014/1358**

Tax information exchange agreements signed but not in force

Marshall Islands	Jersey Exchange of Letters[1]	British Virgin Islands Exchange of Letters[1]
Brazil	Guernsey Exchange of Letters[1]	Turks and Caicos Islands Exchange of Letters[1]
Bermuda Exchange of Letters[1]	Gibraltar Exchange of Letters[1]	Anguilla Exchange of Letters[1]

1 These will amend the existing tax information exchange agreements.

Tax information exchange agreements in force — EU savings directives

Country	*SI*	*Country*	*SI*
Aruba	**2005/1458**	Isle of Man	**2005/1263**
British Virgin Islands	**2005/1457**	Jersey	**2005/1261**
Gibraltar	**2006/1453**	Montserrat	**2005/1459**
Guernsey	**2005/1262**	former Netherlands Antilles (now known as Curaçao, Sint Maarten and BES Islands)	**2005/1460**

International agreements in force to improve tax compliance

Isle of Man, Guernsey, Jersey, Gibraltar	**2014/520**
USA	**2015/878**

Agreements in force covering shipping and air transport profits

Country	*SI/SR & O*	*Country*	*SI/SR & O*
Algeria (air)	**2015/1888**	Iran (air)	**1960/2419**
Armenia (USSR air)*	**1974/1269**	Kyrgyzstan (USSR air)*	**1974/1269**
Belarus (USSR air)*	**1974/1269**	Lebanon	**1964/278**
Brazil	**1968/572**	Moldova (USSR air)*	**1974/1269**
Cameroon (air)	**1982/1841**	Saudi Arabia (air)	**1994/767**
China (air)	**1981/1119**	Tajikistan (USSR air)*	**1974/1269**
Congo Democratic Republic	**1977/1298**	Turkmenistan (USSR air)*	**1974/1269**
Ethiopia (air)	**1977/1297**		
Georgia (USSR air)*	**1974/1269**		
Hong Kong (air)	**1998/2566**		
(shipping)	**2000/3248**		

* HMRC have confirmed that this Arrangement will be treated in the same way as the Convention covering income and capital gains (SI 1986/224). See note 1 p 126.

Agreements in force covering estates, inheritances and gifts

France*	**1963/1319**	Pakistan*	**1957/1522**
India*	**1956/998**	South Africa	**1979/576**
Ireland	**1978/1107**	Sweden	**1981/840**
Italy*	**1968/304**		1989/986
Netherlands	**1980/706**	Switzerland	**1994/3214**
	1996/730	USA	**1979/1454**

* Agreements pre-date UK inheritance tax/capital transfer tax.

Overseas income – basis of assessment

SEE TOLLEY'S TAX COMPUTATIONS 23.1.
(ITTOIA 2005 Pt 8; ITEPA 2003 ss 573–576A, 642, 642A; ITA 2007 ss 809A–809Z10)

	Professions, trades, etc	Pensions	Other income
Non-residents	Exempt	Exempt	Exempt
Residents			
(1) **Foreign domicile**[2]	Remittance	Remittance	Remittance
(2) **UK domicile**	Arising	100%[1]	Arising

1 90% arising basis before 6 April 2017. Pensions paid by the governments of the Federal Republic of Germany, Austria, and from 6 April 2016 the Netherlands, to certain victims of WW2 persecution are exempt.

2 Where from 6 April 2008, an individual not domiciled (or, before 6 April 2013, not ordinarily resident) in the UK who has overseas income (or, for non-domiciles only, gains) in excess of £2,000 claims the remittance basis, he will not qualify for personal allowances or the capital gains tax annual exemption. The claim for remittance basis must be made annually. If the individual is not UK domiciled (or before 6 April 2013, not ordinarily resident) in a year and has been resident in the UK for at least seven out of the last nine tax years and has overseas income or gains in excess of £2,000, there is an additional charge of £30,000. From 6 April 2015 this charge is £60,000 for non-domiciles who have been UK resident for at least twelve tax years in the previous fourteen (£50,000 from 6 April 2012 to 5 April 2015), and, before 6 April 2017, £90,000 for non-domiciles who have been UK resident for at least seventeen tax years in the previous twenty. From April 2017 an individual who has been resident in the UK for more than 15 of the last 20 tax years will be deemed UK-domiciled for tax purposes and hence the £90,000 charge will no longer apply. It is also no longer possible for an individual born in the UK to parents who are UK-domiciled to claim non-domicile status if they leave but then return and take up residency in the UK.

3 A statutory residence test is introduced from 6 April 2013 and ordinary residence is abolished from that date, subject to transitional provisions in certain cases for individuals who were resident but not ordinarily resident in the UK at the end of the tax year 2012–13. Before 6 April 2013 UK-domiciled taxpayers who were not ordinarily resident were taxed on the remittance basis.

Employment income liability of non-resident employees see p 92.

Tax-free (FOTRA) securities

(FA 1996 s 154; FA 1998 s 161; ITTOIA 2005 ss 713, 714; CTA 2009 s 1279)

Interest on all government stock is exempt from tax where the beneficial owner is not resident in the UK. Except in the case of 3½% War Loan 1952 or after, the exemption does not apply where the securities are held for the purposes of a trade or business carried on in the UK.

Social security benefits

Taxable state benefits

		Weekly 9.4.18	*Total 2018–19 (52 weeks)*	*Weekly 10.4.17*	*Total 2017–18 (52 weeks)*
		£	£	£	£
Bereavement benefits — deaths before 6 April 2017[1]					
Bereavement allowance: standard rate		**117.10**	**6,089**	113.70	5,912
Widowed parent's allowance		**117.10**	**6,089**	113.70	5,912
Carer's allowance		**64.60**	**3,359**	62.70	3,260
– Adult dependency increase[7]		**38.00**	**1,976**	36.90	1,918
Employment and support allowance[6]					
–under 25		**57.90**	**–**	57.90	–
–25 or over		**73.10**	**–**	73.10	–
Incapacity benefit[6]					
Long-term (after 52 weeks)		**109.60**	**5,699**	106.40	5,532
– Adult dependency increase		**63.65**	**3,309**	61.80	3,213
– Age increase:	higher rate	**11.60**	**603**	11.25	585
	lower rate	**6.45**	**335**	6.25	325
Short term					
– Under pension age: higher rate		**97.85**	**–**	95.00	–
– Adult dependency increase		**49.60**	**–**	48.15	–
– Over pension age: higher rate		**109.60**	**–**	106.40	–
– Adult dependency increase		**61.30**	**–**	59.50	–
Industrial death benefit[2]					
Widow's pension:	higher rate	**125.95**	**6,549**	122.30	6,359
	lower rate	**37.79**	**1,965**	36.69	1,907
Widower's pension		**125.95**	**6,549**	122.30	6,359
Invalidity allowance[3]					
Higher rate		**22.35**	**1,162**	21.70	1,128
Middle rate		**14.40**	**748**	14.00	728
Lower rate		**7.20**	**374**	7.00	364
Jobseeker's allowance[4]					
Single:	under 25	**57.90**	**–**	57.90	–
	25 or over	**73.10**	**–**	73.10	–
Couple:	both under 18	**57.90**	**–**	57.90	–
	both under 18 higher rate	**87.50**	**–**	87.50	–
	one under 18, one under 25	**57.90**	**–**	57.90	–
	one under 18, one 25 or over	**73.10**	**–**	73.10	–
	both 18 or over	**114.85**	**–**	114.85	–
State pension — retired before 6 April 2016					
Single person (Category A or B)		**125.95**	**6,549**	122.30	6,359
Single person (Category B lower) based on spouse's or civil partner's insurance		**75.50**	**3,926**	73.30	3,811
Adult dependency increase[7]		**68.35**	**3,554**	66.35	3,450
Non-contributory pension					
– single (Category C (higher) or Category D)		**75.50**	**3,926**	73.30	3,811
– single (Category C (lower))		**–**	**–**	–	–
Age addition (over 80) (each)		**0.25**	**13**	0.25	13
State pension — retired after 5 April 2016					
Rate		**164.35**	**8,546**	159.55	8,296
Statutory adoption pay					
Rate[5]		**145.18**	**–**	140.98	–
Earnings threshold		**116.00**	**–**	113.00	–
Statutory maternity pay					
Rate[5]		**145.18**	**–**	140.98	–
Earnings threshold		**116.00**	**–**	113.00	–

	Weekly 9.4.18	Total 2018–19 (52 weeks)	Weekly 10.4.17	Total 2017–18 (52 weeks)
	£	£	£	£
Statutory paternity pay				
Rate[5]	**145.18**	–	140.98	–
Earnings threshold	**116.00**	–	113.00	–
Statutory shared parental pay				
Rate[5,10]	**145.18**	–	140.98	–
Earnings threshold	**116.00**	–	113.00	–
Statutory sick pay				
Rate	**92.05**	–	89.35	–
Earnings threshold	**116.00**	–	113.00	–

1 Paid to widows, widowers and the civil partner of the deceased for up to 52 weeks. For deaths on or after 6 April 2017 bereavement support payments replace bereavement benefits and are non-taxable (see p 135).

2 For deaths before 11 April 1988 only.

3 When paid with retirement pensions. See note below on non-taxable benefits on p 134.

4 Where the allowance exceeds the amount shown above, the excess is not taxable.

5 The allowance is 90% of average weekly earnings if less than the above amount. In the first six weeks the rate of SMP and SAP is 90% of average weekly earnings even if higher than the standard rate.

6 Employment and support allowance replaces incapacity benefits for new claimants on or after 27 October 2008. Only contributory employment and support allowance is taxable. Income related allowance is not taxable.

7 Not available to new retirees or new carer's allowance claimants from 6 April 2010. To be withdrawn completely on 5 April 2020.

8 **A cap is placed on the total amount of benefit** that most people aged 16 to 64 can receive. The cap applies to the total amount that the people in a household receive from certain benefits. From 7 November 2016, the cap is £384.62 a week or £442.31 in Greater London for couples (with or without children living with them), and for single parents whose children live with them, and £257.69 a week or £296.35 in Greater London for single adults who do not have children, or whose children do not live with them. See www.gov.uk/benefit-cap/benefit-cap-amounts.

9 **Universal credit** is being phased in gradually from 29 April 2013 and will be completed by 2021. It replaces some of the benefits above. For current rates see table of non-taxable benefits on p 134. See www.gov.uk/universal-credit.

10 Statutory shared parental pay (ShPP) is available for eligible parents (the mother and her partner) whose baby is due on or after 5 April 2015 or where a child is placed for adoption (the parental equivalents are the primary and secondary adopter) on or after the same date.

Non-taxable state benefits

Weekly rates from		9.4.18	10.4.17
		£	£
Attendance allowance			
Higher rate (day and night)		**85.60**	83.10
Lower rate (day or night)		**57.30**	55.65
Child benefit[3]			
Eldest child		**20.70**	20.70
Each subsequent child		**13.70**	13.70
Child dependency addition			
Paid with state pension; widowed mother's/parent's allowance; short-term incapacity benefit - higher rate or over state pension age; long-term incapacity benefit; carer's allowance; severe disablement unemployability supplement		**11.35**	11.35
Disability living allowance[2]			
Care component	higher rate	**85.60**	83.10
	middle rate	**57.30**	55.65
	lower rate	**22.65**	22.00
Mobility component	higher rate	**59.75**	58.00
	lower rate	**22.65**	22.00
Personal independence payment[2]			
Daily living component	enhanced rate	**85.60**	83.10
	standard rate	**57.30**	55.65
Mobility component	enhanced rate	**59.75**	58.00
	standard rate	**22.65**	22.00
Guardian's allowance		**17.20**	16.70
Incapacity benefit (short-term)[1]			
Under pension age – lower rate (first 28 weeks)		**82.65**	80.25
– Adult dependency increase		**49.60**	48.15
Over pension age – lower rate (first 28 weeks)		**105.15**	102.10
– Adult dependency increase		**61.30**	59.50
Maternity allowance (where SMP not available)			
Standard rate		**145.18**	140.98
MA threshold		**30.00**	30.00
Severe disablement allowance[7]			
Basic rate		**77.65**	75.40
Age-related addition	higher rate	**11.60**	11.25
	middle rate	**6.45**	6.25
	lower rate	**6.45**	6.25
– Adult dependency increase		**38.20**	37.10

See next page for universal credit amounts

Amount payable per assessment period[5] in:		2018–19	2017–18
		£	£
Universal credit[5]			
Universal credit amounts			
Standard allowance	single under 25	**251.77**	251.77
	single 25 or over	**317.82**	317.82
	joint claimants both under 25	**395.20**	395.20
	joint claimants either 25 or over	**498.89**	498.89
Child element[6]	first child	**277.08**	277.08
	second/ subsequent child	**231.67**	231.67
Disabled child additions	lower rate addition	**126.11**	126.11
	higher rate addition	**383.86**	372.30
Limited capability for work element		**126.11**	126.11
Limited capability for work and work-related activity element		**328.32**	318.76
Carer element		**156.45**	151.89
Childcare cost element	maximum for one child	**646.35**	646.35
	maximum for two or more children	**1,108.04**	1,108.04
Non-dependants' housing cost contributions		**72.16**	70.06
Work allowances			
Higher work allowance (no housing element)	single, no dependent children	**Nil**	Nil
	single, one or more children	**397.00**	397.00
	single, limited capability for work	**397.00**	397.00
	joint claimant, no dependent children	**Nil**	Nil
	joint claimant, one or more children	**397.00**	397.00
	joint claimant, limited capability for work	**397.00**	397.00
Lower work allowance	single, no dependent children	**Nil**	Nil
	single, one or more children	**192.00**	192.00
	single, limited capability for work	**192.00**	192.00
	joint claimant, no dependent children	**Nil**	Nil
	joint claimant, one or more children	**192.00**	192.00
	joint claimant, limited capability for work	**192.00**	192.00

1 Incapacity benefit replaced invalidity allowance from April 1995. The benefits are taxable except those paid in the first 28 weeks of incapacity and those paid to persons already receiving invalidity benefit on 13 April 1995 so long as they remain incapable of work.

2 Personal Independence Payment (PIP) started to replace Disability Living Allowance (DLA) for new claims by eligible people aged 16 to 64 from 8 April 2013. PIP will be introduced in stages over a number of years for existing DLA claimants.

3 See note on p 77 regarding the income tax charge arising to certain child benefit claimants from 7 January 2013.

4 **A cap is placed on the total amount of benefit** that most people aged 16 to 64 can receive. The cap applies to the total amount that the people in a household receive from certain benefits. From 7 November 2016, the cap is £384.62 a week or £442.31 in Greater London for couples (with or without children living with them), and for single parents whose children live with them, and £257.69 a week or £296.35 in Greater London for single adults who do not have children, or whose children do not live with them. See www.gov.uk/benefit-cap/benefit-cap-amounts.

5 **Universal credit** is being phased in gradually from 29 April 2013 and will be completed by 2021. It replaces some of the benefits listed in the above tables. An assessment period is a calendar month from effective date of claim. See www.gov.uk/universal-credit.

6 The child element of universal credit is no longer awarded for third and subsequent children born after 6 April 2017. This also applies to families claiming universal credit for the first time after April 2017. The restriction does not apply to disabled children and multiple births.

7 Severe disablement allowance has been replaced with employment and support allowance except for those who reached retirement age before 6 April 2014.

***See next page for* Other non-taxable benefits**

	2018–19	2018–19	2017–18	2017–18
Bereavement support payments — deaths on or after 6 April 2017[1]	**First payment**	**Monthly**	**First payment**	**Monthly**
	£	**£**	**£**	**£**
With children under 20 in full-time education	**3,500**	**350**[1]	3,500	350[1]
Without children under 20 in full-time education	**2,500**	**100**[1]	2,500	100[1]

1 Paid to widows, widowers and the civil partner of the deceased. For deaths on or after 6 April 2017 bereavement support payments replace taxable bereavement benefits (see p 131). Monthly payments paid for up to 18 months.

Other non-taxable benefits include:

Bereavement payment (lump sum £2,000)
Back to Work bonus
Child tax credit (see Tax Credits, p 103)
Christmas bonus (with retirement pension)
Cold weather payments
Housing benefit (income related)
Income support (income related)
Industrial injuries disablement pension
Pension credit
Pneumoconiosis, byssinosis and miscellaneous disease benefits
Social fund payments
Vaccine damage (lump sum)
War pensions
Winter fuel payment
Working tax credit (see Tax Credits, p 103)

Stamp taxes

Stamp duty land tax

(FA 2003 Schs 2A–9; FA 2018 ss 40, 41)

Stamp duty land tax applies to contracts entered into (or varied) after 10 July 2003 and completed after 30 November 2003 and to leases granted after that date (FA 2003 ss 55, 56, Sch 5). With effect from 22 July 2004, it also applies to the transfer of an interest in land into, or out of, a partnership and to the acquisition of an interest in a partnership where the partnership property includes an interest in land. With effect from 19 July 2006, it applies to transfers of partnership interests only where the sole or main activity of the partnership is investing or dealing in interests in land. Stamp duty land tax does not apply in Scotland to transactions with an effective date on or after 1 April 2015, from which date Scottish land and buildings transaction tax applies (see table below), subject to transitional provisions in particular in relation to contracts entered into on or before 1 May 2012. The power to raise stamp duty land tax has been devolved to the Welsh Government from April 2018 (see table below), subject to transitional provisions in particular in relation to contracts entered into on or before 17 December 2014.

Land transactions					
	Residential property[5]	***Rate***[3]	***Higher rate applying to certain purchases***[7]	***Non-residential or mixed property***	***Rate***
Effective date	**From 1.4.16**			**From 17.3.16**	
	On band of consideration[2]			On band of consideration[2]	
	Up to £125,000[3]	**Nil**	**3%**	**Up to £150,000**	**Nil**
	£125,001–£250,000[3]	**2%**	**5%**	**£150,001–£250,000**	**2%**
	£250,001–£925,000[3]	**5%**	**8%**	**£250,001 or more**	**5%**
	£925,001–£1,500,000	**10%**	**13%**		
	£1,500,001 or more	**12%**	**15%**		
	On total consideration[1]				
Non-natural persons[1,6]	**£500,001 or more**	**15%**			
Effective date	4.12.14–31.3.16			4.12.14–16.3.16	
	On band of consideration[2]			On total consideration[1]	
	Up to £125,000	Nil		Up to £150,000	Nil
	£125,001–£250,000	2%		£150,001–£250,000	1%
	£250,001–£925,000	5%		£250,001–£500,000	3%
	£925,001–£1,500,000	10%		£500,001 or more	4%
	£1,500,001 or more	12%			
	On total consideration[1]				
Non-natural persons[1,6]	£500,001 or more	15%			
Effective date	20.3.14–3.12.14			20.3.14–3.12.14	
	On total consideration[1]			On total consideration[1]	
	Up to £125,000	Nil		Up to £150,000	Nil
	£125,001–£250,000	1%		£150,001–£250,000	1%
	£250,001–£500,000	3%		£250,001–£500,000	3%
	£500,001–£1,000,000	4%		£500,001 or more	4%
	£1,000,001–£2,000,000	5%			
	£2,000,001 or more	7%			
Non-natural persons[1,6]	£500,001 or more	15%			

Land transactions				
	Residential property[5]	***Rate***	***Non-residential or mixed property***	***Rate***
Effective date	22.3.12–19.3.14		22.3.12–19.3.14	
	On total consideration[1]		On total consideration[1]	
	Up to £125,000	Nil	Up to £150,000	Nil
	£125,001–£250,000	1%	£150,001–£250,000	1%
	£250,001–£500,000	3%	£250,001–£500,000	3%
	£500,001–£1,000,000	4%	£500,001 or more	4%
	£1,000,001–£2,000,000	5%		
	£2,000,001 or more	7%		
Non-natural persons[1,6]	£2,000,001 or more	15%		
Lease rentals	*On net present value of rent over term of lease (applying a discount rate of 3.5%)*[4]			
Effective date	***Residential property***	***Rate***	***Non-residential or mixed property***	***Rate***
From 17.3.16	**Up to £125,000**	**Nil**	**Up to £150,000**	**Nil**
	£125,001 or more	**1%**	**£150,001–£5,000,000**	**1%**
			£5,000,001 or more	**2%**
1.1.10–16.3.16	Up to £125,000	Nil	Up to £150,000	Nil
	£125,001 or more	1%	£150,001 or more	1%
Premiums The same tax is payable for a premium granted as for a land transaction. Special rules applied before 17 March 2016 to a premium in respect of non-residential property where the rent exceeds £1,000 a year. For transactions before 12 March 2008, the rules applied to all property where the rent exceeded £600 a year.				

1 Rates apply to the full consideration, not only to that in excess of the previous band.

2 Rates are charged on the portion of the consideration that falls within each rate band. Where the change from calculations based on total consideration to those based on band of consideration took place for residential property from 4 December 2014, and for non-residential property from 16 March 2016, in certain circumstances the taxpayer could elect for the new rules not to apply.

3 **With effect from 22 November 2017, residential property purchases by first-time buyers will attract a nil rate of SDLT for purchase consideration up to £300,000. Purchase consideration over £300,000 up to and including £500,000 will attract 5% SDLT. Where the purchase consideration is in excess of £500,000, no relief is due and standard rates above apply.**

4 Rates apply to the amount of npv in the slice, not the whole value.

5 With effect from 19 July 2011, where a purchaser (or a connected person) of residential property acquires more than one dwelling from the same vendor (or a connected person) and makes a claim, the rate of SDLT will be calculated based on the mean consideration for each property, subject to a minimum rate of 1%. For leases granted on or after 26 March 2015 relief may be claimed in respect of superior interests in dwellings subject to a long lease, where the transaction is the lease element of a “lease and leaseback” funding arrangement entered into by a housing association or other qualifying body.

6 From 21 March 2012 a 15% rate applies to certain non-natural persons (ie companies, partnerships with at least one company member, and collective investment schemes) acquiring a residential property where consideration exceeds a specified threshold, which is £2,000,000 from 21 March 2012 to 19 March 2014, and £500,000 from 20 March 2014. Relief is available for certain acquisitions so that the charge is at the lower percentage. See p 65 for the annual tax on enveloped dwellings and capital gains tax charge which also apply to such properties.

7 From 1 April 2016 (for contracts exchanged after 25 November 2015) a higher rate applies broadly to purchases of additional residential property by individuals, and to purchases of residential property by companies and trusts other than bare trusts and interest in possession trusts. It does not apply to purchases of property under £40,000 or to purchases of caravans, mobile homes and houseboats. If there is a period of overlap in ownership of a main residence, a refund of the higher rate can be obtained if the previous main residence is sold within 36 months following the purchase of the new. Relief is available in certain circumstances when someone gets divorced, exchanges a property with a spouse, adds to an existing interest in their main residence or is a child whose affairs are subject to the Court of Protection.

Exemptions and reliefs

No SDLT (or, where relevant, stamp duty) is chargeable on:

(1) transfers to charities for use for charitable purposes.
(2) transfers to bodies established for national purposes.
(3) gifts inter vivos.
(4) certain transfers on divorce or dissolution of a civil partnership.

(5) transfers of property to beneficiaries under a will or an intestacy.
(6) land transfers within groups of companies.
(7) land transferred in exchange for shares on company reconstruction and acquisitions.
(8) certain transfers to or leases granted by registered providers of social housing. (Although the relief is repealed for the old stamp duty rules for instruments executed on or after 6 April 2013, it still applies to stamp duty land tax).
(9) sale and leaseback and lease and leaseback arrangements involving commercial and residential property.
(10) certain acquisitions of residential property by house building companies or property traders from personal representatives, or when people move into a new dwelling or a chain of transactions break down, or by employers involving employee relocations.
(11) for transactions with an effective date before 6 April 2013, transfers on sale of residential property for a consideration of up to £150,000 in disadvantaged parts of the UK. This also applied to leases broadly, on rent where the relevant rental value did not exceed £150,000 and to premiums not exceeding £150,000. No claims can be made after 5 May 2014.
(12) from 1 October 2007 until 30 September 2012 for new zero carbon homes (including flats) with a purchase price of up to £500,000, there was no SDLT charged. Where the purchase price was in excess of £500,000, the SDLT liability on the purchase price was reduced by £15,000.
(13) from 22 November 2017 purchases of residential property by first-time buyers for consideration of not more than £500,000 (see p 138).
(14) demutualisation of building societies and insurance companies.
(15) incorporation of limited liability partnerships.
(16) transfers of land between public bodies under a statutory reorganisation.
(17) compulsory purchase of land facilitating redevelopment.
(18) land transactions in compliance with planning obligations enforceable against the vendor and made within five years of the obligation where the purchaser is one of certain public authorities.
(19) transfers by a local constituency association in consequence of a reorganisation of parliamentary constituencies.
(20) purchases or leases of certain diplomatic or consular premises or headquarters premises of certain international organisations.
(21) from 15 September 2016, transfer of properties into an authorised PAIF or CoACS within an initial period if conditions are met.

Relief from SDLT may also apply on:

(a) right to buy transactions, shared ownership leases and rent to loan transactions.
(b) alternative property finance schemes.
(c) exercise of collective rights by leaseholders.
(d) crofting community right to buy.
(e) certain arrangements relating to land transactions involving public or educational bodies.
(f) acquisitions of interests in land by certain National Health Service bodies.

Land and buildings transaction tax (Scotland)

(Land and Buildings Transaction Tax (Scotland) Act 2013; Land and Buildings Transaction Tax (Amendment) (Scotland) Act 2016; SSI 2015/126; SSI 2017/233)

Land and buildings transaction tax applies in Scotland instead of stamp duty land tax from 1 April 2015.

Land transactions				
Effective date	***Residential property***	**Rate**[2, 3]	***Non-residential or mixed property***	**Rate**[2]
	On band of consideration[1]		On band of consideration[1]	
From 1.4.15	**Up to £145,000**[3]	**Nil**	**Up to £150,000**	**Nil**
	£145,001–£250,000	**2%**	**£150,001–£350,000**	**3%**
	£250,001–£325,000	**5%**	**£350,001 or more**	**4.5%**
	£325,001–£750,000	**10%**		
	£750,001 or more	**12%**		
Lease rentals LBTT is applied to non-residential leases. Residential leases are generally exempt from LBTT with the exception of certain long leases which are qualifying leases. Where a lease is chargeable the amount of tax payable is 1% of the amount of net present value of the rent above £150,000. Licences to occupy property are exempt interests, except licences that are of a description prescribed under Land and Buildings Transaction Tax (Scotland) Act 2013 s 53(1).				
Premiums The same tax is payable for a premium granted as for a land transaction, subject to the exemption for residential leases other than qualifying leases (see above). Special rules apply to a premium in respect of non-residential property where the rent exceeds £1,000 a year.				

1 Rates are charged on the portion of the consideration that falls within each rate band.

2 For land transactions with an effective date on or after 1 April 2016, unless missives were concluded before 28 January 2016, an additional amount of tax equal to 3% of the relevant consideration applies broadly to transactions which consist of or include the acquisition of an additional dwelling by individuals and trusts over which the beneficiary has substantial rights, and to purchases of a dwelling by certain businesses, companies and other trusts. It does not apply to purchases of property under £40,000. If there is a period of overlap in ownership of a main residence, a refund of the higher rate can be obtained if the previous main residence is sold within 18 months following the purchase of the new. From 30 June 2017 relief is available in certain circumstances when two buyers jointly buy a new dwelling and previously lived together as a married couple, civil partners or cohabitants in a dwelling owned by either one of them solely.

3 **A new relief for first-time buyers is proposed to be in place by June 2018 which increases the nil rate band from the current level of £145,000 to £175,000**.

Exemptions and reliefs

There are various exemptions and reliefs from LBTT, all of which currently apply to SDLT (see p 138).

Land transaction tax (Wales)

(Land Transaction Tax and Anti-avoidance of Devolved Taxes (Wales) Act 2017; SI 2017/953; SI 2018/126)

Land transaction tax applies in Wales instead of stamp duty land tax from 1 April 2018.

Land transactions					
Effective date	***Residential property***	**Rate**	***Higher rate applying to certain purchases***[2]	***Non-residential or mixed property***	**Rate**
	On band of consideration[1]			On band of consideration[1]	
From 1.4.18	**Up to £180,000**	**Nil**	**3%**	**Up to £150,000**	**Nil**
	£180,001–£250,000	**3.5%**	**6.5%**	**£150,001–£250,000**	**1%**
	£250,001–£400,000	**5%**	**8%**	**£250,001–£1,000,000**	**5%**
	£400,001–£750,000	**7.5%**	**10.5%**	**£1,000,001 or more**	**6%**
	£750,001–£1,500,000	**10%**	**13%**		
	£1,500,001 or more	**12%**	**15%**		

Lease rentals LTT is applied to non-residential leases and the amount of tax payable is 1% of the amount of net present value of the rent between £150,000 and £2m, and 2% above £2m.	
Premiums The same tax is payable for a premium granted as for a land transaction. Special rules apply to a premium in respect of non-residential property where the rent exceeds £9,000 a year.	

1 Rates are charged on the portion of the consideration that falls within each rate band.

2 A higher rate applies broadly to purchases of additional residential property by individuals, and to purchases of residential property by companies and trusts other than bare trusts and interest in possession trusts. It does not apply to purchases of property under £40,000. If there is a period of overlap in ownership of a main residence, a refund of the higher rate can be obtained if the previous main residence is sold within 36 months following the purchase of the new. Relief is also available where immediately before the purchase the buyer's spouse or civil partner owns a major interest in the same dwelling and that dwelling will be the buyer's only or main residence immediately before and after the purchase.

Exemptions and reliefs

There are various exemptions and reliefs from LTT, all of which currently apply to SDLT (see p 139).

Stamp duty

(FA 1986 Part III; FA 1999 Sch 13)

For contracts entered into (or varied) after 10 July 2003 and completed after 30 November 2003 and for leases granted after that date, stamp duty is abolished for all transfers other than stocks and marketable securities, and interests in partnerships. From 22 July 2004 stamp duty is also abolished for certain partnership transactions involving an interest in land. From those dates, transfers of land are subject to stamp duty land tax (see p 137).

Shares, etc	
Shares put into depository receipts or put into duty free clearance systems[5]	1.5%
Purchase of own shares by company	0.5%
Transfers of stock or marketable securities	0.5%
Takeovers, mergers, demergers, schemes of reconstruction and amalgamation (except where no real change of ownership)	0.5%

1 Stamp duty is rounded to the next multiple of £5.

2 For instruments executed after 11 March 2008 stamp duty is not chargeable where the amount or value of the consideration is less than £1,000.

3 From April 2014 transfers of interests in exchange traded funds will be exempt from stamp duty and stamp duty reserve tax.

4 From 28 April 2014 no stamp duty or stamp duty reserve tax is due on trades in 'recognised growth markets' such as the Alternative Investment Market and the ISDX Growth Market.

5 For options entered into on or after 25 November 2015 and exercised on or after 16 March 2016, where UK securities are deposited with a depositary receipt issuer or clearance service following the exercise of an option, the transfer will be chargeable to stamp duty or stamp duty reserve tax (SDRT) at 1.5% of the higher of the market value or the option strike price at the date the instrument is executed (for stamp duty) or the date of transfer (for SDRT).

Fixed duties

Instruments affecting land transactions	£5

From 13 March 2008 fixed duties are generally abolished other than as above. The £5 rate applies to instruments effected from 1 October 1999.

Stamp Duty Reserve Tax (SDRT)

(FA 1986 Part IV)

Agreements to transfer chargeable securities for money or money's worth (eg renounceable letters of allotment)[1]	0.5%
Chargeable securities put into a clearance service[2] or converted into depositary receipts where the transfer is not an integral part of an issue of share capital[4,7]	1.5%
Dealings of units in unit trusts and shares in open-ended investment companies before 30 March 2014[3]	0.5%
Transfers of foreign currency bearer shares and agreements to transfer sterling or foreign currency convertible or equity-related loan stock issued by UK companies	0.5%

1 If the transaction is completed by a duly stamped instrument within six years from the date on which the charge is imposed, the SDRT will be cancelled or repaid.

2 Where the operator of a clearance service elects to collect and account for SDRT on the normal rate of 0.5% on dealing within the system the higher SDRT charge of 1.5% does not apply.

3 From 6 April 2001 transfers of units in a unit trust and surrenders of shares in open-ended investment companies are exempt when held within individual pension accounts. From 30 March 2014 the exemption applies to all transfers of units in a unit trust and all surrenders of shares in open-ended investment companies, although the charge will remain on non pro-rata in specie redemptions.

4 Following the cases of HSBC Holdings plc and the Bank of New York Mellon Corporation v HMRC and HSBC Holdings plc and Vidacos Nominees Limited v Commissioners for HMRC, SDRT of 1.5% is no longer applicable on issues of UK shares to depositary receipt issuers and clearance services. Claims for repayment of SDRT may be made.

5 From April 2014 transfers of interests in exchange traded funds will be exempt from stamp duty and stamp duty reserve tax.

6 From 28 April 2014 no stamp duty or stamp duty reserve tax is due on trades in 'recognised growth markets' such as the Alternative Investment Market and the ISDX Growth Market.

7 For options entered into on or after 25 November 2015 and exercised on or after 16 March 2016, where UK securities are deposited with a depositary receipt issuer or clearance service following the exercise of an option, the transfer will be chargeable to stamp duty or stamp duty reserve tax (SDRT) at 1.5% of the higher of the market value or the option strike price at the date the instrument is executed (for stamp duty) or the date of transfer (for SDRT).

Interest on unpaid tax

Stamp duty land tax. *From 26 September 2005*: Interest runs from the end of 30 days after the effective date of transaction (normally completion), or the date of a disqualifying event, until the tax is paid. In the case of a deferred payment, interest runs from the date the payment is due until the tax is paid. A penalty carries interest from the date determined until the date of payment. There are proposals to reduce the payment window to 14 days for transactions on or after 1 March 2019.

Stamp duty. *For instruments executed from 1 October 1999*: Interest runs from the end of 30 days after the date the instrument is executed until the tax is paid. Amounts less than £25 are not charged.

Stamp duty reserve tax. *From 1 January 2015*: The harmonised interest regime applies, see p 4.

Before 1 January 2015: Interest was charged from 14 days after the transaction date for exchange transactions and otherwise from seven days after the end of the month of the transaction. Amounts less than £25 were not charged.

Rates: see pp 4, 5.

Land and buildings transaction tax. *From 1 April 2015*: Interest runs broadly from the filing date of the return and is charged at the same rate as under the harmonised interest regime but paid to Revenue Scotland — see p 4.

Land transaction tax (Wales). *From 1 April 2018*: Interest runs broadly from the filing date of the return and is charged at the same rate as under the harmonised interest regime but paid to the Welsh Revenue Authority — see p 4.

Repayment supplement / Interest on overpaid tax

Stamp duty land tax. *From 26 September 2005*: Interest is added to repayments of overpaid stamp duty land tax and runs from the date tax was paid or an amount was lodged with HMRC, or the date a penalty was made, to the date the order for repayment is issued.

Stamp duty. *For instruments executed from 1 October 1999*: Interest is added to repayments of overpaid stamp duty and runs from 30 days after the date the instrument is executed or the date of payment if later. Amounts less than £25 are not paid.

Stamp duty reserve tax. *From 1 January 2015*: The harmonised interest regime applies, see p 4.

Before 1 January 2015: Interest was paid from the date the tax was paid to the date the order for repayment was issued.

Rates: see pp 4, 5.

Land and buildings transaction tax. *From 1 April 2015*: Interest runs from the date the tax, penalty or interest was paid or an amount was lodged with Revenue Scotland, to the date repayment is made. It is paid at the same rate as under the harmonised interest regime but by Revenue Scotland — see p 4.

Land transaction tax (Wales). *From 1 April 2018*: Interest runs from the date the tax, penalty or interest was paid, to the date repayment is made. It is paid at the same rate as under the harmonised interest regime but by the Welsh Revenue Authority — see p 4.

Stamp tax penalties

Offence	*Penalty*
Stamp duty land tax and stamp duty reserve tax	
Inaccuracy in return or other document (FA 2007 Sch 24).	See **Penalties — modernised penalty regime** on p 9
Inaccuracy in return or other document as a result of third party providing incorrect (or withholding) information (FA 2007 Sch 24).	See **Penalties — modernised penalty regime** on p 9
Failure to notify HMRC of an error in an assessment (within 30 days) (FA 2007 Sch 24).	See **Penalties — modernised penalty regime** on p 10
Failure to comply with HMRC investigatory powers with effect from 1 April 2010 (FA 2008 Sch 36).	(*a*) Initial penalty of £300; (*b*) if failure/obstruction continues, a further penalty of up to £60 per day; (*c*) if failure/obstruction continues after penalty under (*a*) imposed, a tax-related amount determined by the Upper Tribunal.
Provision of inaccurate information or document when complying with an information notice with effect from 1 April 2010 (FA 2008 Sch 36).	Up to £3,000 per inaccuracy.
Stamp duty reserve tax – for charges due and payable from 1 January 2015	
Failure to make returns on time (FA 2009 Sch 55)	See **Penalties — modernised penalty regime** on p 11
Failure to make payments on time (FA 2009 Sch 56)	See **Penalties — modernised penalty regime** on p 11
Stamp duty – for instruments executed from 1 October 1999	
Failure to present instrument for stamping within 30 days after execution (or the day in which it is first received in the UK if executed outside the UK) (Stamp Act 1891 s 15B; SI 1999/2537). (Extended to instruments executed from 24 July 2002 for transfers of UK land and buildings, wherever executed (FA 2002 s 114)). From 1 October 2014 HMRC guidance to penalty amounts applies.	Documents submitted late for stamping **on or after 1 October 2014**: If presented within one year after the end of the 30-day period: 10% of the unpaid duty capped at £300. If presented more than one year after the end of the 30-day period but not more than two years after: 20% of the amount of unpaid duty. If presented more than two years after the end of the 30-day period: 30% of the unpaid duty. For delays of one year or more, penalty rate may be higher if there is evidence that the failure to submit documents was deliberate. Before 1 October 2014: If presented within one year after the end of the 30-day period: the lower of £300 or the amount of the unpaid duty. If presented more than one year after the end of the 30-day period: the greater of £300 or the amount of unpaid duty.
Stamp duty land tax – contracts completed after 30 November 2003	
Failure to deliver a land transaction return by the filing date (FA 2003 Sch 10 paras 3, 4).	£100 if return delivered within three months of filing date, otherwise £200. If not delivered within 12 months, penalty up to amount of tax chargeable.
Failure to comply with notice to deliver return within specified period (FA 2003 Sch 10 para 5).	Up to £60 for each day on which the failure continues after notification.
Failure to keep and preserve records under FA 2003 Sch 10 para 9 or Sch 11 para 4 (FA 2003 Sch 10 para 11, Sch 11 para 6).	Up to £3,000 unless the information is provided by other documentary evidence.
Failure (From 1 August 2005) to disclose certain SDLT proposals or arrangements (TMA 1970 s 98C; SI 2005/1868; SI 2005/1869; SI 2010/2743).	(*a*) Up to £600 per day during 'initial period' (but tribunal can determine a higher penalty up to £1 million); (*b*) further penalty up to £600 per day while failure continues. Both the initial penalty in (*a*) above and the secondary penalty in (*b*) above can be increased up to £5,000 per day that failure continues from 10 days after the order is made.
Failure (From 1 August 2005) to provide prescribed information relating to disclosure certain SDLT proposals or arrangements (TMA 1970 s 98C; SI 2005/1868; SI 2005/1869; SI 2010/2743).	(*a*) Initial penalty up to £5,000; (*b*) further penalty up to £600 per day while failure continues. This can be increased up to £5,000 per day after a tribunal has issued a disclosure order.

Offence	*Penalty*
Failure (From 1 August 2005) to provide scheme reference number relating to certain SDLT proposals or arrangements (TMA 1970 s 98C; SI 2005/1868; SI 2005/1869; SI 2010/2743);	(*a*) Penalty of £100 in respect of each scheme to which the failure relates;
for second failure, occurring within three years from the date on which the first failure began;	(*b*) penalty of £500 in respect of each scheme to which the failure relates;
for subsequent failures, occurring within three years from the date on which the previous failure began.	(*c*) penalty of £1,000 in respect of each scheme to which the failure relates.
Land and buildings transaction tax (Scotland) from 1 April 2015	
Inaccuracy in return or document (RSTPA 2014 ss 182, 183)	Careless inaccuracy — maximum 30% of tax lost Deliberate inaccuracy — maximum 100% of tax lost
Failure to make returns on time (RSTPA 2014 ss 160–163)	The penalty rates applying are as for stamp duty reserve tax **Penalties — modernised penalty regime** on p 11, though reductions for disclosure differ. Penalties are payable to Revenue Scotland.
Failure to make payments on time (RSTPA 2014 s 169)	The penalty rates applying are as for stamp duty reserve tax **Penalties — modernised penalty regime** on p 12, though for some types of payment penalty is due as soon as tax is late. Penalties are payable to Revenue Scotland.
Land transaction tax (Wales) from 1 April 2018	
Inaccuracy in return or document (TCMWA 2016 s 130)	Careless inaccuracy — 30% of tax lost Deliberate inaccuracy — 100% of tax lost
Failure to make returns on time (TCMWA 2016 ss 118–121)	Initial penalty £100 Failure continues for more than 6 months — greater of 5% of the tax due and £300 12 months late and return deliberately withheld — greater of £300 or up to 95% of tax due 12 months late and return not deliberately withheld — greater of 5% of the tax due and £300 Reductions for disclosure Penalties are payable to the Welsh Revenue Authority.
Failure to make payments on time (TCMWA 2016 s 122)	5% of unpaid tax Further 5% of any outstanding amount 6 months after return filing date Further 5% of any outstanding amount 12 months after return filing date Reductions for disclosure Penalties are payable to the Welsh Revenue Authority.
Stamp duty reserve tax replaced provisions	
Failure to notify HMRC and pay tax (TMA 1970 s 93, SI 1986/1711 as applied in practice by HMRC; see under 'Penalties and appeals —stamp duty reserve tax' on HMRC website).	*If notified within one year of the payment deadline: the lower of £100 or the amount of the unpaid duty.* *If notified more than one year after the payment deadline: £100 plus up to the amount of unpaid duty, subject to a reduction for mitigating factors* ***Replaced by penalties under FA 2009 Schs 55 and 56 from 1 January 2015***.

Value added tax

Value added tax rates

(VATA 1994 s 2)

	From 4.1.11	
	Rate	*VAT fraction*
Standard rate	**20%**	**1/6**
Reduced rate (see p 150)	**5.0%**	**1/21**
Flat-rate scheme for farmers	**4.0%**[1]	

1 Flat rate addition to sale price.
2 From April 2019 it is proposed that an assignment of a percentage of VAT receipts attributable to Scotland will be made to the Scottish Parliament.

Registration limits

UK taxable supplies

(VATA 1994 Sch 1 para 1, Sch 1A para 1; SI 2017/290)

A person who is UK-established (from 1 December 2012[3], previously both UK and non-UK established persons) and makes taxable supplies is liable to be registered:

(a) at the end of any month, or
(b) at any time, if:

	(a) turnover in the past year[1] *(b) turnover in the next 30 days*[2] *exceeds:*	*Unless, in the case of (a), turnover for next year not expected to exceed:*
1.4.17 onwards[4]	**£85,000**	**£83,000**
1.4.16–31.3.17	£83,000	£81,000
1.4.15–31.3.16	£82,000	£80,000
1.4.14–31.3.15	£81,000	£79,000
1.4.13–31.3.14	£79,000	£77,000
1.4.12–31.3.13	£77,000	£75,000

1 The value of taxable supplies in the year then ending.
2 If there are reasonable grounds for believing the value of taxable supplies will exceed limit.
3 For supplies made on or after 1 December 2012 non-UK established businesses are required to register for VAT regardless of the value of taxable supplies made in the UK.
4 The VAT limit will be unchanged before 1 April 2020.

Supplies from other EC countries ('distance selling')

(VATA 1994 Sch 2)

A business person in another EC country not registered or liable to be registered in the UK is liable to be registered on any day if, in the period beginning with 1 January in that year, the value of supplies by that person to non-taxable persons in the UK exceeds:

1.1.93 onwards	**£70,000**

Acquisitions from other EC countries

(VATA 1994 Sch 3; SI 2017/290)

A person not registered or liable to be registered under the above rules is liable to be registered:

(a) at the end of any month if, in the period beginning with 1 January in that year, the value of taxable goods acquired by that person for business purposes (or for non-business purposes if a public body, charity, club, etc) from suppliers in other EC countries exceeds the following limits; or

(b) at any time, if there are reasonable grounds for believing the value of such acquisitions in the next 30 days will exceed the following limits:

1.4.17 onwards[1]	**£85,000**
1.4.16–31.3.17	£83,000
1.4.15–31.3.16	£82,000
1.4.14–31.3.15	£81,000
1.4.13–31.3.14	£79,000
1.4.12–31.3.13	£77,000

1 The VAT limit will be unchanged before 1 April 2020.

Deregistration limits

UK taxable supplies

(VATA 1994 Sch 1 para 4; SI 2017/290)

A registered taxable person who is UK-established (from 1 December 2012[1], previously both UK and non-UK established persons) ceases to be liable to be registered if, at any time, HMRC are satisfied that the value of taxable supplies in the year then beginning will not exceed:

1.4.17 onwards[2]	**£83,000**
1.4.16–31.3.17	£81,000
1.4.15–31.3.16	£80,000
1.4.14–31.3.15	£79,000
1.4.13–31.3.14	£77,000
1.4.12–31.3.13	£75,000
Unless the reason for not exceeding the limit during that year is that the person will cease making taxable supplies or suspend making taxable supplies for 30 days or more.	

1 For supplies made on or after 1 December 2012 non-UK established businesses are required to register for VAT regardless of the value of taxable supplies made in the UK.

2 The VAT limit will be unchanged before 1 April 2020.

Supplies from other EC countries ('distance selling')

(VATA 1994 Sch 2)

A person registered under these provisions ceases to be liable to be registered if, at any time:

(a) relevant supplies in year ended 31 December last before that time did not exceed following limit; and

(b) HMRC are satisfied that value of relevant supplies in year immediately following that year will not exceed following limit:

1.1.93 onwards	**£70,000**

Acquisitions from other EC countries

(VATA 1994 Sch 3; SI 2017/290)

A person registered under these provisions ceases to be liable to be registered if, at any time:

(a) relevant acquisitions in year ended 31 December last before that time did not exceed the following limits; and

(b) HMRC are satisfied that value of relevant acquisitions in year immediately following that year will not exceed the following limits:

1.4.17 onwards[1]	**£85,000**
1.4.16–31.3.17	£83,000
1.4.15–31.3.16	£82,000
1.4.14–31.3.15	£81,000
1.4.13–31.3.14	£79,000
1.4.12–31.3.13	£77,000

1 The VAT limit will be unchanged before 1 April 2020.

Annual accounting scheme

(SI 1995/2518 regs 49–55)

A business may, subject to conditions, complete one VAT return a year. Quarterly or monthly interim payments to be made.

	Can join if taxable supplies in next year not expected to exceed:	*Must leave at end of accounting year if taxable supplies exceeded:*
1.4.06 onwards	**£1,350,000**	**£1,600,000**

Cash accounting scheme

(SI 1995/2518 regs 56–65)

A business may, subject to conditions, account for and pay VAT on the basis of cash paid and received. It can join the scheme at any time as follows.

	Can join if taxable supplies in next year not expected to exceed:	*Must leave at end of VAT period if taxable supplies in previous year exceed:*	*Unless turnover for next year not expected to exceed:*
1.4.07 onwards	**£1,350,000**	**£1,600,000**	**£1,350,000**

Flat-rate scheme for small businesses

(SI 1995/2518 regs 55A–55V; SI 2017/295)

A business which expects its taxable supplies in the next year to be no more than £150,000 can opt to join a flat-rate scheme. The appropriate percentage below is applied to total turnover generated, including exempt income, to calculate net VAT due. Once in the scheme a business may continue to use it until its total business income exceeds £230,000, and if income does exceed this limit, the business can still remain in the scheme if the income in the following year is estimated not to exceed £191,500.

From 1 April 2017 a 16.5% rate applies to a 'limited cost trader', that is a trader whose VAT-inclusive expenditure on goods used for business purposes (excluding capital expenditure, food and drink for consumption by the business or its employees, and certain vehicles, vehicle parts and fuel) is less than 2% of turnover, or greater than 2% of turnover but less than £1,000 per year. Any trader which is not a limited cost trader continues to use the flat rate based on the categories of business detailed below.

Category of business	*Appropriate %*
	From 4.1.11
Accountancy or book-keeping	**14.5**
Advertising	**11**
Agricultural services	**11**
Any other activity not listed elsewhere	**12**
Architect, civil and structural engineer or surveyor	**14.5**
Boarding or care of animals	**12**
Business services that are not listed elsewhere	**12**
Catering services, including restaurants and takeaways	**12.5**
Civil and structural engineer or surveyor	**14.5**
Computer and IT consultancy or data processing	**14.5**
Computer repair services	**10.5**
Entertainment or journalism	**12.5**
Estate agency and property management services	**12**
Farming or agriculture that is not listed elsewhere	**6.5**
Film, radio, television or video production	**13**
Financial services	**13.5**
Forestry or fishing	**10.5**
General building or construction services[1]	**9.5**
Hairdressing or other beauty treatment services	**13**
Hiring or renting goods	**9.5**
Hotel or accommodation	**10.5**
Investigation or security	**12**
Labour-only building or construction services[1]	**14.5**
Laundry or dry-cleaning services	**12**
Lawyer or legal services	**14.5**
Library, archive, museum or other cultural activity	**9.5**
Management consultancy	**14**
Manufacturing fabricated metal products	**10.5**
Manufacturing food	**9**
Manufacturing that is not listed elsewhere	**9.5**

Category of business	*Appropriate %*
	From 4.1.11
Manufacturing yarn, textiles or clothing	**9**
Membership organisation	**8**
Mining or quarrying	**10**
Packaging	**9**
Photography	**11**
Post Offices	**5**
Printing	**8.5**
Publishing	**11**
Pubs	**6.5**
Real estate activity not listed elsewhere	**14**
Repairing personal or household goods	**10**
Repairing vehicles	**8.5**
Retailing food, confectionery, tobacco, newspapers or children's clothing	**4**
Retailing pharmaceuticals, medical goods, cosmetics or toiletries	**8**
Retailing that is not listed elsewhere	**7.5**
Retailing vehicles or fuel	**6.5**
Secretarial services	**13**
Social work	**11**
Sport or recreation	**8.5**
Transport or storage, couriers, freight, removals and taxis	**10**
Travel agency	**10.5**
Veterinary medicine	**11**
Wholesaling agricultural products	**8**
Wholesaling food	**7.5**
Wholesaling that is not listed elsewhere	**8.5**

1 That is, services where value of materials supplied is less than 10% of turnover of such services; any other services are 'general building or construction services'.

Partial exemption

See Tolley's Tax Computations 408.1, 408.2.

(SI 1995/2518 regs 106–107)

A registered person who makes taxable and exempt supplies is partly exempt and may not be able to deduct (or reclaim) all his input tax. Where, however, input tax attributable to exempt supplies in a prescribed accounting period or tax year is within the de minimis limits below, all such input tax is attributable to taxable supplies and recoverable (subject to the normal rules).

De minimis limits	£625 per month on average and 50% of all input tax for the period concerned

Capital goods scheme

SEE TOLLEY'S TAX COMPUTATIONS 402.1.

(SI 1995/2518 regs 112–116)

Input tax adjustment following change in taxable use of capital goods

Item	*Value*	*Adjustment period*
Computer equipment	£50,000 or more	Five years
Ships, boats or other vessels[1]	£50,000 or more	Five years
Aircraft[1]	£50,000 or more	Five years
Land and buildings	£250,000 or more[2]	Ten years (for adjustment periods commenced before 1 January 2011, five years where interest had less than ten years to run on acquisition)

1 Applies for goods acquired on or after 1 January 2011.

2 Figure reduced to £1 where owner ('O') of item or a person to whom O has granted an interest in that item:
(a) uses that item to make a grant falling within VATA 1994 Sch 9 Group 1 Item 1(ka) (self-storage facilities excluded from exemption);
(b) decides, no later than 31 March 2013, to treat the item as a capital item; and
(c) makes a written record to that effect, specifying the date of the decision.

Adjustment formula where adjustment period begins on or after 1 January 2011

$$\frac{\text{Total VAT on item}}{\text{Length of adjustment period}} \times \text{adjustment percentage}$$

The adjustment percentage is the percentage change in the extent to which the item is used (or treated as used) in making taxable supplies between the first interval in the adjustment period & a subsequent interval. (The first interval generally ends on the last day of the tax year in which the input tax was incurred.) For goods acquired on or after 1.1.11 total VAT includes any non-business VAT & the extent to which a capital item is used for business purposes must be determined when ascertaining taxable use for each subsequent interval.

Zero-rated supplies

A zero-rated supply is a taxable supply, but the rate of tax is nil (VATA 1994 Sch 8).

Group 1 – Food
Group 2 – Sewerage services and water
Group 3 – Books etc
Group 4 – Talking books for the blind and disabled and wireless sets for the blind
Group 5 – Construction of buildings etc
Group 6 – Protected buildings
Group 7 – International services
Group 8 – Transport
Group 9 – Caravans and houseboats
Group 10 – Gold
Group 11 – Bank notes
Group 12 – Drugs, medicines, aids for the disabled etc
Group 13 – Imports, exports etc
Group 15 – Charities etc
Group 16 – Clothing and footwear
Group 18 – European Research Infrastructure Consortia (from 1 January 2013)
Group 19 – Women's sanitary products (from a date to be appointed)

Reduced rate supplies

(VATA 1994 Sch 7A)

Group 1 – Domestic fuel and power
Group 2 – Installation of energy-saving materials
Group 3 – Grant-funded installation of heating equipment or security goods or connection of a gas supply
Group 4 – Women's sanitary products (to be reduced to zero-rated from a date to be appointed)
Group 5 – Children's car seats and bases
Group 6 – Residential conversions
Group 7 – Residential renovations and alterations
Group 8 – Contraceptive products (from 1 July 2006)
Group 9 – Welfare advice or information (from 1 July 2006)
Group 10 – Installation of mobility aids for the elderly (from 1 July 2007)
Group 11 – Smoking cessation products (from 1 July 2007)
Group 12 – Caravans (from 6 April 2013)
Group 13 – Cable-suspended transport systems (from 1 April 2013)

Exempt supplies

(VATA 1994 Sch 9)

Group 1 – Land

Group 2 – Insurance

Group 3 – Postal services

Group 4 – Betting, gaming, dutiable machine games and lotteries

Group 5 – Finance

Group 6 – Education

Group 7 – Health and welfare

Group 8 – Burial and cremation

Group 9 – Subscriptions to trade unions, professional and other public interest bodies

Group 10 – Sport, sports competitions and physical education

Group 11 – Works of art etc

Group 12 – Fund-raising events by charities and other qualifying bodies

Group 13 – Cultural services etc

Group 14 – Supplies of goods where input tax cannot be recovered

Group 15 – Investment gold

Group 16 – Supplies of services by groups involving cost sharing (from 17 July 2012)

EC Sales Lists

(SI 1995/2518 regs 2, 21–23)

All VAT-registered businesses in the UK must provide HMRC with details of goods and services supplied to a VAT-registered customer in another EU country. The requirement for returns is as follows:

Supplies of		Frequency
Goods	Supplies of goods are in excess of £35,000 (£70,000 before 1 January 2012) in any of the current or last four quarters	Monthly
Goods	Supplies of goods are below £35,000 (£70,000 before 1 January 2012) per quarter in the current and previous four quarters	Quarterly on 31 March, 30 June, 30 September and 31 December
Services supplied to a business where the place of supply is where the customer belongs		Quarterly as above
Goods and services where a business is required to submit monthly lists for goods		Monthly for all supplies, or monthly for goods and quarterly for services
Goods or services supplied by a business completing annual VAT returns	Total annual taxable turnover does not exceed £145,000; annual value of supplies to other EU countries not more than £11,000 (and do not include *New Means of Transport*)	On application — annual on agreed due date
Goods only supplied	Total annual taxable turnover does not exceed the VAT registration threshold plus £25,500; annual value of supplies to other EU countries not more than £11,000 (and do not include *New Means of Transport*)	On application — annual in simple format on agreed due date

The due date for returns is 21 days after the end of the period if submitted online and 14 days after the end of the period if submitted on paper.

Country	Code
Austria[10]	AT
Belgium	BE
Bulgaria	BG
Croatia[13]	HR
Cyprus[9]	CY
Czech Republic	CZ
Denmark[2]	DK
Estonia	EE
Finland[3]	FI
France[4]	FR
Germany[5]	DE
Greece[11]	EL
Hungary	HU
Ireland	IE
Italy[6]	IT
Latvia	LV
Lithuania	LT
Luxembourg	LU
Malta	MT
Netherlands[12]	NL
Poland	PL
Portugal[7]	PT
Romania	RO
Slovak Republic	SK
Slovenia	SI
Spain[8]	ES
Sweden	SE

1 Countries not listed in the table above are not part of the EU VAT area and so sales to those countries should not be included on the EC sales list. The following are not part of the EU VAT area; Andorra, The Channel Islands, Gibraltar, Mount Athos, San Marino, and Vatican City. The UK and the Isle of Man are part of the EU VAT area, but sales to these should not be included on the list.

2 Does not include the Faroe Islands and Greenland.

3 Does not include Aland Islands.

4 Includes Monaco; excludes Martinique, Guadeloupe, Reunion, St Pierre & Miquelon, and French Guiana.

5 Does not include Busingen and Isle of Heligoland.
6 Does not include communes of Livigno and Campione d'Italia and the Italian waters of Lake Lugano.
7 Includes the Azores and Madeira.
8 Includes the Balearic Islands but excludes Ceuta, Melilla, and the Canary Islands.
9 Includes British sovereign base areas of Akrotiri and Dhekelia, but excludes those areas in United Nations buffer zone and to the north of that where the Republic of Cyprus does not have effective control.
10 Includes Jungholz and Mittelberg.
11 Excludes Mount Athos.
12 Excludes Antilles (now Curaçao, Sint Maarten and BES Islands).
13 Croatia joined the EU on 1 July 2013. Supplies of goods, or services subject to the reverse charge, to a VAT registered customer in Croatia, must be included in the ESL.

Intrastat

(SI 1992/2790)

All VAT-registered businesses in the UK must complete boxes 8 and 9 on the VAT return showing the total value of goods supplied to and acquired from other EC member states respectively. Businesses with a total value of such supplies (dispatches) or acquisitions (arrivals) exceeding a threshold must make supplementary declarations containing further information each month. Thresholds are set for each calendar year and recent thresholds are shown below. If a person's dispatches or arrivals in the previous calendar year exceeded the current year's threshold, supplementary declarations must be made for the full current year. If the cumulative total of dispatches or arrivals in a year exceeds that calendar year's threshold, supplementary declarations must be made for the rest of the year, starting in the month in which the threshold is exceeded. Additional delivery terms information must be provided on the supplementary declaration only if the annual value of arrivals or dispatches exceeds the delivery terms threshold, and the information must be submitted from the start of the next calendar year. If the delivery terms threshold for arrivals is exceeded, but not that for dispatches, delivery terms must be provided for arrivals only, and vice versa. From April 2012 declarations must be submitted electronically and will be due 21 days after the end of the month in which there is EU trade to declare.

Year	**Supplies (dispatches) threshold per calendar year**	**Acquisitions (arrivals) threshold per calendar year**	**Delivery terms threshold per calendar year**
From 1.1.15	**£250,000**	**£1,500,000**	**£24,000,000**
1.1.14–31.12.14	£250,000	£1,200,000	£24,000,000
1.1.10–31.12.13	£250,000	£600,000	£16,000,000

Some of the EU country codes and the areas included for intrastat purposes differ from those used for EC sales list purposes. The intrastat codes are as follows.

Country	*Code*
Austria	AT
Belgium	BE
Bulgaria	BG
Croatia[12]	HR
Cyprus[9]	CY
Czech Republic	CZ
Denmark[2]	DK
Estonia	EE
Finland[3]	FI
France[4]	FR
Germany[5]	DE
Greece[10]	GR
Hungary	HU
Ireland	IE
Italy[6]	IT
Latvia	LV
Lithuania	LT
Luxembourg	LU
Malta	MT
Netherlands	NL
Poland	PL
Portugal[7]	PT
Romania	RO
Slovak Republic	SK
Slovenia	SI
Spain[8]	ES
Sweden	SE
United Kingdom[11]	GB

1 Andorra and Liechtenstein are both outside the customs territory (and therefore the statistical territory) of the EU.
2 Does not include the Faroe Islands.

[3] Includes Aland Islands.
[4] Includes Monaco, but excludes all French Overseas departments and territories. Martinique, Guadeloupe, Reunion, Mayotte, and French Guiana are part of the statistical territory of France but because customs documentation is still required for exports to, or imports from, these territories HMRC continue to collect trade statistics from that documentation and it must not be declared on the intrastat.
[5] Includes Isle of Heligoland but excludes Busingen.
[6] Does not include communes of Livigno and Campione d'Italia, the Italian waters of Lake Lugano and the Vatican. Livigno is part of the statistical territory of Italy but because customs documentation is still required for exports to, or imports from, this territory HMRC continue to collect trade statistics from that documentation and it must not be declared on the intrastat.
[7] Includes the Azores and Madeira.
[8] Includes the Balearic Islands but excludes Ceuta, Melilla, and the Canary Islands. The Canary Islands are part of the statistical territory of Spain but because customs documentation is still required for exports to, or imports from, these territories HMRC continue to collect trade statistics from that documentation and it must not be declared on the intrastat.
[9] Includes UK sovereign base areas but excludes Northern Cyprus.
[10] Includes Mount Athos.
[11] Includes the Isle of Man and the Channel Islands but excludes Gibraltar.
[12] Croatia joined the EU on 1 July 2013. Dispatches and arrivals to/from Croatia should be included from this date.

VAT Mini One Stop Shop (VAT MOSS)

(VATA 1994 Sch 4A paras 15, 16; SI 2014/2726; HMRC Brief 46/2014)

From 1 January 2015 the place of supply for business-to-consumer (B2C) supplies of broadcasting, telecommunications and e-services (digital services) is determined by the location of the consumer. The changes affect all businesses that supply digital services to consumers (ie private individuals), whether or not they are registered for UK VAT, because there are no registration limits for digital service supplies made to consumers outside the UK. Any business supplying digital services to a consumer in another member state therefore has to charge VAT on the supply in that member state and register for VAT in that member state. Supplies of digital services to businesses only (including the self-employed) are not affected by the changes.

To avoid having to register for VAT in every EU member state where digital services are supplied, a business may opt to use the VAT Mini One Stop Shop online service (VAT MOSS). Using the VAT MOSS online service means a business can submit a single calendar quarterly VAT MOSS return and payment covering all its EU digital service supplies. If the business registers for the VAT MOSS online service in the UK, HMRC will send an electronic copy of the appropriate part of the VAT MOSS return, and the related VAT payment, to each relevant member state's tax authority.

Car fuel

SEE TOLLEY'S TAX COMPUTATIONS 406.1.

(VATA 1994 ss 56, 57, Schs 4, 6; FA 2013 Sch 38)

Where an employer pays mileage allowances, he may use the advisory fuel rates on p 84 to calculate the input VAT to reclaim on the fuel element. Receipts must still be retained.

VAT-inclusive scale figures can be used to assess VAT due on fuel provided at no cost (from 11 December 2012, previously at below cost) for private journeys by registered traders or their employees, where the fuel has been provided from business resources. The figures represent the tax-inclusive value of the fuel supplied to each individual and relate to return periods beginning on the dates shown. If the trader or employer opts to use the scale figures he must use them for all supplies of fuel for private use made for no consideration in the prescribed accounting period. From 17 July 2013, the scale charge may also be used as an alternative to accounting for VAT on the required open market value where the fuel is supplied for a consideration below that value.

	12 months £	*3 months* £	*1 month* £
From 1 May 2018: CO_2 band			
120 or below	562	140	46
125	842	210	70
130	900	224	74
135	954	238	79
140	1,013	252	84
145	1,067	266	88
150	1,125	280	93
155	1,179	295	98
160	1,238	309	102
165	1,292	323	107
170	1,350	336	111
175	1,404	351	116
180	1,463	365	121
185	1,517	379	125
190	1,575	393	130
195	1,630	407	135
200	1,688	421	140
205	1,742	436	145
210	1,801	449	149
215	1,855	463	154
220	1,913	477	159
225 or above	1,967	491	163

	12 months £	3 months £	1 month £
1 May 2017–30 April 2018: CO_2 band			
120 or below	563	140	46
125	842	211	70
130	901	224	74
135	955	238	79
140	1,013	252	84
145	1,068	267	88
150	1,126	281	93
155	1,180	295	98
160	1,239	309	102
165	1,293	323	107
170	1,351	337	111
175	1,405	351	116
180	1,464	365	121
185	1,518	379	125
190	1,577	393	131
195	1,631	408	136
200	1,689	422	140
205	1,743	436	145
210	1,802	449	149
215	1,856	463	154
220	1,914	478	159
225 or above	1,969	492	163

	12 months £	3 months £	1 month £
1 May 2016–30 April 2017: CO_2 band			
120 or below	467	116	38
125	699	175	58
130	747	186	61
135	792	197	65
140	841	209	69
145	886	221	73
150	934	233	77
155	979	245	81
160	1,028	256	85
165	1,073	268	89
170	1,121	279	92
175	1,166	291	96
180	1,214	303	101
185	1,259	314	104
190	1,308	326	108
195	1,353	338	112
200	1,401	350	116
205	1,446	362	120
210	1,495	373	123
215	1,540	384	128
220	1,588	396	132
225 or above	1,633	408	135

	12 months £	3 months £	1 month £
1 May 2015–30 April 2016: CO_2 band			
120 or below	536	133	44
125	802	200	66
130	857	213	70
135	909	227	75
140	965	240	80
145	1,016	254	84
150	1,072	267	88
155	1,123	281	93
160	1,179	294	97
165	1,231	308	102
170	1,286	320	106
175	1,338	334	111
180	1,393	347	115
185	1,445	361	119
190	1,501	374	124
195	1,552	388	129
200	1,608	401	133
205	1,660	415	138
210	1,715	428	142
215	1,767	441	146
220	1,822	455	151
225 or above	1,874	468	155

	12 months £	3 months £	1 month £
1 May 2014–30 April 2015: CO_2 band			
120 or below	627	156	52
125	939	234	78
130	1,004	251	83
135	1,064	266	88
140	1,129	282	94
145	1,190	297	99
150	1,255	313	104
155	1,315	328	109
160	1,381	345	115
165	1,441	360	120
170	1,506	376	125
175	1,567	391	130
180	1,632	408	136
185	1,692	423	141
190	1,757	439	146
195	1,818	454	151
200	1,883	470	156
205	1,943	485	161
210	2,008	502	167
215	2,069	517	172
220	2,134	533	177
225 or above	2,194	548	182

	12 months £	*3 months* £	*1 month* £
1 May 2013–30 April 2014: CO_2 band			
120 or below	675	168	56
125	1,010	253	84
130	1,080	269	89
135	1,145	286	95
140	1,215	303	101
145	1,280	320	106
150	1,350	337	112
155	1,415	354	118
160	1,485	371	123
165	1,550	388	129
170	1,620	404	134
175	1,685	421	140
180	1,755	438	146
185	1,820	455	151
190	1,890	472	157
195	1,955	489	163
200	2,025	506	168
205	2,090	523	174
210	2,160	539	179
215	2,225	556	185
220	2,295	573	191
225 or above	2,360	590	196

Value added tax interest and penalties

Default interest

(VATA 1994 s 74)

Interest runs on the amount of any VAT assessed (or paid late by voluntary disclosure):

- from the reckonable date (normally the latest date on which a return is required for the period in question);
- until the date of payment (although in practice it runs to the date shown on the notice of assessment or notice of voluntary disclosure if paid within 30 days of that date).

The period of interest cannot commence more than three years before the date of assessment or payment.

The rates of interest are as follows:

Period	*Rate*
from 21 November 2017	**3.00%**
23 August 2016– 20 November 2017	2.75%
29 September 2009–22 August 2016	3.00%

Interest on VAT overpaid in cases of official error

(VATA 1994 s 78)

Where VAT has been overpaid or underclaimed due to an error by HMRC, then on a claim HMRC must pay interest:

- from the date they receive payment (or authorise a repayment) for the return period in question;
- until the date on which they authorise payment of the amount on which interest is due.

This provision does not require HMRC to pay interest on an amount on which repayment supplement is due.

The rates of interest are as follows:

Period	*Rate*
from 29 September 2009	**0.50%**
27 January 2009–28 September 2009	0.00%
6 January 2009–26 January 2009	1.00%

Repayment supplement – VAT

(VATA 1994 s 79)

Where a person is entitled to a repayment the payment due is increased by a supplement of the greater of:

(i) 5% of that amount; or
(ii) £50.

The supplement will only be paid if:

(a) the return or claim is received by HMRC not later than the last day on which it is required to be made;
(b) HMRC do not issue a written instruction making the refund within the relevant period; and
(c) the amount shown on the return or claim does not exceed the amount due by more than 5% of that amount or £250, whichever is the greater.

The 'relevant period' is 30 days beginning with the receipt of the return or claim or, if later, the day after the last day of the VAT period to which the return or claim relates.

Penalties and surcharges

Offence	*Penalty*
Inaccuracy in return or other document (FA 2007 Sch 24)[1].	See **Penalties — modernised penalty regime** on p 9.
Failure to notify obligation to register for VAT, change in supplies made by person exempted from registration, acquisition affecting exemption, acquisition of goods from another member state and unauthorised issue of an invoice (FA 2008 Sch 41).	See **Penalties — modernised penalty regime** on p 9.
Inaccuracy in return or other document as a result of third party providing incorrect (or withholding) information (FA 2007 Sch 24).	See **Penalties — modernised penalty regime** on p 9.
Failure to inform HMRC of an error in an assessment within 30 days of the date of the assessment (FA 2007 Sch 24).	See **Penalties — modernised penalty regime** on p 10.
Failure to comply with HMRC investigatory powers with effect from 1 April 2009 (FA 2008 Sch 36).	(*a*) Initial penalty of £300; (*b*) if failure/obstruction continues, a further penalty of up to £60 per day; (*c*) if failure/obstruction continues after penalty under (*a*) imposed, a tax-related amount determined by the Upper Tribunal.
Provision of inaccurate information or document when complying with an information notice (FA 2008 Sch 36).	Up to £3,000 per inaccuracy.
Failure to submit a return electronically if required to do so by SI 1995/2518 reg 25 for prescribed accounting periods starting on or after 1 April 2012. Before 1 April 2012, failure of a *specified person* to make a *specified return* using an electronic return system for prescribed accounting periods ending on or after 31 March 2011 (SI 1995/2518 reg 25A). 'Specified person' was broadly a person registered for VAT on or after 1 April 2010, or one registered before that date who at 31 December 2009 or any later date has an annual VAT exclusive turnover of £100,000 or more. Penalty will only apply to prescribed accounting periods ending on or after 31 March 2013 where the person is required to make an electronic return only as a result of the removal of the turnover test from 1 April 2012.	Annual VAT exclusive turnover of: £22,800,001 or more — £400 £5,600,001 to £22,800,000 — £300 £100,001 to £5,600,000 — £200 £100,000 or under — £100
Failure to submit return or pay VAT due within time limit (where a return is late but the VAT is paid on time or no VAT is due, a default is recorded but no surcharge arises) (VATA 1994 s 59)[2]. Failure to pay tax due under the payment on account scheme on time (VATA 1994 s 59A).	The greater of £30 and a specified percentage of outstanding VAT for period, depending on number of defaults in surcharge period: first default in period 2%, second default 5%, third default 10%, fourth and further defaults 15%. (Surcharge assessments are not issued for sums of less than £400 unless the rate of the surcharge is 10% or more.) **Due to be replaced by penalties under FA 2009 Schs 55 and 56 from a date to be appointed.**
Issuing incorrect certificate stating that certain supplies fall to be zero-rated or taxed at the reduced rate (VATA 1994 s 62).	Difference between tax actually charged and tax which should have been charged.
Material inaccuracy in EC sales statement (VATA 1994 s 65).	£100 for each material inaccuracy in two-year penalty period (which commences following notice of second material inaccuracy).
Failure to submit an EC sales statement (VATA 1994 s 66).	Greater of £50 or a daily penalty (maximum 100 days) £5 for the first, £10 for the second, £15 for the third or subsequent failure in the default period.
Breach of walking possession agreement (VATA 1994 s 68).	50% of VAT due or amount recoverable.
Failure to preserve records for prescribed period (VATA 1994 ss 69, 69B).	£500.
Failure to preserve records specified in HMRC direction (VATA 1994 ss 69, 69B).	£200 for each day of failure (maximum 30 days).
Breaches of regulatory provisions, including failure to notify cessation of liability or entitlement to be registered, failure to keep records and non-compliance with any regulations made under VATA 1994 (VATA 1994 s 69).	Greater of £50 and a daily penalty (maximum 100 days) of a specified amount depending on number of failures in preceding two years: £5* per day if no previous failures; £10* per day if one previous failure; £15* per day if two or more previous failures.
Where failure consists of not paying VAT or not making a return in the required time.	*1/6, 1/3 and 1/2 of 1% of the VAT due respectively, if greater.

Offence	*Penalty*
Breaches of regulatory provisions involving failure to pay VAT or submit return by due date (VATA 1994 s 69).	Greater of £50 and a daily penalty (for no more than 100 days) of a specified amount depending on number of failures in preceding two years: greater of £5 and 1/6 % of VAT due if no previous failures; greater of £10 and 1/3% of VAT due if one previous failure; greater of £15 and 1/2% of VAT due if two or more previous failures.
Failure to comply with the requirements of the investment gold scheme (VATA 1994 s 69A).	17.5% of the value of transactions concerned.
Import VAT (FA 2003 ss 24–41):	
– failures relating to non-compliance	maximum penalty of £2,500
– evasion.	maximum penalty equal to VAT sought to be evaded.
Evasion of VAT: conduct involving dishonesty (VATA 1994 ss 60, 61). Does not apply to acts or omissions relating to an inaccuracy in a document or failure to notify HMRC of an under-assessment (to which penalties under FA 2007 Sch 24 apply).	Amount of tax evaded or sought to be evaded (subject to mitigation).
Transactions connected with fraudulent evasion of VAT (VATA 1994 ss 69C–69E).	30% of potential lost VAT.
Failure to notify the use of a designated avoidance scheme (VATA 1994 Sch 11A paras 10, 11).	*15% of the tax avoided (applies to businesses with supplies of £600,000 or more).* ***Replaced from 1 January 2018, see below***.
Failure to disclose certain schemes within 30 days of the due date or the first return affected (VATA 1994 Sch 11A paras 10, 11).	*£5,000 (applies to businesses with supplies exceeding £10 million).* ***Replaced from 1 January 2018, see below***.
Failure from 1 January 2018 to notify details of, or notify use of, a notifiable proposal which enables a person to obtain a tax advantage within 31 days of the making of the proposal (F(No 2)A 2017 Sch 17).	Penalty up to £600 per day in 'initial period' A continuing penalty not exceeding £600 for each day on which the failure continues after imposition of initial penalty (but a tribunal can determine a higher penalty up to £1 million).
Failure from 1 January 2018 to provide HMRC with the reference number and related information in relation to notifiable arrangements above (F(No 2)A 2017 Sch 17).	Penalty not exceeding £5,000 in respect of each scheme to which the failure relates For second failure within three years of first, penalty not exceeding £7,500 in respect of each scheme For subsequent failures within three years of previous, penalty not exceeding £10,000 in respect of each scheme.

1 In relation to VAT MOSS returns, a penalty under FA 2007 Sch 24 only applies when the recipient of the supply is in the UK. If an inaccuracy on a UK return relates to a supply to a recipient in another member state, there is no penalty under UK legislation, but a penalty may apply in that other member state in which the recipient is located. If an inaccuracy on (say) a French VAT return relates to a supply to a recipient in the UK, there could be a penalty under UK legislation.

2 In relation to VAT MOSS returns, a penalty for a late return or late payment could be charged by each member state in which the supplies are deemed to be made.

Index

T

U

V

W

Z